THE
SQUEEZE

James Dale Davidson

SUMMIT BOOKS
NEW YORK

Designed by Stanley S. Drate
Manufactured in the United States of America
1 2 3 4 5 6 7 8 9 10

Library of Congress Cataloging in Publication Data

Davidson, James Dale.
The squeeze.

1. United States—Economic conditions—1971-
2. Cost and standard of living—United States.
3. Middle classes—United States.   I.   Title.
HC106.7.D38   330.973   79-28411

ISBN 0-671-40084-3

Acknowledgments

Someday, when a junior-college professor produces his dissertation, "The History of the Thank-You Note Through the Ages," I hope there is a passage in his volume explaining how easy it is to fail to thank everyone to whom thanks are owed. What follows is proof.

As are all books, this is a collective endeavor of many people. In the first instance, I am indebted to a wide variety of persons, living and dead, who are quoted throughout this text and whose thoughts are otherwise in evidence. They fashioned the conceptual tools from which this book was built. I could never have been clever enough or energetic enough to proceed without them. I feel especially indebted to F. A. Hayek. His illuminating and discerning insights into all the social studies helped raise my interest in economic theory to the same level of impractical excitement which I once experienced as a juvenile poet. To the late playwright Maxwell Anderson I give thanks for emphatically stating that government is a business. I also extend special thanks to Z. A. Pelczyniski, John Flemming, William Bonner, Lewis Lehrman, Scott Burns, James Webb, Matt Valencic, and Paul Craig Roberts. They and others have contributed ideas and suggestions which found their way into this book.

Undoubtedly, their thoughts would have been better and more fluently represented had I not been preparing this volume, under a deadline, at a very hectic time in my life—as I was in the crucial stages of trying to organize the convening of a constitutional convention to reform federal fiscal policies.

Under such circumstances, I could never have proceeded without the willing help of a number of fine friends. Mark Hulbert, Jane Dittenhoffer, and Kathy Britton provided imaginative and exacting research assistance. My brother and my father helped by shuttling rough drafts to and from typists. Karen Chace, Margaret Payne, Marty Webber, Cathy Briskie, and especially Lois Leyda did exemplary jobs producing a legible typescript and pleasantly tolerating what were at times frantic deadline pressures. I also thank Elizabeth Philip, Rita Smith, Leonard Liggio, Theron Raines, Jim Silberman (for betting money that I had something to say), Paul Bresnick (for helping me to say it better), and my mother, for providing me with valuable suggestions, encouragement and logistic support.

I also thank Milton Friedman for serving as a Dutch uncle in commenting on a typescript draft of this volume. His vigorous criticisms helped me both to avoid some errors which otherwise would have been set in print, and to strengthen my case at some points where we disagree.

As is customary, the division of responsibility stops where fault begins. The credit for what is good in this book stretches far and wide, while its defects are, I suppose, mine.

For my parents

Contents

CONTENTS

Part III
BREAKING THE GRIP

Part I
PERSPECTIVES

"And now," observes Adam, "we must again try to discover what sort of world this is. . . ."

—*Nathaniel Hawthorne*

1

Awakening from the American Dream

It takes time to ruin a world, but time is all it takes.
—*Bernard DeFoutenelle*

—". . . you can't even keep your home."

—"I started out my first year with sixteen cows, and by the end of the year I had eight . . . we had to eat or sell them to get us through."

—"Ten years ago I would have thought what we are making now is a fortune, but we are just able to give our kids the normal things . . . nothing above the average."

—"If you wait to have a baby until you can afford it, you never will . . . we could not survive just on my husband's salary."

—"There is not going to be any relief for the middle class . . . I don't think that there is any relief in sight."

—"I don't even have an extra five dollars for pin money. Before, with both of us working, there was not always this kind of problem."

—"We see it coming. God help this country if they keep pushing us against the wall."

These are the voices of a disturbed America. The men and women who are the common citizens of the world's great middle-class nation feel squeezed and hurt. Many no longer expect to end their lives in a better material condition than they began. This represents a reversal of the central fact of the American experience—the conviction that anyone can attain a better life through tenacity, enterprise, and thrift. That expectation peopled America, and that hope attracted immigrants to build a new race on a new land. They dug, plowed, hoed, and built from nothing the mightiest commercial civilization in history. The effort was animated by the self-confident premise that life's prospects were essentially good. This made penniless ambition bankable. It made room for invention—and growth. It created what Walt Whitman hailed in *Leaves of Grass* as "a better, fresher, busier sphere," which gave the adventuresome, exploratory spirit room to grow.

Now our spirits are faltering. Perhaps this is merely the sociological equivalent to freak weather, a cold day in July, which will pass. If so, Americans will soon be back at their business—imagining life's prospects to be bigger and greater than sober analysis says they are. Yet if we are not in a self-correcting phase, but are entering into a new condition, the effect would be impossible to exaggerate. If, as the evidence suggests, the middle-class aspiration to advance, to become whatever one's sense of adventure allows, has been squelched, it will soon lead to the loss of much else.

The reversal of centuries of experience and hope that tomorrow holds a greater promise than today would not only diminish the prospects for new-car sales and drop the stocks of baby-food companies, it would also dull our personalities. It would erase the "right" look that Robert Frost once discerned on the faces passing his window. Consider what he wrote after trying to "Figure out whether American men or women swing their arms more freely." Frost said, "There cannot be much to fear in a country where there are so many right faces going by. I keep asking myself where they all come from, and I keep thinking that God was just making them up new around the next corner."[1]

Today, we may no longer be so free-spirited and confident. The faces one meets on the street tell of the cares which weigh heavily upon the average person. If God is on the next corner, he is probably watching for purse snatchers and muggers, like everybody else; queued up waiting for a bus that is late. . . . Not many people wear "right faces" home from jobs that yield declining spending power. Not many people, wherever one stands, turn out of the grocery store smiling when their twenty-dollar shopping bag can be carried easily with one hand; when the overtaxed and inflated dollars which they must budget buy less and less each day. The good, solid citizens on the way to the bank to draw down their savings do not swing their arms as freely as they used to do. They are not only afraid of crime, they are intimidated and victimized at many turns by actions which are perfectly legal. When nothing works the way it should, when a man is on foot because his automobile is in the repair shop and he fears it will be in even worse condition upon its return, when illness or injury strikes and that hurt is compounded by the greater financial hurt to come, then the man on the street loses something more than money.

The professions have so augmented their incomes through legislation, regulation, and litigation that the law itself has become the public enemy. In today's street there is a lawyer on every corner, and as the eighteenth-century wit Charles Caleb Colton said, "There is no room for justice; . . . the claimant expires of wrong in the midst of right, as mariners die of thirst in the midst of water."

The crisis in American life is not merely a matter of impressions. Whatever one sees out his window or reads from the faces on street corners, there has been a real reduction in the spending power of the average family. "Making ends meet" is now the greatest personal difficulty facing Americans. To be sure, individuals are still worried about their health, their careers, the tribulations of rearing children, boredom in retirement, crabgrass, the difficulties of losing weight, and the rise of suburban venereal disease. But given all these woes to choose from, more individuals are floundering over difficulties of personal finance than any other problem. According to a Gallup poll, no other concern even comes close. People are earning higher incomes, but it costs them ever more to live. They feel that they should be enjoying increased standards of living. Instead they must skimp and watch the expenditure of every penny.

With real purchasing power declining, a continuation of current trends would cut the average family's real wealth in half by 1985.

That would be a peril of the first magnitude for American life, made all the more difficult by the fact that it is covert. It is more a mathematical expectation of a long, protracted discomfort than an immediate danger that makes the adrenaline flow. If a thief were to come directly into your home and begin to move out your furniture, you would be excited, angry, and most likely ready to fight that easily comprehended wrong. But let something similarly impoverishing happen over years, decades, and the process slakes rather than excites the animal spirits. We can sense that somewhere the mill wheel is turning, propelling the mechanism which works against us. But it is all abstract and invisible.

It is nothing you can see coming, nothing you can measure against the normal physical and emotional tools with which evolution has fitted human beings to combat danger. Under such conditions, it is little wonder that optimism and even comprehension falter.

America's middle class is being steadily impoverished. Yet the squeeze is hardly heralded or understood. Frustration and discontent have a million voices, but they tell a million different stories. Each of us holds a private perspective on a difficulty which is now too large to be seen as a private matter.

The factors contributing to the squeeze on the middle class are so complicated that we cannot hope to understand them in all their details. The best that can be attained is clarification. We can lay some of the matters which are the cause of our hurt within the reach of explanatory principles. That is the purpose of these essays. They are an attempt to see the crisis of the middle class in a new light; at the very least to draw thought and attention to the plight of the average middle-class individual. He deserves no less. He has been the stalwart and the builder of the greatest commercial civilization that the world has yet seen. He is the man for whom we can borrow Arthur Miller's words from *Death of a Salesman*: "I don't say he's a great man. Willy Loman never made a lot of money. His name was never in the paper. He's not the finest character that ever lived. But he's a human being, and a terrible thing is happening to him. So attention must be paid. He's not to be allowed to fall into his grave like an old dog. Attention, attention must finally be paid to such a person."

2
The Rise and Fall of Progress

> . . . among the ideas which have held sway in public and private affairs for the last two hundred years, none is more significant or likely to exert more influence in the future than the concept of progress.
>
> —*Charles A. Beard*

Analysis of the prospects for America's middle class cannot proceed far without an examination of the method and doctrine of progress. The fact that Americans, perhaps more than any other people, have persistently believed in progress has much to do with why the impoverishment of the middle class is a phenomenon we have been so slow to recognize. Only now is it becoming a matter for serious discussion— years after evidence pointing in that direction ought to have been obvious. Our inherent optimism, our inherited belief in an ever-brighter future, has served to obscure our perception of our present situation.

Put simply, Americans have traditionally believed that the future will almost necessarily be better than the present. We have abused our health—smoked, gorged, and guzzled, in anticipation that medical science would spare us the consequences. It is the same idea upon which almost every monster movie is based. When Godzilla is taking over Tokyo and "civilization crumbles" as the cast of thousands trample one

19

another, the moral of the tale is never in doubt. There must always be one calm scientist in a basement somewhere who will save 90 percent of the uncomprehending multitude by the last reel.

This is the doctrine of progress in action. It is a doctrine of fate. It is the assumption that things are bound to get better in the future, not for any particular reasons, but because a general betterment is the destiny of history.

"Belief in progress," Baudelaire said, "is a doctrine of idlers. . . . It is the individual relying upon his neighbors to do his work." That may be, yet belief in progress has made much sense. The notion that life will materially improve has corresponded closely enough to real developments over the last several hundred years to justify its recent status as an article of second-nature wisdom. Indeed, the doctrine of progress could never have come into being had there been no practical basis for expecting continuously more of the future. Such a notion could not be sustained by brute optimism, as analysis will demonstrate.

There are only a handful of possibilities for the future: things will get better; things will get worse; or—the more realistic assessment— some things will get better, even while others get worse. In almost every culture which has entertained the notion of the future at all, one of the first two notions has dominated.

During the early part of the Christian epoch and even as late as the beginnings of the Industrial Revolution, the future held a negative potential, at least insofar as the material conditions of life were concerned.

As an apocalyptic religion, Christianity found its first audience among the dispirited populations of the Roman Empire. In those times, belief that the world might come to an end was encouraged by a rapid decline in the material conditions of life. Tax collectors had so plundered the population that farmers and other productive individuals simply stopped producing rather than continue to pay the imperial taxes. So many taxpayers disappeared during the reign of Diocletian (284–305) that laws were passed to compel them to stay on the job. Farmers were prohibited from leaving the fields. Other occupations were made hereditary, with severe penalties for those who attempted to escape. Nevertheless, people by the millions literally fled into the arms of the barbarians. Whole communities were depopulated in what once had been the most productive regions of the empire. As more and more land passed out of cultivation, the food-distribution system broke down. People in cities starved. Other millions died in plagues, which seemed to prove that natural and human disaster go hand in hand. In short order the popula-

20

tion under Roman rule fell by more than twenty million. Commerce of all kinds dwindled and living conditions fell sharply, not to recover to their previous level for almost a thousand years.

During the centuries which followed, there was little to contradict the negative attitude of the public toward the future. Because trade routes had been shortened and agricultural productivity had declined, economic relations were for the most part more primitive in medieval times than they had been in the ancient world. The few urban populations which remained eked out a precarious survival, being almost wholly dependent upon local food supplies. Whatever material comforts the average person could enjoy, foremost among them the simple provision of food and water, never lasted long enough to be the foundation of further advancement. Between the ravages of weather and marching armies, life was, as Hobbes aptly described it, "short, brutish, and mean."

People fully believed that the world was "coming to an end." Almost any disturbance in nature of the seriousness of a thunderclap or a shooting star was sufficient to instigate an epidemic of apocalyptic terror. This was so for centuries. In the year 999, for example, a sizable percentage of European economic activity ceased. Craftsmen dropped their trades. Serfs left the fields. People from all walks of life sold or abandoned everything and trudged together in a motley horde to Jerusalem, where they prayed and waited for the hour of doom.

Similarly remarkable demonstrations of a negative public attitude toward the future were repeated, though later on a less grand scale, until the Industrial Revolution. As late as 1806 the people of Leeds, England, and its environs were winding up their worldly affairs and preparing to depart in the greatest haste for the Holy Land. It seems that a local hen was laying eggs on which appeared the words "Christ is coming." Those who examined the eggs were incited to a rare pitch of religious enthusiasm. Sure enough, the eggs did say: "Christ is coming." The whole community would have been depopulated, had not some skeptics turned up to investigate. They discovered that the hen's owner had been inscribing the freshly laid eggs with a corrosive liquid and then cramming them back into the chicken's body. While the animal lovers were appalled, most people laughed and were relieved to get back to their business.[1]

By the early nineteenth century, faith had abated enough so that the public had begun to look more favorably upon the material prospects of life. This was due not so much to an inherent antagonism between religion and progress as to the fact that the decline of Christian faith coincided with a development that made gradual material advancement possible: *the accumulation of capital.* Only as capital began to be accumulated did the public learn to expect more of tomorrow than today. The seeds of the modern doctrine of progress were sown.

Not force of intellect, nor hard work, but the successive employment of ever more capital has been the basis of the unprecedented prosperity of the modern age. That accumulation, more than anything else, was responsible for the ever-improving quality of material life that has characterized the past two centuries of world history, and virtually all of American history. Yes, of course, genius has been known at all times of human history. Even our ancestors who struggled before civilization began must have been capable of prodigious mental accomplishments to have endured at all. It would tax the ingenuity of the modern individual to figure out how to survive in the same rude environment which supported primitive man. But no, it is not the alacrity with which we think, nor our tolerance for hard work—which is now a fraction of what has been common in the past—which accounts for the self-defrosting refrigerator and the microwave oven.

Practically everything that the ordinary person holds dear and which permits us at least the illusion of dignity during our period on earth has resulted from the accumulation of capital. That gave us more time, which allowed a better preparation for newer, more elaborate, more profitable work. Today, one thousand teamsters with Diamond Reo rigs and CB's can move more goods over an American highway in a week than all the workers in China could have toted in the same time a century ago.

Capital accumulation not only aids the teamsters in exercising man's "propensity to truck," it gives each person a "free ride" to a higher income simply by increasing the number of opportune uses for his time. *The greater the accumulated surplus from previous generations, the more valuable an individual's labor*—even if he performs a function which has remained unchanged or is physically less exacting than similar trades in the past. For example, butlers today, where they can be found, are exceedingly well paid. Yet they do far less actual labor and have fewer responsibilities than the butlers of four hundred years ago, whose yearly wages were one-tenth or less of those paid today. The increased prosperity of butlers bears no relation whatever to the actual, physical activities of butlering. They are paid better wages because their employers must offer them at least as much as they could earn from the next most opportune use of their time. *Because capital accumulation increases the productivity of some labor, it indirectly increases the value of all labor.* Butlers are richer today, whether they own capital or not, simply because someone, it hardly matters who, has contributed to a general capital accumulation. If there were massive *dis-savings* and a general capital consumption, butlers would be poorer again, no matter how properly they served the tea.

The great upsurge in life expectancy in the modern world is due, in large measure, to improved nutrition and public sanitation made possible by capital accumulation. Even today, when scientific and medical knowledge can be carried almost instantaneously around the globe, those areas where the highest mortality persists are precisely those which have witnessed the least capital accumulation.

By the same token, one can reckon that a good measure of the world's scientific and even literary accomplishment is owed to the fact that capital has progressively reduced human drudgery and freed the inquiring spirits of individuals who would have otherwise been, at best, successful peasants, and at worst might never have survived at all in the hand-to-mouth economies of the past.

As long as capital accumulation continues, it is a fair surmise that the general material conditions of life will improve. Thus the doctrine of progress upon which the world obtains its warrant for being lazy arises as a consequence of capital accumulation.

Of course, people do not make that connection. It took hundreds of years, once capital accumulation had begun, for the public anticipation of the future to change. When the word "progress" first gained currency in English, it could and frequently did have negative connotations. "Progress" described the movement of anything running its course, such as the progress of a disease, which carried the patient through various stages of suffering to the final outcome, recovery or death. Only after capital accumulation had continued for centuries, more or less unabated, did the modern consciousness arise incorporating the assumption that tomorrow is bound to be better than today.

A strict scrutiny of all the facets of life would reveal that the doctrine of progress has only limited application. The same would be true of the supposition that everything is bound to decline. It is a plain descriptive truth that while some things get better, other things may be getting worse. Even during the last two centuries, which by almost indisputable account have been times of the most dramatic progress, some things have not improved. Violin-making, for example, has been on the decline since the time of Stradivari. So have many other crafts.

Not many examples of blown glass produced today match those from seventy-five years ago.

If one were to survey every aspect of human endeavor, the catalog of material things that have not improved during recent centuries of general improvement could be extended to some length. But it would take more than a slight effort to prepare the list. And that is significant. The fact that one would have to pause and puzzle over the matter, that thinking of exceptions to progress takes an effort of imagination, is indicative of why a realistic approach to anticipating the potential of the future is unlikely ever to be accommodated to the limitations of the human mind. We have, in effect, been blinded by the brightness of the future we have come to expect. But we must not allow our faith in progress to blind us to the facts of contemporary economic life in America. The average citizen's capital is *not* accumulating. On the contrary, it is being eaten away at such a rate that if the present pace continues, the average American family's real wealth will be cut in half just five years from now.

3
The Information Deficit

The Master said: "Yu! Shall I teach you the meaning of knowledge? When you know a thing to recognize that you know it; and when you do not, to know that you do not know—that is knowledge."

—*Confucius*

One of the primary causes and manifestations of the squeeze on the average individual is the fact that society is operating on an increasing information deficit. The sheer number of facts and theories which the average person needs to have at his command in order to guard his interests is growing far faster than his ability to collect and understand them. Dozens of systems with which everyone must deal in his workaday life are not only multiplying their demands for cold cash, they are increasing their costs in another way—by constantly hiking the volume and complexity of the information one must master to successfully cope with them. Politicians, bankers, bureaucrats, lawyers, doctors, tax collectors, and others are like vampires preying upon the ignorant. Most people cannot act nimbly enough to escape through tax loopholes. They do not know where they are. They cannot cross-examine the propositions upon which the doctor and the hospital treat and bill them. They cannot penetrate the murk of bureaucracy or speak the special, exploitative language of the lawyer.[1] This is very much a part of what ails America.

It is an essential condition for continued progress that the evolution of society not overload the mental capacity of the average human being.

This means that the information prerequisites for successful participation in the various spheres of life must not be changed with a dizzying speed. They must be stable enough and clear enough to be open to general understanding. This is the condition which enables people to survive by making do with the least feasible amount of thought. The philosopher Alfred North Whitehead contended that "civilization advances by extending the number of important operations which we can perform without thinking about them. Operations of thought are like cavalry changes in a battle—they are strictly limited in number, they require fresh horses, and must only be made at decisive moments."[2]

He was certainly right in suggesting that substantial thinking is uncomfortably near to being a heroic effort. Indeed, individuals often evidence an almost amazing reluctance to think about their own aspirations and deepest desires. That is why we do not speak nonsense when we say of someone, "He has finally found himself." It is commonplace for people to spend years of their adult lives without realizing what they want to do or be. How much more difficult, then, is it to come to grips with the multitude of intentions, aspirations, and actions that comprise other people's lives?

The fact that we act under the handicap of a permanent information deficit is one of the least obvious of the fundamental aspects of life. In this, we are beneficiaries of what might be called the "activating delusion." However little we know, even when our ignorance is complete, we habitually assume that we know enough. As Santayana cleverly observed: "By nature's kindly disposition, most questions which it is beyond a man's power to answer do not occur to him at all."

In the millennia of human development before society was organized on a grand scale, knowing enough simply to survive may have been nearly all one needed to know. But as human affairs have become increasingly interdependent, the factors which affect every individual have multiplied a millionfold. A revolution in Zaire, famine in Southeast Asia, the inert gas in our spray deodorant, and a multitude of other things that we could neither know nor recognize could singly, or together, lead to our undoing.

With so many of the factors which affect the individual located at some physical distance from him, the demands upon his attention are growing far faster than can ever be met. We have, necessarily, developed ways of obtaining the widest possible utilization of the least amount of information and thought.

One mental shortcut which has found increased institutional, if not individual, use is the compilation of statistics. Tabulations are available enumerating almost anything—from the batting averages of shortstops to the average age of television sets of farm families. Such compilations are undoubtedly illuminating in some respects. Unfortunately, they have merely lessened the information deficit; they have not eliminated it. Charts of numbers, useful abstractions that they are, tend to stand in the way of a fully humanistic comprehension of the quality of life and where it is tending. This is because these statistics are precisely that—abstractions.

One never bothers to think twice about 400,000 households, a 7.2-percent increase in the cost of living, declining new-housing starts, a $500-billion federal expenditure, or a tremor of 3.7 on the Richter scale. In spite of the familiarity of such figures, few people have personal, vivid realizations of what they mean. Such magnitudes do not correspond to what we know in life.

That is one reason why it is exceedingly difficult to keep track of what is becoming of our world and to understand what the actions of people around us imply for our own lives. To the extent that the average person thinks at all about the abstract factors which have a substantial impact upon his life, he generally seeks to make do with the least amount of mental exertion.

It is a matter of simple economizing. People prefer not to waste their thoughts, so they confine them, largely, to fields which promise a direct application. This is why individuals seldom have practical ideas except upon practical subjects. Thinking about something is usually not worth all the grunting and groaning unless it yields a sufficient return. Almost always this means that people understand best and think most exactly about their work. Almost by definition, that is the sort of thought which yields the most tangible benefit. If another line of thought yielded greater returns, the individual would most likely adopt it as his line of work. This suggests that a jeweler, as a rule, does not spend a great deal of time reading the operating manuals for a Caterpillar tractor. By the same token, neither a jeweler nor a tractor driver is likely to take a day off to puzzle over an encyclopedic array of facts and theories to discover, as nearly as possible, whether a politician's claim about what constitutes progress is really substantiated by the facts. Instead, one relies upon the thoughts of other people—upon general notions that are "in the air."

This points directly to the permanent limitation on the successful operation of politics. Most people give very little thought to the whole range of phenomena which the word "politics" describes. In fact, it is probable that more careful attention is paid, over a year's time, to such questions as where to spend a vacation or whether to stop for a fried-chicken dinner than is directed toward understanding politics. Substantial percentages of the population do not even know the names of the candidates who offer themselves at elections, let alone understand the underlying issues which infringe upon the plausibility of various political decisions.

Indeed, a government-financed study conducted by the University of Texas flatly concluded that less than one half of America's adult population—48 percent—is proficient in "awareness of government." Almost 26 percent were judged "functionally incompetent." The remaining 26 percent were reported to be "just getting by" as citizens. Some 20 percent could not read well enough to decipher the meaning of this widely seen phrase: "We are an Equal Opportunity Employer." Another 14 percent, or about 16.5 million adults, were judged unable to make out a personal check.[3] There is more to the study, but none of it points to a very lively hope that the public as a whole could consciously control the politicians.

Politicians control us because we cannot know the facts. No citizen, no matter how brilliant and dedicated, can examine the particulars of political action to sort out all the details in the context in which the politicians present them. Not only do politicians call upon us to know what they have in fact done—to recognize changes in the tax laws or to see the meaning of a water project or sugar subsidy—we must also grasp possibilities which are counter to fact. If we are to protect ourselves at the ballot box, we must be able to foresee the meaning of potential changes before they occur. When the government proposes building nuclear-power plants, the citizen must penetrate the murky claims and counterclaims of rival sets of nuclear engineers to figure out what nuclear construction might mean someday in the future.

Under such conditions, it is hardly surprising that many people have ceased to think about politics altogether and many of those who remain active citizens rely upon partisanship to avoid thinking. Instead of trying to sort out a million complexities, people can choose sides and let the difficult questions take care of themselves. Thus, ideas become "conservative" or "liberal." Candidates or policies are good or bad, according to how they are judged by our crowd, whether it is a political party, the women's caucus, or merely readers of *The New York Times*.

THE INFORMATION DEFICIT

In the past, it may well have been that the tendency of mind to polarize on a "them-and-us" basis was useful. When small bands of human beings fought one another in primitive warfare, a disposition to partisanship may have made sense. Under such conditions, the tendency of members of the group to stick together, to be partisan, would undoubtedly have had a substantial survival value. As we are the descendants of those who did survive, perhaps we are not wholly immune to instinctive pressures toward partisanship. However that may be, there can be little doubt that the partisan inclination is a powerful force deflecting people from thinking about political and economic topics in ways that might more nearly reflect an informed respect for their own interests.

There is an almost relentless effort to simplify everything; to make the multitude of happenings which comprise "public policy" a matter of partisan labels, stereotypes, and buzz words. More than anything else, this is applied laziness. It is a consequence of our reluctance or inability to comprehend the developments around us in all their particulars. So we simplify, reduce them to a few emotionally charged categories toward which we already have defined attitudes. If an individual is a Democrat and certain issues have been defined in a favorable light by Democratic leaders, that fact alone may spare him from the intricate reasoning and research which would be necessary to independently assess the matter. And it will do the same for his neighbor the Republican. Ideas, complex issues, and programs are unceasingly forced into partisan contexts, when they are addressed at all, simply because that division between "them" and "us" assists people to escape thinking.

There is probably not one person in a hundred, however partisan he may be, who could deliver a coherent explanation of his party's program. No one can say precisely what distinguishes a "conservative" and a "liberal." Still less can anyone offer an exact example of a policy, program, or propensity to injustice which can at all times and places distinguish the Left from the Right. Remove the names and dates, refurbish the buzz words, and one crowd would find something to applaud in the other's pronouncements. However unpleasant it is to contemplate, a Mussolini oration on forceful action to cut unemployment could well be delivered to a Democratic conclave in Massachusetts, and a Stalin attack upon the "sentimentalism" of demands for material equality could warm the hearts of the richest capitalists on Wall Street.

This is not to imply that political abstractions are devoid of content. Rather it is to say that we have shifting grounds for debate. While there

29

is all but unanimous agreement among people in locating the meanings of words which refer to tangible objects, such as "a tweed jacket" or "a mason jar," this is not the case with political vocabulary. Even terms in the widest use and of undoubted importance have many different meanings, as any competent dictionary would report. Words such as "freedom," "equality," and even "democracy" are applied to describe relationships which are in essence diametrically opposite. Raymond Williams, professor of drama at Cambridge University, has illustrated this in great detail in his book *Key Words: A Vocabulary of Culture and Society*. As Professor Williams clearly documents, every political and economic term which matters is invested with emotional importance and is subject to manipulation. Use of persuasive definitions and conscious attempts to turn descriptive terms into expressions of praise or ridicule are part of the normal operation of politics. Opponents are quick to label any unpleasant doctrine "reactionary," "radical," "socialistic," "fascistic," or merely "doctrinaire" or "ideological." For every person who has something to say about the abstract complex of rules and actions which comprise society, there is someone else who has some self-interested reason to make others believe that the ideas in question are zany and wrong, prevailing, as Walter Scott had it, "with none save hot-brained boys and crazed enthusiasts."[4]

All these factors—the inability of the human mind to be aware of more than a minute fraction of events unfolding in the world; the incomprehensibility of statistics, especially of the sums involved in the bookkeeping of a modern society; the recurring human desire to form judgments in terms of key words and emotionally charged slogans and programs—conspire to make it very difficult for the average person to develop a realistic understanding of the way the world is tending. Even in the best of times, political discourse tends to be uninformative. To say of someone that he is making a "political speech" is in essence to warn that what he says should not be taken seriously.

Yet whatever we say or believe, political actions do have consequences, some of which develop independently of those the politicians intend or the public expects. The slogans and fantasies of politics give way to specific actions which affect our lives. That the effects are obscure and the connections less than obvious does not make them any less real. In the end, when the disparity between political illusion and reality becomes too drastic to be sustained, there must be a revolution in thinking. That means going beyond slogans and questions of partisanship—

to think anew about economic relationships which are ordinarily too difficult to grapple with. We must make this effort if we are to retain, let alone improve, our quality of life.

In America, as indeed in the entire Western world today, the people are being steadily impoverished, not only in spite of political gestures toward prosperity but also because of them. As politics dominates more and more aspects of life, the information deficit upon which society operates increases. The rhetorical and political allegiances which have brought us to this condition no longer work. Even without the ability to comprehend what is happening in all its details, we should at least see enough to grasp this, and perhaps begin to sever those distorting allegiances.

The evidence of impending failure is all about us to take to heart, if we will. This evidence is not merely statistical. It can be read in a thousand ways in any shopping center: the disquiet, the now declining expectations, the deep hunch that what one buys will not perform as it ought to, and that what one repairs will not stay repaired. And it is more—the recognition that additional money is not enough when hamburgers sell at steak prices and all the while the farmers go bust.

Something is wrong. The survival of the progressive way of life and of the middle class itself may be at stake. When survival is the issue, it is worth the effort of thinking anew. We must transcend the current political context by seeking a new, more vivid understanding of the factors which bear on a satisfactory evolution of society.

4

The Illusions of Politics

We must regard industrial and commercial life, not as a
separate and detached region of activity, but as an organic
part of our whole personal and social life; and we shall
find the clue to the conduct of men in their commercial
relations, not in the first instance amongst those characteristics wherein our pursuit of industrial objects differs from
our pursuit of pleasure or of learning, or our efforts for
some political and social ideal, but rather amongst those
underlying principles of conduct and selection wherein they
all resemble each other. . . .

—*Philip H. Wicksteed*

Contemporary politics does not have an answer for the declining living
standards of the middle class. As already indicated, the problem is not
a matter of conservative-liberal partisanship. If it were that simple, we
should have a fifty-fifty chance of seeing all the evils undone. Sooner
or later, the losing party would win, institute its programs, and prosperity would be restored. Unfortunately, the actual conduct of government under all parties seems to be very much the same. While it would
be grandiloquent to say that it does not matter who is elected, in most
cases it matters so little that the task of a citizen trying to preserve the
quality of his life with a ballot is akin to that of a child trying to spell
with the wrong blocks. He can never get it right. One reason is that we
lack a public philosophy to describe adequately what goes on in a
mixed economy.

33

Almost every politician who enters office carries with him intellectual baggage which impedes his ability either to perceive or to implement policies which are good for the public. He believes that he is someone set aside from the mass of men. He believes that there are two distinct sectors of life—the public and the private—operating on different principles, and he is a leader of the public sector, whose job it is to rein in the greed of unfettered production and operate institutions based upon different motives—community, equality, and fair play. The politician, so he tells himself, and so he is told, has more important things to occupy his attention than grabby, material necessities. He and the government to which he is attached are referees. Their job is to make the rules to suit the public good and see that all the players act accordingly. This is a view that is about 10 percent accurate and 90 percent deluded—because even today, two hundred years into the industrial age, we have yet to adopt a truly modern approach to understanding political economy.

What conventional economics largely ignores is that politics is as much a route to wealth as is production. You or anyone else who can attain the assent of a few hundred politicians can radically and substantially alter the profitability of almost any activity. A firm producing a superior shoe polish at an attractive price can be bankrupted by any of 101 provisions of the Shoe Polish Reform Act of 1983. By the same token, the worst shoe polish ever produced, as far as quality and price are concerned, can nevertheless be the most rewarding if its principals can coddle or connive politicians into subsidizing it. Those politicians can give the firm gobs of money, choke off competition, or buy tons of the stuff for GI's to curse over when they black the Army's boots.

Such developments are by no means unheard of. They are at the heart of economic life today, as anyone should realize who reads the newspapers. The fact is, however, that most academic economists do not explicitly recognize these developments, or to the extent that they do, they treat the consequences of political activity as a special case. Once this is realized, it becomes clear why so much so-called sophisticated economic reasoning proves to be well wide of the mark. The premise from which the logic proceeds is too narrow by half. It proposes that individuals, motivated by self-interest, will participate in the process of production to maximize their profits—*within the rules.* Investors, managers, and workers all are supposed to join in producing better goods and services at lower prices, not because they have a religious dedication to the well-being of others, but because in so doing they bring home the bacon. The more they can satisfy the needs and desires of consumers, the higher their profits and the more readily they can afford the eggs and the milk, as well as the marmalade and the English muffins.

The catch here is the assumption that the rules have already been determined. If this were true, conventional economics would have more to tell us about what goes on in the real world. But politicians are constantly changing the rules under which people act. New rules, regulations, and laws are being churned out in an almost incomprehensible volume. It is obvious, therefore, that the rules are *not* determined. Not only can they be changed, they are in a constant state of upheaval. Since the actions of politicians in changing the rules under which society operates are more significant than anything else in determining what rewards people may obtain and keep in their workaday activities, no theory of human action which excludes politics from the equation can illuminate what goes on in today's mixed economy.

The current theoretical orthodoxy is simply anachronistic. It is more suited to the predemocratic era. Hundreds of years ago, when the first extended efforts were made toward understanding how people's actions fit together in productive activity, economists could have safely assumed that the rules were determined. Even persons whose counterparts in today's society could elect presidents really had no share in power. Political office was almost exclusively a hereditary privilege. Only once in a very great while did someone who was not born to power rise to the position where he could actually change the laws of the society in which he lived. Certainly the up-and-coming Europeans of the eighteenth century had scant opportunity to become kings of their countries. Nor did they expect, unless they were court intimates, that the king and his party would intervene to change the laws on their individual account. Under those conditions, there was a sanction in experience for the notion that productive activity was the way for an individual to maximize his profits. He had no other choice. That being the case, the distorting effects of excluding politics from economic analysis were much less severe.

Furthermore, the tendency to think in terms of a society in which the rules were set on a permanent basis was reinforced by the strong rationalist bias of the Enlightenment. The supposition that there are self-evident truths to which all rational men assent in a scientific way tended to obscure the genuinely difficult problem of why individuals obey rules. Utilitarians, such as Bentham, who set out to define the conditions of law under which a society could prosper economically, assumed all too readily that the general good would be such a lively goal in a society of rational actors as to make for universal assent to the rules. According to the Utilitarians, each individual would support rule-making for general prosperity because it would be in his long-range interest to do so. But this is not necessarily true, as the late Oxford political theorist John Plamenatz has pointed out:

> . . . not only Bentham, but others, too, have taken it for granted that, if it is in someone's interests that a rule be generally obeyed, it must also be his long-term interest to obey it himself. This, in strict logic, is not true. For example, if a man has been for a long time a successful thief, and has good grounds for confidence in his own skill for continued success, it is not in his interest, not even in long-term interest, to observe the rule requiring him to abstain from what belongs to others. Yet it is within his interest that the rule be generally obeyed. For if it is not obeyed by the great majority of people the social order on which he, as much as the honest man, depends to achieve his purposes (or to maximize the satisfaction of his wants), will disintegrate. His long-term interest is that the rule be generally obeyed except by himself and his partners in crime, if he has any.[1]

The thief maximizes his profits when the rules allow an exception for him. If he could, he would explicitly amend the law to grant himself a license to steal. This would improve his standing, from a self-interested perspective, by reducing his exposure to punishment while still granting him the benefits of having others conform to the rules. And it is not the thief alone who has an interest in seeing that rules are changed to benefit him. When a method is available through politics for an individual to adapt the rules of society in a way specifically directed to his own cause, then the rules themselves are *means* to *ends*.

Our thinking about how society works must take this into account. When the rules of society become means to an end, they become the logical equivalents to shops, barns, factories, mines, or anything else which is a means to economic advancement, from the herbalist's hoe to the rock star's tight pants. What this suggests is that *politics can create new forms of property which can be of just as much economic value as any tangible item of production.* As former Supreme Court Justice William O. Douglas commented:

> We are living in a society where one of the most important forms of property is government largesse which some call the "new property."

> . . . The payrolls of government are but one aspect of that "new property" . . . multifarious forms of contracts are another part. So are subsidies . . . disbursements by government for scientific research . . . "social welfare."[2]

This new political property will be just as much subject to competition as any other object of value.

This being true, it is no longer even a tolerable distortion to assume that politicians and bureaucrats operate outside the economic structure as something akin to "referees" or "arbiters" of unbridled economic competition. On the contrary, they are participants in the competition, just like everyone else.

These observations are important because they go to the heart of much of the current confusion about prosperity and how to attain it. The realization that the politician and bureaucrat are not imposing their wills upon the economy from the outside, but rather are part of the whole structure of it, points toward a more modern view of economics. That means acknowledging the fact that the politician and bureaucrat, no less than the steel baron and auto salesman, pursue their own self-interest. For too long we have assumed that because the ostensible goals of politicians were to "serve the public interest," they were somehow doing only that. Their decisions, theoretically at least, were to be based upon an informed regard for the well-being of all, rather than on what was good for them personally. But there is no evidence to prove the politicians or bureaucrats incorporate a higher regard for the interest of others in their decisions than do people in any other walk of life. Because they are just people, they act as all people do. Political theorist Morris P. Fiorina put it this way:

> Most people most of the time act in their own self-interest. This is not to say that human beings seek only to amass tangible wealth, but rather to say that human beings seek to achieve their own ends—tangible and intangible—rather than the ends of their fellow men.[3]

This is not to say, of course, that individuals must always be remorselessly selfish in the narrow sense of the word. To note that all action is self-interested is not to foreclose the possibility that strangers will rescue widows from burning buildings, parents will sacrifice for their children, and many human beings are devoted enough to ideals of justice and freedom to fight against tanks with cobblestones. All this is true without detracting from the usefulness of analyzing behavior in

37

terms of self-interest. Rewards and costs may be psychic as well as material. Indeed, it is recognition of the fact that man is a complicated being—with desires and preferences which point in several directions—that gives the fullest understanding of the admirable aspects of human nature. It is far meaner to assume that in large categories of man's behavior, his action is not his own, which is to say that much which is noble in his values is imposed from outside himself. To assume that if man is self-interested he must be narrow and cruel is not only mistaken, it is a slur on human character. To think in terms of self-interest is merely to focus upon the connections between all actions: they arise from the preferences and goals of individuals and are taken with a view to their relative costs and rewards.

If, as we assume, the man who manufactures Shinola is primarily in business to obtain a high standard of living for himself and his family, we would be wrong to assume less of the politician and the bureaucrat. Most people, most of the time, enjoy having more rather than less. They want to attain the highest standard of living they can. So while they may be and probably are well-intentioned toward their fellows, they will be generous only when their interests allow. They will not be saints or fools. Neither the purveyor of Shinola nor the bureaucrat at his desk will generally and routinely act so as to reduce his own income and quality of life. That is the way the world works.

People are generally interested in bringing as much capital as possible under their effective control. To do so, they are willing to recognize implicitly that politics is as much a road to advancement as any form of productive activity. When politics can transform the rules of society, creating new, abstract forms of property, this creates opportunities which individuals will seize no matter what their actions imply for overall social well-being. Most people do not care, really, how the capital which they employ came into being. Nor do they care who the theoretical owner of the capital may be. What counts for most people is the practical effect. Whether their prosperity is based upon legal ownership of tangible capital or *de facto* control of intangible assets created through politics, they will take the best opportunities which circumstances offer.

As a practical matter, this is the philosophy of even so benighted an authority as Leonid Brezhnev, whose dozens of limousines, country estates, and all but infinite entertainment budget give him a power to dispose of wealth which is the equal of any man's. Even if he is absolutely sincere in supporting the *legal* abolition of the private ownership of capital, he still remains one of the earth's wealthiest men by virtue of his *de facto economic* ownership of just about any object which it is within the resources of the Soviet system to produce. This is a matter which can be better understood by referring to the analysis of Aleksander Bajt, one of Yugoslavia's Marxist economists. Bajt is known for his explicit admission that the legal control of capital by the state need not prohibit economic ownership. He says:

> According to Marx's economic and social doctrine, there have to be distinguished, from the viewpoint of relations of production which form the social content of an economy, property in the *economic* and property in the *juridical*, or legal sense. . . . In the economic sense of the word, the owner of a factor is the one to whom the income of this factor flows. . . . [T]he legal structure of property does not necessarily reflect its economic counterpart. The legal owner, let us say of a house, may be one person, and the economic owner quite another person, for instance the tenant who, as a result of legal regulations, does not pay a rent which is higher than depreciation, does not pay, in other words, any price for services he employs. He is, in effect, the economic owner of the house.[4]

To this we might add, even if the state is the legal owner of a palace, the economic owner may be Mr. Brezhnev.

Dozens of people everywhere have realized that one can control capital without technically owning it. Almost everyone, from the Guru Maharaji to the assistant deputy to the assistant in the Department of Health, Education and Welfare wants to bring more capital under his disposal rather than less. And this does not necessarily mean legally owning the productive implements. Comrade Brezhnev has proven that. So have the managers of many of America's biggest corporations. They do not legally own more than an infinitesimal percentage of the assets they control. They merely profit from them. The legal owners figure so slightly in the operation of most of the larger, established businesses that for many practical purposes they might as well not exist at all. Mutual life-insurance companies are theoretically owned by the policy-holders. Yet this does not prevent the capital they accrue from increasing the living standards of the managers. This is not the result of any form of misfeasance or malfeasance. It is simply a reflection of the fact that one does not need to own capital to enjoy it. He need only control it.

One reason that so many denominations of unorthodox religious faiths spring up is that they offer an appealing way for individuals to control capital—without necessarily holding it in legal ownership. In

1964 a Californian named Kirby Hensley began to mass-market this insight by establishing the Universal Life Church. After studying Section 501 (c) (3) of the Internal Revenue Service Code of 1954, Hensley incorporated his home as a tax-exempt religious institution. When the IRS application was approved, Hensley began to confer ministerial degrees upon his friends and neighbors in exchange for a charitable contribution of two dollars apiece. By deeding their property to the Universal Life Church they could avoid many of the legal liabilities which fall upon "owners"—such as taxes—without forgoing the use of the capital. The fact that the Universal Life Church is one of the faster growing religious denominations in the United States demonstrates that there is wide popular familiarity, even among persons of modest means, with the fact that *it is the control of capital, not the legal ownership, that counts.*

Once this is realized, it becomes clear why a new way of looking at the search for fortune is needed. We cannot continue to pretend that individuals will seek to amass the greatest possible store of wealth through economic production, not when there are more rewarding alternatives at hand. When the opportunity presents itself to obtain higher rewards through participation in politics or profiting from political decisions, the average person will do so.

5

The Three Species
of Capital

> Entrepreneurs have left the frontier and now dwell in tent
> camps on the edge of government. A tycoon is someone
> like Joseph Califano, who knows how to corner a market
> of federal funds. The rest toil to shape legislation that
> shows the necessity of purchasing 100 new jet fighters or
> maintaining a moribund domestic industry like shoes or
> sugar. Fortunes are made by correctly anticipating a gov-
> ernment regulation.
>
> —*The editors of* Harper's

For the purposes of this analysis, it seems useful to assume that an individual seeking to make his way in the world has three choices: he can throw his lot with *productive capital*; he can turn toward *static capital*—what the Germans call *sachwerte;* or he can seek the rewards which politics substitutes for tangible capital—what financial writer Scott Burns has called, doubtless with apologies to Emerson, *transcendental capital*.

Productive capital includes any investment which has as its object the creation of additional goods and services for sale in the market-place. A stamping press would be productive capital. So would a share in the ownership of the stamping press, or in the company which produces stamping presses. A television transmitter, a bowling alley, a tractor, a carpenter's tool chest, even a poet's pen would all be examples of productive capital. And of course, one need not be the owner of tangible assets in order to cast his lot with production. Every individual owns his own time, which he invests as he sees fit, sometimes by working in productive enterprises.

While production is obviously the basis of all capital accumulation, productive activity is not always rewarding. In fact, over the past decade in America it has been decreasingly so. Fifty thousand dollars invested in stocks in 1968 had maintained only about half that spending power by 1978. Investors in corporate bonds had lost about 40 percent of their 1973 wealth five years later. The average worker in the productive sector actually experienced a decline in purchasing power so that his real disposable income is several hundred dollars lower than it was in 1968. As the rewards for production have shrunk, most people who have sought to maintain their livelihoods through production have suffered.

By contrast, static capital is not invested with a view toward producing anything. It includes any tangible item of value which is not employed in the production of additional goods and services. A diamond, a rare stamp, a Honus Wagner 1913 baseball card, a bar of gold, or perhaps, in some sense, even the family home, could be examples of static capital. These are investments which are essentially unproductive. They are not intended to yield any tangible output. The diamond jewelry is itself the ultimate product.

It is in the nature of things that very few individuals can derive their livelihoods solely from the trading of static capital. In the first instance, only persons of considerable wealth could hope to attain sufficient appreciation from the holding and exchange of static assets in order to yield a comfortable living. This means that in practical terms, most individuals who rely upon static capital accumulation do so only partially. Most must depend primarily upon productive capital, or the third alternative, transcendental capital. This is not to say, however, that nonproductive investments of tangible wealth do not yield substantial returns. A study by Salomon Brothers revealed that wealth invested in Chinese ceramics over the last decade obtained a compounded annual rate of growth of 19.2 percent. Investments in gold yielded 16.3 percent; coins 13 percent; diamonds 12.6 percent; silver 9.1 percent. Since consumer prices rose by an average of less than 7 percent a year, static capital provided a substantial positive rate of return. The Salomon Brothers study does not exaggerate. Better rates of return have been realized in many static capital investments. One thousand dollars invested in 1966 in an average American stamp collection was worth $10,799 by 1976. A thousand-dollar emerald from 1966 was worth between $4,000 and $6,000 ten years later. A Siam ruby worth between $25 and $50 in 1966 had risen to $800 in value by 1976. A $50,000 collection of antique automobiles in 1966 was worth on the average $262,000 in 1976. These returns dwarf what was obtained in typical productive capital investments during that same period. Even the family home has appreciated in value far more than any of the productive factors which contribute to the building of the home. Each $10,000 invested in a home in 1966 was worth almost $20,000 by 1976, and the appreciation is continuing to accelerate.

These developments have hardly gone unnoticed. More than six million investors have dropped out of the stock markets to shift their investments into nonproductive, tangible assets. Money which in the past would have been invested in equity markets or otherwise placed in productive savings has been put into static capital, as alert individuals have taken advantage of the higher returns which these investments have offered.

But as we shall see, by far the most profitable method of accumulating wealth these days is in the form of transcendental capital. This form of wealth is not capital at all in the conventional sense, it is merely a substitute by which an individual enjoys returns on the capital owned by someone else.

A pure form of transcendental capital would be a general requisition order authorizing the bearer to confiscate whatever he needed or desired under the spurs of severe penalties. Such writs have been fairly common in the past, especially during periods of war. For example, in 1512 the Raetian Republic (which once occupied the area now comprising the Swiss canton of Graubünden) seized the rich Tellina Valley (now part of northern Italy). The conquerors wasted no time in organizing plunder on a wide scale. "One judge," as a recent history put it, "passed an arbitrary sentence of death on anyone who appeared before him, for whatever reason. It is a tribute to the catalyzing effect of fear on human generosity that this particular individual amassed in 15 months a fortune surpassing that of his most imaginative colleagues."[1] Since the judge's threat was entirely credible, backed as it was by a conquering army, the hapless residents were obliged to yield up anything which excited the interest of someone favored with an order from the judge. Any documentary evidence of his pleasure was bought and sold just like any other object of value. Indeed, the transcendental-capital claims were more valuable than the actual property that was the object of the plunder. The nominal owners of capital under such circumstances were largely the owners of liabilities. Persons favored with the judge's writs could demand almost anything of their victims and obtain it under penalty of death. The skyrocketing value of transcendental capital under those circumstances reduced the worth of actual productive assets. Only persons who had wealth which could be easily moved and hidden were able to survive the occupation without being reduced to poverty. Gold coins, which could be buried or carried away, were worth much more than a fine business or a productive farm.

Thankfully, the ways in which the proprietors of transcendental capital extract their profits have become more subtle through the intervening centuries. Their claims are now organized on a less terrible basis. Yet the same principles obtain.

If this is not often discussed frankly, perhaps it is for the reason suggested by the seventeenth-century wit Sir George Savile, Marquis of Halifax. "A man," he said, "that should call everything by its right name would hardly pass the streets without being knocked down as a common enemy." This is at least partially true. Most of the time, most people prefer not to recall that the basis of political power is force— the force policemen will exert in escorting you to the penitentiary if you do not submit to the claims of transcendental capital as most of us pale and flabby souls do. To consider an informing example, the IRS may say that our tax system is one of "voluntary compliance." But life cannot be so far emancipated from fact. As the late Joseph Schumpeter wrote: "The theory which construes taxes on the analogy of club dues or the purchase of the services of, say, a doctor only proves how far removed this part of the social sciences is from scientific habits of mind."[2] Politics today, as in the past, is still the business of plunder, now modified through the forms of law so that we seldom execute resisters. Yet one form of capital punishment remains: *The increasing value of transcendental claims reduces the worth of every productive asset, drawing away and consuming hundreds of billions of dollars annually.*

If matters have become more subtle since the unabashed plunder of the Tellina Valley in the ruder past, they have also become more complicated. The penetration of politics into almost every aspect of normal life has multiplied transcendental-capital claims almost beyond numbering. Since politicians in power must garner the votes of about 20 percent of the adult population, they are obliged to share the spoils as widely as possible. Not only are millions of persons dependent directly upon government for their livelihoods, millions of others have their current income enhanced or guaranteed by a transcendental-capital claim.

Firms such as Lockheed and General Dynamics have attained payments in excess of hundreds of millions simply to guarantee their continued profitable existence. When they cannot sell their products or count on the returns from productive investments to keep cash in the till, they can count on politics. Public Law 85-804 enables them to draw upon other people's incomes to subsidize their expenses.

And not merely government contractors, but as a practical matter, almost any well-connected corporation in a pinch could draw upon political income. Already, government agencies at all levels spend the equivalent of $2,000 per family to purchase otherwise unsold or unsalable goods from corporations. In effect, if not by law, most of the very largest corporations enjoy a transcendental-capital claim which they could exercise in a cash-flow crisis. For example, during its liquidity difficulties of the early 1970's, the Chrysler Corporation reportedly averted bankruptcy only through intervention inspired by the Federal Reserve. In the fall of 1979, Chrysler was again standing in line in Washington. Even without a crisis, the transcendental-capital claims of existing business institutions have the force of law in the form of regulations, quotas, tariffs, and other legal measures to direct income in ways other than would be the case with open competition. And not just industries: doctors, lawyers, and other professionals also profit mightily from regulations which grant them an effective claim upon productive wealth.

It is hard to think of these common political favors and privileges as transcendental-capital claims. How can a regulation be the capital equivalent of money in the bank or some tangible productive implement, such as a spray-painting machine or a computer?

Part of the difficulty in appreciating the value of transcendental capital is the fact that it is seldom for sale. Except for government bonds, one cannot usually obtain a transcendental-capital claim on an impartial, straightforward basis.

An exception to this rule is the taxi medallion. It is a grant of regulatory power, a license which permits a driver to operate a vehicle for hire. These medallions sell for very high prices—for tens of thousands of dollars. In fact, the transcendental-capital cost of operating a taxicab is typically greater than the productive cost. You could buy or rent an automobile, fill it with gas, install a meter, and turn out into the streets for customers for a fraction of the cost of purchasing a taxi medallion in a city like New York or Chicago.[3] If other transcendental-capital claims, such as licenses to do business, tariff exclusions, and government pension benefits, were put up for sale, they too would command very great prices indeed.

Among the more depressing transcendental-capital claims are those which are, in effect, subsidies for the incompetent or the incapacitated. They include such familiar expenditures as welfare payments, unemployment compensation, and a wide variety of income-transfer programs which have come to include federal disability payment for just about any form of hurt.

For persons with a narrow range of opportunities, the attractiveness of succumbing to subsidized incapacity can be great. In most instances, qualification is easy to establish, and can be maintained without a taxing effort. While the typical rewards are low, the programs are so poorly policed that there are opportunities for enterprising claimants to obtain overpayments, with minimal prosecution, even for overt fraud. In one case, Linda Taylor of Chicago allegedly collected $400,000 in a five-year period by using wigs and disguises to establish fifteen false identities. According to reports, she passed herself off variously as a black, white, Chicano, or Filipino woman between the ages of twenty and fifty. For her virtuosity at bamboozling the welfare board, she enjoyed all the trimmings of the high life: luxury automobiles, lavish penthouse apartments, and foreign vacations, all financed from an income greater than that received by 99 percent of America's families.

Admittedly, Miss Taylor's case is out of the ordinary. But it is instructive of the fact that opportunities for substantial transcendental-capital gains do exist in programs of income redistribution. Fraud of that magnitude indicates widespread abuse. Robert Carlson, former commissioner of welfare for HEW, indicated several years ago that there were then at least 900,000 totally ineligible welfare recipients drawing benefits. In Michigan a cross check of welfare rolls with payrolls of just two major corporations turned up 6,000 possible cases of fraud. In New York City, a comparison of welfare rolls with census data indicated that there might be as many as 100,000 phantom children enrolled in the AID program. These examples only begin to tell the story. A 1976 study of welfare recipients in the city of Washington, conducted by the Department of Human Resources, found that 54 percent of the general welfare recipients were ineligible.

Whether these unhappy individuals were technically meant to be receiving disability subsidies or not, most were clearly enjoying something less than a handsome living. Yet welfare benefits are not to be sniffed at as inadequate when they are more rewarding than the opportunities available in productive activity. In thirty-four counties of the state of New York, for example, the state's basic welfare grant, plus food stamps and other subsidies for incapacity, exceed the after-tax income of the average blue-collar worker. In Hamilton County, recent figures showed it was $2,834 more profitable to receive welfare than to be employed. For the state as a whole, the average tax-free benefits to four-member welfare households came to $7,742, or about one dollar a day less than the after-tax income of the state's average blue-collar worker.

As these figures suggest, individuals in many cases can realize increases in their purchasing power while freeing their time completely by qualifying for a disability subsidy. As of 1977, workers in their early twenties with as little as 1½ years participation in the labor market could retire and receive benefits 38 percent higher than their after-tax income prior to disability. The average benefit was $517 monthly tax-free, with a maximum as high as $1,051.

There are still higher rewards for the administrators of income-redistribution programs. They qualify for substantial current salaries, which all but uniformly exceed the averages available for persons participating in production. Furthermore, the administrators have not been above profiting from the lax controls which they impose upon the programs in their charge. In New York City, 805 cases of welfare cheating by city employees were uncovered in one recent six-month period.[4] In Washington, D.C., nineteen employees of the Department of Human Resources were accused of collecting part of $300,000 in welfare fraud. In California, several former social workers were convicted of running a night school for welfare cheaters. They employed techniques they had learned while working in welfare departments to help their students to maximize fraudulent income. They showed people how to successfully create aliases, employ false telephone numbers and fake addresses, and earn income for the support of nonexistent dependents. In exchange for these tutorials, the social workers collected a commission of between 20 percent and 50 percent of their graduates' welfare income, earning $300,000 in three years. There are many examples such as these illustrating a point which should by now be obvious—that when one offers people money for being incapacitated, he is creating a market for incapacity which will produce its own supply. By most accounts, being paid for what one cannot do is easy money. The long-run tendency of people to succumb to the lure of easy money is more than a match for any fitful efforts at policing the eligibility of recipients.

Unemployment compensation is another subsidy to incapacity which has grown in attractiveness over the years. Almost half of those included in the normal unemployment statistics were neither laid off nor fired. Labor Department studies suggest that as many as one in five people collecting unemployment compensation choose to remain unemployed. One reason is that some families can increase their take-home pay by quitting their jobs and collecting tax-free unemployment benefits, which are often supplemented by welfare payments and food stamps.

The realization that unemployment compensation can represent an attractive alternative to employment and productive enterprise is not confined to those who read Harvard economist Martin Feldstein's papers. *Fortune* magazine reported that some senior labor-union members are now bargaining for the right to be laid off first. If so, they are merely catching up with many of their fellows who routinely depend upon unemployment compensation to finance extended periods of leisure. The state of New York has mailed more than 20,000 unemployment checks to southern Florida and other vacation spots in a single week. Instead of the unemployment compensation representing an insurance payment to buffer people during short lapses between jobs, the situation has been effectively reversed for many. Many now work only for short times between unemployment. One man even set up his own company to qualify himself for unemployment benefits. He would pay just enough into the system to meet the minimum requirement, "fire" himself, and then collect unemployment for the maximum period of time. His efforts prove that transcendental capitalists understand the spirit of enterprise.

All this is no more than is known in every garage and barber shop. Yet, even with malingering raised to a pitch of invention of the sort which has not been seen since the death of Thomas Edison, it is a plain fact that neither normal welfare nor unemployment provides a sufficient income to support typical recipients at a truly superior standard of living. With the total available benefits varying widely between states, an average effective income of more than $8,000 is difficult to obtain, even with the combination of food stamps, general state welfare as-sistance, aid to families with dependent children, railroad unemployment insurance, trade-adjustment allowances, city and county welfare benefits, low-income-housing allowances, subsidies to heads of households, and general aid to the Indians. Assuming that all of these benefits in cash and kind are tax-free, they are equivalent to the annual yield on a sum of less than $150,000 in capital. Of course, this is more than the average participant in production owns, so even the lowest transcendental capitalist has, in the economic sense, a superior claim to America's wealth. Yet it is far less than can be obtained in the most rewarding of the programs to subsidize incapacity. If one is to become a true tycoon of transcendental capital, he must devote *time* to qualify for the disability subsidies available to government employees.

Consider the possibilities open to policemen in Washington, D.C. In one recent year, 97 percent of all retiring policemen and firemen in the District of Columbia were granted disability status, with their retirement income essentially tax-free. One of these former policemen is Johnny Arellano. He joined the Washington police force, worked for a few years, and retired on disability with a bad back at age thirty-one. His tax-free monthly income amounts to $500, about what one could obtain from $100,000 in capital. This amount will increase as inflation adjustments expand Arellano's monthly payments. Precisely what value this inflation insurance will have is impossible to know, but it is bound to be considerable, more than you could buy in any known private annuity. True, Arellano paid for his income by suffering the misfortune of back trouble. But this has not altogether left him incapacitated. In fact, if the advertisements of a local outdoor-equipment and sporting-goods store were accurate, Mr. Arellano was doing his best to stay active. One ad shows Arellano posing with a backpack. He is described as a

> . . . resident authority on bike touring. His next trip: Williamsburg, Virginia, to Seattle! Right now, though, he's busy with cross country skiing. A native American, Johnny has seen lots of this country's wilderness. . . .

If this lends to an impression that Arellano may be spectacularly fit in spite of his disabilities, he denies that this involves anything wrong. As he told *The Washington Post*, "I am just trying to lead a normal life. Why shouldn't I?"[5]

Indeed, Arellano's transcendental-capital gains have not been extraordinary. They have been *below average*, which is what makes his case so interesting by way of illustration. For his dozen or so years on the Washington police force, he accumulated an annual transcendental-capital gain which amounted to about $6,500. The typical retiring D.C. policeman who left the force at age forty-five with nineteen years service obtained an annual transcendental-capital gain of $20,107.93. That is the amount of productive capital he would have had to save each year in order to accumulate the typical D.C. policeman's expected-lifetime retirement income of $700,000. Since as of January 1, 1977, 82 percent of the city's retired police officers and 83 percent of the retired firemen were considered disabled, most of their incomes will be tax-free. This, of course, makes the productive-capital equivalent even greater. To obtain $700,000 in after-tax return would necessitate, even on conservative assumptions, an annual savings of $28,725. That is big money, more than twice the average annual after-tax income of the typical person participating in production.

Clearly, the transcendental-capital gains available through qualification for government disability claims are among the more lucrative financial possibilities in today's economy. It is little wonder that the number of persons discovering incapacitating disabilities multiplies tremendously upon qualification for benefits. Almost no difficulty is too trivial to be considered. One man actually retired on disability from the Washington police force with a "stiff trigger finger."

Sounds illegal, doesn't it? It is not. In fact the retirement boards in question have approved 98 percent of the disability applications for whatever reason. It is routine and automatic. As one budget officer told *The Washington Post*: "It's not a matter of taking advantage of loopholes. The door is wide open."[6] Everyone, from Johnny Arellano to former city Police Chief Maurice J. Cullanane has walked right through it. Cullanane retired on a $31,000-a-year tax-free pension to compensate him for a knee injury he received when kicked by a demonstrator in 1968. If Cullanane lives to be sixty-nine, which is the normal life expectancy for a man his age, he will receive more than one million dollars, thus making the demonstrator's kick the most valuable piece of athletic footwork since Pele first won the World Cup for Brazil.

This is not to say that Chief Cullanane did not suffer a perfectly genuine injury. Indeed, this may have been the case with all these retiring civil servants. However, it is at least as plausible that many of the disabilities which beset so many apparently rugged policemen and firemen are magnified out of proportion because of the transcendental-capital gain which incapacity creates. Life is full of bumps and bruises which cumulatively drive us toward disability. How easy it must be to find some accident or affliction which still hurts when we are paid tens of thousands and even hundreds of thousands to do so. Put plainly, when the spirit is willing, the flesh is weak.

This is a truism which by no means applies only to Washington, D.C.'s finest. One federal civil servant who retired on the grounds that he was disabled, for example, earned an average of almost $64,000 a year in a new job after his disability. A Civil Service Commission report showed that another disability pensioner had earned a total of $100,943 in 1975 and 1976 while drawing a substantial disability pension. Disability claims have become so lucrative that private consultants have sprung up to advise government employees on how to obtain disability settlements and pensions. One consultant alone, working in a single naval shipyard, was reportedly responsible for inducing 2,500 claims, 90 percent of which were approved. One retired civil servant, then seventy-five years old, received an award of $42,000 to compensate him for hearing losses related to his job—even though he had not been exposed to any noise louder than an office typewriter since 1929.

While the disability settlements for government employees can in some instances approach magnificent proportions, they are by no means the only substantial forms of transcendental capital available. The normal salaries and pension benefits which can be obtained through government far outstrip what can be earned on the average by devoting oneself to production. For example, the average federal pay for civilian workers in 1977 exceeded the average pay for people engaged in production, by at least 22 percent—$13,936 to $11,092. This difference is compounded by government fringe benefits, which exceed those in productive life by more than 50 percent. The typical federal employee, for example, receives almost twice as much vacation pay—$1,140—as the typical employee of business—$636. Government sick leave is more than 200 percent more generous than what can be had from most private firms. And this is just the beginning of the disparity.

Federal employees may retire with full benefits at age fifty-five; military personnel, even earlier. One living a normal life span would expect to receive $465,000. By contrast, a commission chaired by former budget director Charles J. Zwick determined that the average nongovernment pensioner will retire with benefits averaging only 40 percent of final pay—at age sixty-two. From that point, he can anticipate lifetime benefits of only about $135,000 in 1978 dollars. His plan will not be protected against inflation. This means that continuation of a 7-percent average inflation for the next decade would reduce every thousand dollars the nongovernment pensioner receives to less than $500 in purchasing power. Meanwhile, the political pension is fully protected. In fact, from 1965 to 1976 the typical retiree from a government job had his pension increased 156 percent while the cost of living rose by 80.4 percent.

So while government employees begin with pension benefits that are three to four times higher than what can be had in productive life, this is only the beginning. As inflation accelerates, so does the advantage of securing a government pension claim.

This advantage is compounded by the fact that there are at least sixty-eight federal pension plans to choose from, and the same individual can qualify for benefits under several. Military employees, for example, can retire as early as age thirty-eight and receive 50 percent of their base pay, so they have the leisure to qualify for additional government checks. At least 125,000 persons have done so, going back on the government payroll again as "double dippers." Most of these are also entitled to Social Security, as indeed are more than half of all federal civilian retirees. These "double dippers" are the only ones for whom Social Security represents a profitable investment. Because most federal workers are not subject to Social Security tax in the normal course of events, they do not pay during all their working lifetimes as do people in the productive sector. Nonetheless, by taking odd jobs or finding employment after early retirement, more than half of all government pensioners are able to qualify for Social Security benefits anyway. They can take advantage of a quirk in the law that was supposed to benefit low-income workers. Since the benefits are distorted to pay more to those who contribute less, the "double dippers" can end up with a 100-percent to even 500-percent return or more on the money they invest. By contrast, the average young person working in the productive sector, subject to Social Security tax all his life, would have to live to be more than one hundred years old to recover the principal capital amount—without interest—that Social Security taxes will confiscate during his working lifetime. Further, more than two-thirds of all nongovernment pension plans reduce the pensioner's benefits when Social Security is also received. This does not happen in government.

It is possible right now for one sufficiently alert to the fine art of dipping into the government till to scoop out more than $75,000 annually. Those with real ingenuity are not "double dippers" but "triple dippers," taking in military, civil-service, and Social Security checks. Somewhere, there are assuredly "quadruple dippers," federal judges who receive full pay for life, $65,000, plus civil-service retirement pay, plus military pay, plus Social Security. Who knows what the limit is?

The advantages of investing one's life in the pursuit of transcendental capital are so numerous and so substantial from a purely material viewpoint that they are beyond denying. Not only does transcendental capital grow more rapidly and assuredly in value, it is almost never subject to expropriation. Since all those who run the government have an almost equal share in continuing to deal themselves the spoils of political power, the transcendental-capital claims are about as well-guaranteed as anything in this unpredictable world could be. They do not even seem to arouse the envy of the neighbors. Political debate focuses almost entirely upon the supposed inequities and defects in the ownership of productive capital while glossing over far more gross disparities in the accumulation of transcendental capital. To make matters even more jolly for the transcendental capitalist, his invisible capital gains are almost never subject to taxation. While he is qualifying for his annuity by putting in time on the job, his invisible savings are compounding tax-free. This is why the most enterprising—those who have the sharpest eye for a dollar—go into government. That is where the rewards are.

The trouble with this is that *transcendental capital does not represent an asset to society, but a liability.* Every transcendental-capital gain attained by shrewd individuals pursuing their own interests is another claim upon wealth enforced through government action. To what does this lead? To *The Squeeze: the continued reduction in the value of productive activity as more and more burdens are loaded upon those who do produce.*

The explosive growth of transcendental capital has brought at least seventy million persons—almost a third of the entire population—to depend upon government for their income. Some estimates place the number even higher. Whatever the precise figure, there can be little doubt that the total claims now aimed at production are almost unimaginable. They include all the public debts of government agencies, as well as political loan and credit guarantees. They also include such liabilities as flood, mud-slide, and riot insurance, nuclear-accident indemnity, and contingent liabilities for crop failures They include the unfunded liabilities in the sixty-eight federal-government retirement or pension plans, as well as the present value of projected Social Security outlays. The total of these obligations is at least *$15 trillion*, or a sum roughly equal to what would be required to spend £900,000 per hour for every hour, day and night, from the birth of Christ to the present moment.

According to the Conference Board, this is a sum considerably in excess of the total value of everything else which exists in the United States. All tangible assets, every piece of land, public and private, every battleship, Ping-Pong ball, diamond ring, woman's shawl, and all the accumulated presidential and congressional and courthouse papers which have been deposited in every library and warehouse in the country, amount to a value of $6.2 trillion, or $28,611 per person. In other words, *transcendental-capital claims now dramatically exceed the total value of all the wealth in the United States.*

We have created a situation in which the most effective way for an individual to pursue his immediate economic interest is to create liabilities against production. In essence, we have created a competition to consume. And our economic orthodoxy is largely blind to this. The accepted method of perceiving economic orthodoxy is largely blind to this. The accepted method of perceiving economic activity—a Gross National Product computation—measures expenditures alone. Thus the economy can appear to be growing, not only from an increase in productive wealth but from an increase in expenditure resulting from the liquidation of wealth. Because the returns from the transcendental capital have long exceeded what can typically be obtained in production, much of the increase in our Gross National Product in recent years has been financed by a liquidation and drawing down of the accumulated reserves from productive activity in the past. The Gross National Product increases as more and more and more dollars pass through people's hands, yet the average individual suffers a decline in his real standard of living.

The way people live—the prices for lobster dinners and Alka-Seltzer, the distribution of Rinso Blue and cabins in Aspen—are all the outcome of *competition*, not only between economic producers, but between the various means to wealth. When production is rewarded, that makes for an increase in total wealth and consequently a greater abundance of material comfort for everyone. That means "progress." It means doing more for less. On the other hand, when the rewards for meeting challenges and performing well in productive tasks are reduced and even lowered below those available to persons staking out a transcendental-capital claim upon the production of others, then many of the more discerning, talented, and enterprising people become transcendental capitalists.

That is a major reason that government has become the largest growth entity in the Western world in recent decades. Politics is where the rewards are. The many individuals who wait in line for every employment opening in the federal government realize this. They recognize that the surest opportunity to obtain superior incomes and enjoyment of physical comfort which they seek for themselves and their families is to cast their lot with politics.

The shrewd dealers may indeed increase their private wealth and material well-being as transcendental capitalists. Individual business institutions, even whole industries, can prosper by substituting transcendental capital for productive capital as the basis of their income. Doctors, lawyers, and others can employ politics to wrench ever more resources from the remaining members of the public. But the magic which produces prosperity for these individuals does not rank with the miracle which fed the multitudes with five loaves and two fishes. It is a sleight of hand: a false shuffle by which some people live at the expense of their neighbors. Even if the neighbors do not decisively object, they will soon lack the resources needed to maintain the system.

That society cannot consume what it does not produce is by no means a startling revelation. Yet its implications have been unnecessarily obscured in our public philosophy. So long as we modeled our thinking on the notion that politics is a separate and different realm from economics, where different and more noble motivations apply, we could not see clearly enough how greed is stimulating a squeeze on production. The pursuit of self-interest by individuals does not stop short just because the means that they employ, the transcendental capital, cannot be straightforwardly bought and sold. The bureaucrat or politician who leaves his post to prospect for gold has not suddenly undergone a transformation. He, as much as anyone else, is the same character whether he is sitting behind the desk in his official capacity or shopping for a mortgage for a bigger and better home on his day off. In either case, he wants more rather than less. He is no detached arbiter of the excess of greed and the profit motive in the productive sector. He is part of them, first and last. Profiting through politics is not only possible, it is the overwhelming phenomenon of our time.

Part II
THE SQUEEZE

The menacing spectre of state bankruptcy drew ever nearer. The old remedy was prescribed: reduction in the value of the currency and increased taxation. . . . Thus began the fierce endeavour of the State to squeeze the population to the last drop. Since economic resources fell short of what was needed, the strong fought to secure the chief share for themselves with a violence and an unscrupulousness well in keeping with the origin of those in power. . . .

In these disturbed and catastrophic decades of the third century countless people, especially of the bourgeois middle-class, were impoverished, even ruined, and these were precisely the men who had brought into being and maintained the economic prosperity of former times. The wasteful policy of the State, the constant interference with private economic life, and the inflations, amounted to a landslide beneath which a vast amount that was of value was crushed out of existence.
  —*The Cambridge Ancient History,*
  Vol. XII

A people without history
Is not redeemed from time. . . .
  —*T. S. Eliot*

6

The Money Squeeze

> . . . of all the contrivances for cheating the laboring classes
> of mankind, none has been more effective than that which
> deludes them with paper money.
>
> —*Daniel Webster*

Samuel Butler (II) noted that "the three most important things a man
has are, briefly, his private parts, his money, and his religious opinions."
It would be a great sensual and spiritual misfortune if the average person knew no more of the other two points of this trinity than he does
about money. Nothing else which is so important is so little understood.
In fact, *the average American family is losing hundreds of dollars in
purchasing power each year because of inflation made possible by a
general misunderstanding of money.*

To see how you are being squeezed, you must look at money in a
new light. That means looking beyond the fact that you want more of
it. Everyone is so anxious to put money to his own use that he forgets
that it serves a function other than merely commanding resources.
Money is wonderful, not just because it enables us to pay for our loaf of
Pepperidge Farm bread and the peanut butter we put between the slices
but also because money in use provides a kind of communications net-
work. It enables people to take advantage of more information than is
obtained from Walter Cronkite, *The New York Times*, radio news bul-
letins, the mails, telegraph, smoke signals, the beating of drums, and,
indeed, any other form of communication.

The movement of prices, up and down, feeds you an incredible array of information about how the world is working. A simple change in price can reduce complicated networks of facts to useful information which can help you make day-to-day decisions in your life. If tuna fish have suddenly become scarce in the world, then the price of tuna fish will rise. All things being equal, you will make an appropriate decision to eat less tuna salad, without having to be burdened with learning all the details of all the possible combinations of cause and effect which have led to smaller tuna catches. This is the great and little-understood advantage of money. As Nobel laureate F. A. Hayek put it:

> How little the individual participants need know in order to be able to take the right action. In abbreviated form, by a kind of symbol, only the most essential information is passed on and passed on only to those concerned. It is more than a metaphor to describe the price system as a kind of machinery for registering change, or a system of telecommunications which enables individual producers to watch merely the movement of a few pointers as an engineer might watch the hands of a few dials, in order to adjust their activities to changes of which they may never know more than is reflected in the price movement.[1]

The basic use of money, then, is something which requires a substantial effort of imagination to understand. *We are so preoccupied with obtaining money and spending it that we tend to take for granted the basic service which money provides: the provision of information.* It should be emphasized, however, that the fact that money is a marvelous information device also makes it a great invention for purveying misinformation. *When money is unsound, when inflation reduces the value of every dollar you have, it not only makes you poorer, it conveys unsound information.* In this respect, monetary manipulation has become a sort of mind control.

Because we tend to see money from a personal perspective, we assume that more money makes us richer. From an individual perspective, this may be true. But it does not necessarily prove true for the whole system. This is what the average person is discovering to his pain today. He has more money than ever before, but he is poorer than he was a decade ago. The average worker in the private sector earned almost $11,000 in 1978, but he had no more spending power than he did in 1967, when he was earning about $5,000 a year. In addition to losing income, the average individual has suffered a decline in his total financial assets—cash, checking accounts, savings, pensions, insurance policies, stocks and bonds, and other forms of wealth. The value represented in those assets has been partially transferred to other individuals, or lost completely.

Most analyses of the effects of inflation miss this important point. They focus on income, primarily because income statistics are easily gathered. The comparison of income adjustments from year to year suggests that people are staying abreast of inflation. This is not true. While pay is adjusted upward to at least partially compensate for the decline in purchasing power, this is not true of *overall wealth*. Much of any asset denominated in dollars is necessarily lost. The insurance company cannot effectively index your life insurance—it can only charge more for the policy. Banks cannot pay interest rates high enough to offset the effects of inflation—it is illegal. Not only is there no mechanism for indemnifying all the millions of individuals for their losses; the very attempt to offset inflation's effects would be contrary to inflation's *raison d'être*. The purpose of inflation, *as it has been throughout history, is to transfer capital from some persons to others.*

Inflation is caused by the creation of additional money. The more that is created, the less each individual unit of the currency is worth. Because people who control the issuance of money can profit handsomely by creating more, inflation has been common throughout history. Even before paper money supplanted coinage as the primary form in circulation, politicians who controlled the mints were able to profit by reducing the value of each coin.

Consider this description of the late Roman inflation:

> The State resorted to repeated debasement and increase of the currency in circulation. The mints worked with feverish activity. The gold coinage remained pure, but the coins became smaller and smaller, and in the end were only accepted by weight. After 256 the silver currency of the Empire in its chief denomination, the Antoninaius, lost 75 percent, and ultimately 98 percent, of its silver contents; in other words, it became silver-washed copper.[2]

Every time the mints melted down and recast the coins, that action produced substantial profits for the political elite. When the silver content of what had previously been one coin was spread, after constant debasement, to fifty, the only result to be expected was that it would take about fifty of the new coins to equal the value of one of the old. Since the public was constantly forced to accept newly debased money at face value, average people bore the loss, while the lucky few who controlled the government enjoyed fantastic profits. These profits were shared out with an increasingly well-paid military and an increasingly large welfare population. At one time, a third of Rome's 1,200,000 residents were nominal freemen dependent on Imperial handouts. They served the ruling elite, in turn, as the mob which bestowed its fickle favors upon the emperor and his party.

Inflation of the currency was continued on a wide scale by the feudal potentates of the Middle Ages. Every lord, duke, or earl found that having a mint was almost as important to his occupation as having a sturdy, damp dungeon. Each would claim the exclusive right of issuing money in his own locale. By recalling the coins which had circulated in the reigns of his predecessors, and debasing them during restrike, the noblemen normally secured substantial profits.

But no money manipulator in the course of history had the totally free hand which monetary authorities enjoy today.

None of the princelings or kings really had sufficient power to enforce a hyperinflationary reduction in the value of money. There were so many coins of different origins in circulation in the same area that the competition prohibited anything other than slow, moderate inflation. Nonetheless, such coin as the maravedi, which had once been a dinar of 65 gold grains, was debased so much that it became too small to circulate. Thereafter, it became a silver coin comprising 27 grains. Eventually this coin passed out of existence after declining to only 1.5 grains of silver, which made it about as minuscule as a coarse piece of sawdust. (There are 480 grains to one ounce.)[3]

While European potentates seeking to profit from inflation were essentially limited to what silver and gold could be shaved from the coinage, the early invention of paper in China made it possible for the political elite there to profit from repeated hyperinflations. When Marco Polo visited China, he reported that paper money was the "means whereby the Great Khan may have, and in fact has, more treasure than all the kings in the world." Thankfully for the Europeans, the rulers there did not take this report to heart. Although the first paper mill was established in Western Europe in 1189 at Hérault in France, most of the early European experiments with nonmetallic money involved attempts to create a leather currency. These failed to become the basis of a profitable inflation.

As long as coin was the primary money in circulation, the degree to which governments and their allies could profit from creating money was limited. It was a relatively simple matter for the public to realize when coins became smaller. Even when debasement involved a change in the metallic composition of the coins, with junk alloys replacing portions of the gold and silver, it was always possible, as Archimedes had shown in the third century B.C., to determine whether coins were pure. Although many people were undoubtedly misled, especially when the currency was only slightly reduced in value, the primary profits from medieval inflation did not really depend upon hoodwinking the public. For most people, it was plain at a glance what was happening. The ruler was pocketing the gold and silver yielded by shaving the coins.

With the emergence of paper money in the West during the late seventeenth and early eighteenth centuries, inflation began to take on a more modern form. Increasingly, the profits from the inflationary enterprise began to depend not merely upon the pinching of gold but also upon misleading people into spending money in new ways. This involved, as it does today, the engineering of a vast *credit expansion* operated through a banking system.

One of the most notorious and instructive of the early modern inflations was John Law's Mississippi scheme. After Louis XIV died in 1715, the entire French economy was left in turmoil. The famed "Sun King" was barely cold in his grave before a long-suppressed clamor against high taxes spread throughout France. A review of the national finances showed that the debt amounted to three billion livres. This was grave indeed, because only three million livres were available to pay the interest on that staggering obligation. It was so plainly impossible for the burden to be met that a faction of the French court led by Duke St. Simon advised the regent that the only hope to save France from revolution would be to immediately convoke the Estates General and declare the nation bankrupt. This sensible advice was rejected in favor of an immediate debasement of the currency. All the coin in France was restruck at the same value but with a one-fifth reduced content of gold or silver. By this means seventy-two million livres were obtained to temporarily stave off bankruptcy.

At this point, a Scot adventurer and soldier of fortune, John Law, arrived on the scene and proposed that he be entrusted with establishing a bank to issue paper money. In spite of the fact that Law could scarcely speak French, the leaders of the government were immediately attracted to his scheme. On May 5, 1716, Law's bank was established by royal edict. Law turned to the public with a flourish, issuing paper notes which he announced would be payable on demand at face value. Branches of his bank opened all over France, and he obtained an immediately favorable reaction. While government securities issued by Louis XIV sold at a steep discount of almost 80 percent, Law's notes incredibly commanded a premium above their face value. The public was gulled. Law wasted no time turning his initial success into a fantastic series of monopoly privileges. His bank obtained the exclusive right to sell tobacco in France, the exclusive right to refine precious metals, and was renamed "The Royal Bank of France."

At the same time, Law announced a credit issue, trading on his company's exclusive privilege of conducting commerce in the province of Louisiana and along the Mississippi River. He told the public that the territory abounded in precious metals and other riches which assured great success to his company. To give his issue added glitter, Law also obtained a royal patent as the exclusive tax collector and coiner of money. The public fell for this heady speculation: 200,000 shares of capital stock were sold. Immediately thereafter, while enthusiasm still ran high, the bank issued one billion livres in paper notes. These were followed by still further depreciation of the coin. The result was a speculative inflation of stupendous proportions, what would today be known as an inflationary boom.

For a period, all went well. Then the inevitable reaction set in. Early in 1720, members of the public began to experience difficulty converting Law's paper money to specie. Numerous laws were passed in swift succession restricting the redemption of paper money for gold. By May 27, 1720, the Royal Bank of France stopped payment in specie. In the ensuing panic over the next few weeks, dozens of persons were crushed to death trying to crowd through the doors of banks to cash in their depreciating paper money. Law managed to save himself by escaping through Belgium with little more than the clothes on his back.

As Elgin Groseclose has written, Law's story is worth noting because he may be regarded as "the foster father of modern paper money."[4] The artificial "boom" that was touched off by Law's massive bank-credit expansion provided a primitive example of how inflation can be profitable to those who control it. *By inducing people to act under the influence of misinformation provided through the money system, inflationists could profit from speculation in the sale of stocks, land, and other items at artificially high prices.*

The limits to inflation were thus no longer set by chemistry. The sheer physical impossibility of reducing the value of a coin by more than a few hundred percent was no longer a factor restricting inflations. With the emergence of a complex system of bank credit it became possible for the first time to attain essentially "invisible" inflations. Additional paper money could be created without altering the physical appearance of the new notes. This provided the creators of inflation a flexibility they had lacked when coinage was the most important aspect of the money supply.

This new inflation was made all the more attractive by the fact that it was a thousand times more difficult to comprehend than the rude debasements of coinage of earlier times. Henceforth, as Groseclose put it, "It was the complex baffling and deceptive subjects of central banking, reserve ratios, and credit controls that were to entangle the understanding of men and vitiate control of the money mechanism."[5]

Law's system of inflation is essentially the same as the inflation that squeezes us today. But contemporary inflation is at once more refined and more fantastic than "classical" inflation: our central bankers have devised more reliable ways of keeping the credit expansion under way, so in that respect our inflation is more refined: it is more fantastic, in that the expansion of currency and debt in modern America has grown out of all proportion to anything envisioned by John Law.

To better understand how the system works, consider another tale out of the past, the story of the creation of the Bank of England. In the late seventeenth century, a big-time banker named William Paterson had a bright idea. He figured out how he could obtain a 139-percent return on his money each year. His method was simplicity itself. He collected seventy-two thousand pounds in gold and silver coin, almost all of it borrowed, and formed a bank to print paper money receipts for 16⅔ times the value of his coin. He immediately lent the funny money— £1,200,000—to the King of England, who used it to finance a war. Since the king paid an interest of 8.3 percent, Paterson received £100,000 annually in interest on an actual capital of £72,000. It was a great deal for Paterson, and the king did not complain. But it wasn't so great for everyone else. Since Paterson actually had only six percent as much gold as he needed to redeem his notes, he was clearly defrauding the taxpayers, whom the king obligated to retire Paterson's inflationary loan. When people started grumbling, the king simply granted Paterson a monopoly privilege to print paper money. Thus the Bank of England was established, and along with it, a principle that inflationists have clung to ever since: *the best way to bring paper money into circulation is to finance government deficits.*

That is how our inflation works. When the government builds a huge budget deficit, our central bank, the Federal Reserve, covers it by buying government bonds (whatever cannot be sold to the public). But unlike anything in normal experience, the Fed spends money that never existed before. It creates brand-new checkbook money which is deposited with the banks. The banking system as a whole is then privileged to create six to ten times as much money in loans. This is inflation. If the Fed completely monetized a deficit of $50 billion, the banks could end up lending and collecting interest on $300 billion or more.

The new money that is created reduces the value of each older dollar that exists. It is rather like what would happen to the value of an art print if the artist, instead of limiting the edition, continued to issue more whenever he pleased. If, for example, there were one hundred prints and the artist decided to crank out ten more, the value of each previously existing print would decline by about ten percent. All things being equal, this is what happens to the dollars you hold. If the money supply is expanded by ten percent, you can expect your dollars to be worth about ten percent less.

This is not to say, of course, that there is an absolutely arithmetic relationship between an increase in the money supply and the decline in the value of the dollar. Nor does inflation affect everyone the same way. The new dollars created by the banks are not equally distributed to every citizen. They are directed through the allocation of credit to benefit some individuals at the expense of others. In the first instance, almost all inflation today begins with heavy government borrowing. This is because the government is the most credit-worthy of borrowers, as well as the most powerful. Its bonded obligations provide the necessary reserves which expand the money supply. Government involvement also assures that the necessary political support exists to proceed with credit expansion.

The newly created money is first spent by the persons who hold transcendental-capital claims: government employees, welfare recipients, and politically favored interests which depend upon the government to purchase their unsold products. Because they get the newly created money first, they get to spend it before prices have risen.

Eventually, the newly created money dribbles through the system to the point where nearly everyone is enjoying some increased increment of cash. Prices, by this time, may have begun to rise, but no one is quite sure how high they will go. It is at this point that the effects of inflation in creating misinformation through the price system generate actions which otherwise would not have taken place.

Consider the case of the Joneses—a typical family, subject to no more than the normal blunders and imbecilities. The Joneses have experienced an increase in apparent income from $10,000 to $11,000 a year. It may be that $11,000 this year will prove to be worth no more and possibly less than $10,000 was last year. However, the Joneses have no direct way of measuring this. An inflated dollar looks much the same as one of the past. It does not get smaller. It does not change color. Our typical family cannot bite it, weigh it, or subject it to any physical test to determine how much it has been inflated. The result is that our family is misinformed, just as many hundreds of millions have been misinformed since inflation was first thrust upon the modern world.

Examine further how this misinformation works its damage. When the Joneses thought they had an income of only $10,000 to spend each year, they preferred not to buy a swimming pool. They saw how far their income could go and concluded that rather than own a pool, they would prefer to save some of their earnings and spend other money on more clothes for their children, a better vacation, dining out on weekends, or perhaps a subscription to *Better Homes & Gardens*. Since their income has apparently risen, however, they decide that they can afford a swimming pool. So they borrow money and conclude the purchase. They are only one of tens of thousands of families who are simultaneously misled into similar mistakes. Many persons like them undertake expenditures which they have been manipulated into making because inflation has conveyed false information through the money system.

It should be clear at this point that we are focusing on the swimming pool industry for purposes of illustration only. The kind of consumer error we consider here would not be concentrated in just one area of the economy. All kinds of expenditures would be affected. What we single out is descriptive of a general process in which all kinds of firms in many industries suddenly begin to realize larger than ordinary profits. The early stages of inflation provide a condition in which almost every business succeeds and hardly any fails.[6] Under such conditions, swimming pools galore are purchased. Swimming pool makers are taken by surprise by all the buying. They have geared their capacity to the previous, undistorted level of demand.

Since people want to buy more pools than the pool makers could currently produce, the misinformation is relayed along in a new form to further manipulate people's behavior. The pool builders are just as duped as the pool buyers. They act to meet the artificial demand by ordering more of the components which go into swimming pools. This spreads the misinformation still further—by inducing the manufacturers of pool pumps and vinyl linings to increase production. They too are surprised by the intense demand for swimming pools. In order to accommodate their customers, they break ground on a new factory to manufacture pool products. They are able to borrow money to finance construction cheaply because credit expansion has kept interest charges artificially low. This compounds the error. They hire hundreds or thousands of new workers who are trained to produce and service these swimming-pool pumps. Some of the workers who are hired are persons of low skill who might barely be worth as much as the minimum wage.

One effect of inflation in making the dollar worth less is to effectively lower the minimum wage. This particular effect is good for the unemployed as it enables them to find work. This is true not only with businesses which are *misled* into additional hiring, but elsewhere as well. But that is really another story. To the extent that inflation lowers the barriers to employment—by reducing wage rates to the point where people can be hired—it is really just circumventing counterproductive laws.

Prices eventually rise. It becomes apparent to the Jones family that prices have risen so much as to reduce the value of the dollar by a full dime. The family recognizes that it is no richer than it was before. Yet this is not the end of the matter. The members of the family are in a predicament. They have borrowed money to purchase the swimming pool. They must make a monthly payment. How can they afford to do so? Only by dipping into their savings, canceling their subscription to *Better Homes & Gardens*, taking their vacation at home, doing without new shoes for the children, and eating macaroni three times a week.

Meanwhile, their next-door neighbors, who had been eyeing the new swimming pool and imagining that they too could afford one, decide not to buy one after all. They also have discovered that they have less real spending power than they had been misled to believe. Consequently, they call the pool company and cancel their order for an oval-shaped pool with diving board. Many other pool buyers follow suit. The managers of the pool company realize that in spite of their earnest efforts, the sudden spurt of sales which they had enjoyed will not continue. This means that the new employees they hired to dig pool foundations must be fired. Two hundred miles down the road at the pool-pump maker's headquarters, an entirely new factory is being built to fill a nonexistent demand for pool pumps. Either work on the new plant will be halted and all its employees fired, or the firm will attempt to limp along, carrying its extra costs and higher debt load in the hope that pool sales will in the long run recover.

This chain of events is extended all the way along the structure of production. The manufacturers who produce the equipment, the machine tools, stamping presses, and forges used by the pool-pump makers face exactly the same difficulty. They have committed their resources, borrowed money, hired new employees, and obtained raw materials to manufacture more of the capital goods which produce the pool pumps. They were misled, just as makers of the pool pumps were misled, as indeed were the swimming-pool dealers and the customers themselves. All of these individuals were manipulated, misled into taking actions which they would not have taken otherwise—if not for the misinformation conveyed by the inflation of the money supply.

This is the process known as an "inflationary boom." A flurry of activity is generated, all of it misguided, by the impression which inflation creates—that one is richer than he really is.

The false prosperity created through this process cannot last. Hayek comments:

> Inflation thus can never be more than a temporary fillip, and even this beneficial effect can last only as long as somebody continues to be cheated and the expectations of some people unnecessarily disappointed. Its stimulus is due to the errors which it produces. It is particularly dangerous because the harmful after effects of even small doses of inflation can be staved off only by larger doses of inflation.[7]

As soon as the funny money works its way completely through the system and shows up in price increases and a higher cost of living, people realize that they have erred and have no choice but to curtail their spending. If no further action were taken, all the pool dealers and their employees, pool-pump makers and their employees, and all the higher-order capital-goods manufacturers and their employees would face a stiff correction. Since they were misled and manipulated into investments they ought not to have made, they might see these investments fail. The workers could lose their jobs, and the businesses would be lucky to avoid bankruptcy. This phase of the inflationary process is known as recession or depression.

If the process ended right there, everyone could adjust and go about his business, some substantially poorer than they were before, others, the perpetrators and beneficiaries of inflation, richer.

Unfortunately, there are many reasons why the process is not allowed to develop into so clear-cut a resolution. The inflationists have more to gain by continuing the process than by allowing the correction to occur, and paradoxically, they normally enjoy the political support of those whom the inflation has most thoroughly gulled. The Jones family and the swimming-pool industry, having been misled once, may now support the decision by political and banking authorities to compound the inflation by accelerating the growth of money supply. This postpones the day of reckoning by continuing to mislead members of the public into believing that they are richer than they are. As in the first round of the process, for the inflation to succeed in purveying misinformation, it must be greater than anticipated. The Jones family, which first bought the swimming pool, has learned from past experience to expect a 10-percent inflation. To have effect, the renewed inflation must be 11 percent or higher. If it is, many people will be fooled again. The Joneses' next-door neighbor may then go through with his purchase of the oval pool with diving board, and all the way down the line, more resources and human energy will be misdirected.

The longer the inflation process continues, the more fully it shifts rewards away from productive capital to the transcendental capitalists who both perpetrate and profit first from the inflation. The politicians, and other government employees, use inflation to stake out greater claims on the country's existing wealth. For one thing, inflation automatically increases your tax bite. Even if your income rises so as to keep exactly "even" with inflation, the effect of progressive income-tax rates is to take an ever-larger bite from your real disposable income. We shall see in the next chapter, when inflation increases by 10 percent, your taxes increase an average of 16 percent. This gives the politicians more of your wealth to spend and lets them increase the returns from transcendental capital, even as productive capital declines in value.

Inflation not only takes resources away from production, it provides a convenient rationale for increasing the total compensation of those who are allied with government. When the value of the dollar is declining, everyone wants a cost-of-living adjustment. That makes the public more disposed to sympathize with government pay hikes. But what the public seldom realizes is that government employees, who appear to suffer along with the rest of us at the supermarket, are already substantially overpaid. Their inflation-generated salary-and-fringe-benefit increases actually enable them to prosper from inflation.

The facts bear this out. A survey of government compensation all the way back to 1929 shows that government employees were better paid than the rest of us during all the years when inflation was high. The only time that they have fallen behind the average in the productive sector, and then only marginally, was during the decade of the 1950's— when inflation was low. Since the mid-1960's, when inflationism really began to take hold, there has been a dramatic escalation in the total compensation of government employees.

Inflation also dramatically increases the rewards of those with transcendental-capital claims outside of the government. Politically favored firms obtain higher subsidies with inflation. Doctors, lawyers, and others who profit through transcendental-capital claims have multiplied those claims upon wealth as inflation has increased. (These developments will be considered in greater detail later.)

This wide-scale shifting of rewards from productive to transcendental capitalists is perhaps the most significant effect of inflation. But without the banks, this effect could never be achieved. Banks are the most commercial of transcendental-capitalist institutions; their charters empower them to create money by expanding debt.[3] We have already seen part of the way in which this newly created money misguides the public into altering economic activity. The changes in the economy which are the consequence of these misinformed actions greatly reduce the scope for productive activity and diminish the returns from the productive investment of capital.

Today's money is "pure credit" money. Most new dollars which come into existence are created as instruments of debt. As brokers of debts, bankers have a proprietary interest in a steady inflation of the money supply. Generally speaking, the more debt that the banks can bring into circulation as money, the higher their profits. The only limitations on the banks are the rules of prudence established by the Federal Reserve Board; these rules have the primary effect of guaranteeing that the banks obtain the optimum return from managed inflation. Bankers today do not want the kind of wild blow-off which occurred when John Law and his Royal Bank of France inflated too much, too quickly. An inflation of 100 percent annually, for example, under current circumstances, would surely yield a lower return than a controlled inflation

71

of five percent, because the public would be less misled by so staggering a change, and the banks themselves would be hard pressed to maintain their liquidity under such conditions.

The role of the Federal Reserve in this situation is like that of a dealer in a game of poker who can surreptitiously create new chips at will and dish them out to his favorite player. The dealer has to be reasonably conservative about it or the victims will become aware of what is happening, grow disgusted, and quit. The art is to create just enough funny chips so that the favorite player wins and pockets the largest possible pot. An exact determination of the point of diminishing returns is, of course, a technical and empirical question. The important point is that the banks profit as brokers of debt by inflating to their point of diminishing returns.

Through the magic of fractional reserve banking and compound interest, the commercial banks have a hefty incentive to promote new debt. This debt gives the banks a leverage to command real assets far in excess of the money capital originally invested by the banks' owners. By creating money, the banks can dole out the new checkbook money to credit-worthy borrowers. The borrowers then command the assets which are bid away from those who lack access to the system of credit.

Inflation, therefore, no less than taxation, is an instrument for the redistribution of income and wealth. That is inflation's purpose. Increases in the money supply benefit those who receive the newly extended credit at the expense of others who pay for it through devaluation of all their assets denominated in dollars. While it may not be strictly true to say that the overall structure of credit involves a "plan" of redistribution, it certainly involves a pattern of redistribution. Real wealth is transferred between the winners and losers. The primary winners, along with the government, are the debtors. The big losers are the creditors.

Generally speaking, the larger the entity (the greater its cash flow and higher its total assets), the more deeply it will be able to go into debt. Since the overall financial advantage in an inflationary period lies with those who are able to obtain tangible assets through debt finance, there is a different test for the prosperity of a firm under inflation than in an economy with a stable currency. It is not merely the firm's ability to serve customers and deliver goods in the market which generates rewards; it is also the degree to which it can manage indebtedness. As already suggested, static capital assets, which produce nothing, provide an appreciably higher return than almost any productive activity during a period of inflation. As long as inflation accelerates, idle land, buildings, diamonds, gold—practically anything of tangible value—can be a profitable investment, even though it produces nothing. This is why firms in a period of rising inflation do not need to concentrate as fully as they would otherwise upon satisfying the consumer. One economic historian put the matter in perspective while describing the consequences of one of the twentieth century's more famous monetary expansions: "The inflation worked to the advantage of the great firms, which could profit more easily from the changeable conditions of the market, adapting sale price to the monetary depreciation using bank credit and directing to their own advantage the economic and financial policy of the State. . . . Great firms . . . bought under favorable conditions industrial companies, packets of shares, land and buildings."[9]

Today's conglomerate is the most vivid example of the "great firm" using inflation to speculate through the purchase of tangible assets. Managing conglomerates is in some respects akin to the juggling of static capital investments by an individual. Instead of dealing in such tangible assets as gold, Oriental rugs, antiques, rare books, and the like, the managers of a conglomerate juggle businesses. These businesses are valued, like gold or art, primarily because their value is not denominated solely in terms of currency. One can go into debt to purchase a business, and if inflation is high enough, make a profit even without doing a notably good job of pleasing the consumer. This is not to say that most conglomerates fail to please consumers, but they may not try as hard to please during periods of inflation as they otherwise might.

With the benefits of inflation falling so clearly to the debtors, it may be wondered why any would want to be a creditor. The answer is complicated. Many become creditors indirectly when their pension funds and insurance policies are invested in dollar-denominated instruments. Some, such as those accumulating a down payment for a house, save money in order to qualify as larger-scale debtors. Some save because they anticipate inflation. But most creditors remain creditors involuntarily. The realization that money deposited in a bank is rapidly expropriated through inflation has led to a decline in voluntary savings. Nearly a quarter of American families, 23 percent, no longer have any savings at all. This is almost three times the number without savings five years earlier. Furthermore, four out of every ten American families are reducing their savings. The growth of deposits at commercial savings banks declined by 50 percent from January 1977 to the fall of 1978. Yet many are creditors anyway. Whatever their personal inclinations, *people are forced through the tax laws to lend money to the government.* Income-tax withholding forces those who earn salaries to pay their tax bills before they are due. And a substantial percentage of payroll-tax revenues are converted to service government debt instruments which depreciate with inflation.

The tax laws have also been arranged to enhance popular dependence upon the banking institutions. In the first instance, the high tax rates dramatically reduce the prospects for accumulating capital, as will be emphasized later. Literally hundreds of billions which could be available to finance productive investment are subtracted from the total available and consumed. This reduction of the capital stock—or conversion, if you will, of productive capital to transcendental capital—increases the dependence upon debt. As the tax rates rise, an ever larger proportion of economic activity is financed with borrowed rather than invested funds.[10]

The tax code further supports this tendency through differential rates favorable to the service of debt. A business which borrows money it needs may deduct the cost of obtaining the money—the interest payments—directly from its taxable income. On the other hand, a business which attracts investors cannot deduct the dividends which are the analogous payment for the use of the money. Thus, it is more expensive to operate using invested rather than borrowed funds. This not only leads to further dependence on the part of businesses and individuals upon debt, it also discourages individual investors from making funds available for new productive ventures.

Thanks to this unholy alliance between the tax laws and inflation, the average return from investment in production may now be negative. Even new businesses which do not fail tend to operate through a write-down in the real value of their capital—as the decline over the last decade in even the high-quality Dow Jones stocks would indicate. For the smaller corporations, the loss also has been great.

It is clear that a long-term currency inflation has a wide-ranging effect upon production. The type of economy which is dependent upon debt creation and debt service is necessarily different from the economy which rewards savings and production. The management of business enterprises is transferred out of the hands of entrepreneurs and into the hands of bureaucrats who are "hired hands"—experts, not owners. The corporate managers are encouraged to convert economic activity to a debt finance basis because expansion of the invested-capital base of any corporation threatens the jobs of the current executives. Each new issue of stock could become part of a new control block that could place the corporation in other hands.

The whole process involves connections similar to those in the old song: "The knee bone's connected to the thigh bone, the thigh bone's connected to the hip bone . . ." Government creates currency inflation through the banks. The currency inflation converts the basis of economic success from productivity to the juggling of debt. This contributes to great conglomerates. The tax laws, designed to encourage indebtedness and thus promote the inflation, contribute to making invested savings, the alternative to debt finance, in the aggregate unprofitable. Tax laws further sever the control by independent owners of the corporate entities and vest more of the control in bureaucratic management. Thus an economy based on debt turns out to be bureaucratic.

In a time of inflation, the government can be assured that most of the economically shrewd operators in society will gain a stake in continued inflation because the prime means to prosper in the situation is to go deeply into debt for the purchase of tangible assets. Everyone who does this aligns his economic interest with that of the inflationists. By now, many average Americans have done just that. Consumer indebtedness has been rising 50 percent faster than income. From 1976 to 1978 consumer indebtedness rose by 16.4 percent. Residential-mortgage obligations, which now total more than $750 billion, rose by 18.1 percent. And corporate indebtedness rose by 11 percent to slightly more than $1 trillion. Since late 1975, the total debt in the American economy has risen 42 percent, to about $4 trillion. Total debt expansion has risen far faster than the growth of the economy, and as of this writing the repayment cost relative to income was greater than at any time in America's history.

It is one of the unhappy ironies of inflation that it must be generally unanticipated before individual investments, especially of the sort made by ordinary people, can profit from it. Once everyone begins to count on the idea that inflation will continue at 13 percent for the next 20 years, the current price of everything will be bid up to a level that reflects that expectation. For example, when people go deeply into debt to buy a home, farmland, or some similar "inflation hedge," they are paying, at the moment they buy, a price that incorporates an anticipation of future inflation. Those who go into debt expecting windfalls on their property due to inflation will be mistaken unless the actual inflation rate exceeds what is expected, or some other factor intercedes to increase the value of their investment in real terms. Thus, a 13 percent inflation each year, if it is foreseen, will not provide annual appreciation in the real value of a property equal to an unexpected 5 percent inflation in the past. Only inflation that proves to be greater than expected will have an impact in raising a property's real value.

Those who have recently gone into debt with the thought that inflation will necessarily make their purchases profitable, may not have waited for the other shoe to drop. Seeing that many have profited by going in over their heads in the past, later buyers have followed suit. But there is no guarantee that they are correct. Far from it. Unless they are benefiting from subsidized interest rates that are below the level of inflation, they may end up paying the full price in real terms for what they have bought. They may end up with losses.

Just as inflation in its early stages causes profits to be higher than normal, so after it has been anticipated in its later stages, inflation engenders greater than normal losses and bankruptcies. In fact, inflations are ordinarily followed by depressions. Unless the value of money keeps falling at a faster and faster rate, beyond the level expected, there will no longer be great windfalls. There will be great losses. Professor Hayek describes the process this way:

> The stimulating effect of inflation will thus operate only so long as it has not been foreseen; as soon as it comes to be foreseen, only its continuation at an increased rate will maintain the same degree of prosperity. If in such a situation prices rose less than expected, the effect would be the same as unforeseen deflation. Even if they rose only as much as was generally expected, this would no longer provide the exceptional stimulus but would lay bare the whole backlog of adjustments that had been postponed while the temporary stimulus lasted.[11]

The money squeeze on the average person has reached a point where there is almost no doubt that his standard of living must decline even further. Borrowing at the prodigious rates that have been witnessed in recent years cannot be sustained. The average family now spends 23 percent of its current income to service past debt. Since one-fifth of all families have no debt at all, many must be shouldering burdens approaching 50 percent. When inflation dramatically worsens, the consumer will no longer be able to service an additional debt burden. At that stage he will be forced to stop borrowing. He will no longer be able to afford automobiles, appliances, or swimming pools. The inevitable result will be recession—likely a recession that could topple the entire multitrillion-dollar pyramid of debt.

The masters of today's sophisticated inflations—the politicians and banks—are thus threatened with the same end as John Law's Royal Bank of France, whose gaudy credit speculation came to an end in 1720. Faced with severe recession, the U.S. government, like the eighteenth-century French government, would undoubtedly do all in its power to prevent a collapse of the credit structure. This means the Federal Reserve would print money. A liquidity crisis developing at home or abroad could move the government into a paper-money binge of hyperinflationary proportions.

To get an idea of how wild and destructive such inflations can be, with prices rising by the hour, and the paper-money notes printed in truly astronomical denominations, consider what has actually happened to other countries in this century.

The German experience is well known. Three hundred paper mills and about two thousand presses worked around the clock to stamp out ever more worthless currency in higher and higher denominations. After a time, the money was no longer printed on both sides. It was a waste of ink. Housewives bumped along the sidewalks with wheelbarrows full of paper money. In one noted case, a woman parked her treasure outside a shop and rushed in with an armload of banknotes to purchase a small utensil. When she returned a few moments later, she found that she had been robbed. Someone had stolen her wheelbarrow. The money it contained was in the gutter. Even the thieves wanted tangible assets, not paper. When the printing presses were finally turned off, the public was invited to redeem the old money for new. The ratio was one trillion paper marks to one gold mark.

An even more severe inflation began in China in July 1937. It was approximately 150 times worse than the hyperinflation in Germany after the First World War. And unlike the German inflation, which was concentrated into a few desperate years, the Chinese inflation lasted more than a decade. Prices increased by 151.73×10^{12}.[12] Robert P. Martin, a foreign correspondent in Shanghai during the height of the monetary disaster, wrote:

> I remember one time carrying 17 lbs. of money to four different offices just to pay month-end bills. . . .

Only the totally unemployed weren't millionaires. The cost-of-living index introduced to offset inflation quickly topped the monthly one million Yuan level per individual and then rose higher and higher. No one saved or even tried to. By mid-summer, stores had been stripped of everything worthwhile as people sought security in commodities. One of the city's major department stores had nothing on its ground floor other than a few unsold top hats. . . .

It was impossible to find out how the desperately poor and unemployed managed to keep living. You could see children waiting at kitchen doors of restaurants to get a few morsels of garbage. Women in filthy rags swept up the few grains of rice on the docks and junks where sacks had been hauled. And for the first time, people who could speak English—probably school teachers—became beggars.[13]

General Laurence S. Kuter, along with some other American military officers, served in China in 1948. A few days before Peking fell to the Communists, he and his companions went out for dinner. He recounts the story:

The party had what may have been the last elegant Peking-duck dinner at the Wagon-Lits, where, it was claimed, the ceremony originated. As soon as the guests were seated in a private dining room, a big fat white duck was led around the table set for six. As the last course, duck soup was served from a large tureen in the center of which was the stark skeleton of the duck. For this elaborate dinner, the cost was 50 million (Chinese) dollars.[14]

Probably the worst inflation in history occurred in Hungary after the Second World War. In a little more than a year, Hungarian prices increased by 399.62×10^{27}. To get a view of how vast such an inflation was, consider this: a collection of old one-pengo notes (the unit of Hungarian currency) large enough to have matched the new values would have piled up two thousand miles high and stretched out past the moon, past Mars, past the superior planets, out to the nearest star and beyond, all the way across the Milky Way—a distance of 100,000 light-years. In other words, it would have taken a stack of one-pengo notes six billion high and as wide as the galaxy to maintain the purchasing power of one pengo prior to the inflation. Obviously the Hungarians quickly stopped printing one-pengo notes. In fact, they achieved a kind of celebrity among inflators by raising the numbers on their banknotes to a higher power than the world has seen before or since:

in July 1946 a note for *one hundred quintillion pengos* was issued in Budapest.

This kind of gaudy hyperinflation, carried out until the money supply is measured in the trillions, quadrillions, or quintillions, like the distances to stars, is not directly relevant to the American situation—at least not now. What will happen with the almost certain arrival of the credit crisis is beyond telling. It is unlikely (though not impossible) that the dollar will be emptied of all value, as were the currencies of Germany, Hungary, Greece, and China. Our worst inflation is more likely to resemble what frequently happens in Latin America, where protracted increases in the money supply range in the double- and triple-digit levels, rather than in the ten-digit range.

In the good years, such inflations can fall to 20 percent. In bad years, prices may explode by 50 percent, or even 100 percent and more. In Uruguay, the inflation rate has averaged almost 70 percent through the decade of the seventies. In Argentina, prices rose at a 175-percent rate through the first half of 1978.

Even though the numbers involved in such inflations are comprehensible, it is hard to imagine what they mean in personal terms. The little that is left of the middle class in such inflationary economies survives by working two or three jobs and skimping on everything. As one Uruguayan put it: "The key to survival is cutting your expenditures to the absolute minimum—food, utility bills, transportation, those sorts of things." This means no luxuries, and scarcely even venturing from the house. A resident of Montevideo described the conditions under which he lives in this way: "The general rule is no recreation, or hardly any. People do not gather at neighborhood bars anymore to talk politics and soccer. Eating out even once a month is a luxury, and a cinema or theater is even more of a luxury. That's why the streets of the city are practically deserted after nine o'clock at night."

V. S. Naipaul's account of inflation in Uruguay details an even bleaker picture of the economic, political, and spiritual condition in a country "grown sad" after decades of inflation.

> The army—essentially rural, lower middle class—is in control and rules by decree. Interest rates have dropped to around 42 percent, with the taxes; . . . inflation this year has been kept down to 60%. "Prices don't rise here every day," a businessman said, "they also rise every night. . . ."

The shops have little to offer; . . . the three or four fair restaurants that survive in a city of more than one million—do not always have meat; and the bread is made partly of sorghum. . . .

Out of a work force of just over a million, 250,000 are employed by the state. PLUNA, the Uruguayan airline, used to have 1000 employees and one functioning airplane. The people at ANCAP, the state oil company, tried to get to the office before it opened; there were more employees than chairs. . . .[15]

That is life after long-term inflation. It is the kind of life to which we may be moving. We have picked up the Latin-American habit of deep personal indebtedness. We have begun to index pensions on labor contracts. *We are trying to accommodate ourselves to a condition which could destroy us.* Already our average inflation rate for the decade has surpassed that of Venezuela. The Latins who once hoarded American dollars as a partial protection for themselves against the fantastic money-supply increases in their own lands dumped the dollar with the same alacrity as the international bankers. They now hoard Swiss francs in Buenos Aires, Rio, and Bogotá.

The dollar's value has shrunk to about half of what it was a decade ago. With inflation at 10 percent, it will be cut half again in a little more than seven years; at the rate of 13 percent annually, the dollar would be halved in little more than five years. *When you need to quadruple your paper money every decade—just to break even—the increasing inflation can mean only one thing: a lower standard of living.*

As the dollar declines in value, workers postpone retirement, more wives go to work, and more heads of households take second and even third jobs. All values are disrupted. Prices of necessities—shelter, food, and clothing, health care—steadily increase, leaving less for the luxuries which enhance life. Furthermore, it becomes all but impossible for anyone to advance economically. Said an eighty-four-year-old Minneapolis man: "I saved when I was young. But the average couple today earning $24,000 or $25,000 can't save a nickel." Inflation creates a great shuffle of paper that keeps more dollars passing through your hands but allows you to keep less.

Not everyone is in a position to adjust adequately to the decline in the value of money. Those who are less agile or less adept become permanent losers. And even those who are able to somehow keep their incomes rising are faced with a challenge they must meet with the ceaseless rigor of galley slaves: to adjust all their information perceptions to compensate for the fluctuations in the value of money.

That we flag under such conditions is all but inevitable. Inflation disorients. It shatters our inherent expectations that hard, productive work and savings are the means to material progress and advancement. Inflation leads to an inversion of middle-class virtues. Thrift is penalized, consumption rewarded. The steady, hardworking citizen becomes the gull of the debtor and the speculator. Money itself becomes a speculation. It is no longer a commodity of positive value, but rather a circulating instrument of other people's debts. With the entire monetary system teetering upon an inverted pyramid of debt expansion, not even full-time students of monetary affairs can predict what the value of the dollar will be in six months.

Will the impending liquidity crisis lead to a collapse of the debt structure and thus a devastating deflationary depression? Will world political and banking authorities succeed in escalating the monetary expansion to a still-higher and possibly runaway level?

Who can answer such questions? The greatest experts and speculators may, but the average person cannot. Whatever becomes of the gyrating value of money in the unknowable future, that average person is almost bound to lose. He cannot change his expectations from day to day, as the outstanding profiteers from monetary disruption must. He cannot move from one side of the market to the other, being a buyer of dollars in the morning and a seller in the afternoon. He is always a buyer of dollars. He sells his services at work for dollars. He deposits dollars at his bank. Only by indirection can the average person be a seller of dollars—by going deeply into debt. But once in debt, as the average American is today, he cannot emerge from debt in an afternoon as he might need to if a liquidity crisis threatened to collapse the money supply.

It takes months or years for the average person to adjust to monetary changes. With the system becoming ever more vulnerable to increasingly trivial events, the reaction time for adjustments necessary to protect purchasing power has been reduced to a matter of days or hours. Whatever happens under such disorderly conditions will inevitably result in a tighter stranglehold on America's middle class.

The simple fact is that the real assets do not exist, under current conditions, to fulfill the expectations of Americans about their future purchasing power. Too many people have been eyeing the same resources to provide the future basis of their standard of life. In this, we are like a thousand housewives all planning to pick the same bough of apples for our pie. Instead of apples, however, we are counting dollars, and those dollars are merely circulating instruments of debt by which we have placed overlapping mortgages on the same tangible assets. Money that was borrowed into existence is deposited and becomes the foundation of new borrowing that brings still more dollars into existence. Consumer debt, mortgage debt, corporate debt, and even more staggering debt by government at the state, local, and federal level, are all predicated upon the survival of the same inflated values. With production unrewarding, and productivity declining, it is hard to see how we shall suddenly produce enough new wealth to satisfy the already existing claims on future purchasing power. We have been misled by monetary manipulation into abandoning our tools and spending more than we earn. Someday there will be a reckoning that could make the already great costs imposed by monetary manipulation seem trivial.

7

The Tax Squeeze

Man, biologically considered . . . is the most formidable
of all the beasts of prey, and indeed the only one that
preys systematically on his own species.

—*William James*

Most Americans sense instinctively the unhappy truth about taxation.
When they see the subject coming, they duck the other way as they
would avoid a bully, and for the same reason. No one wants to suffer
an injustice he is powerless to resist. Taxation imposes such an injustice.
Its details are like slaps in the face, reminders that we are victims. For
that reason, most Americans choose not to know what the tax man is
actually doing to them.

Another reason we tend not to think about taxes is that the process
of understanding taxation carries us away from the concerns of normal
life into the realm inhabited by accountants. Unless one intends to be
fitted out for a green eye shade and keep company with CPA's, that, too,
is an unwelcome prospect.

This social dilemma points to another—the question of how to
handle the many political implications of the issue. To crack taxation's
secrets and not utter them would be nearly impossible. Yet the secrets
themselves could be embarrassing, as many secrets are. Not the least
of the embarrassment could be the prospect that one's neighbors, with
whom he intended to share party chatter, could be the profiteers of
injustice. Almost any desirable circle of acquaintance would include

some of the transcendental capitalists who benefit from taxation's great inequity.

John C. Calhoun, onetime vice-president of the United States, described the tax-victim/tax-beneficiary distinction in this way:

> Whatever amount is taken from the community in the form of taxes, if not lost, goes to them in the shape of expenditures or disbursements. The two—disbursement and taxation—constitute the fiscal action of the government. . . .
>
> Such being the case, it must necessarily follow that some one portion of the community must pay in taxes more than it receives back in disbursements, while another receives in disbursements more than it pays in taxes. It is, then, manifest, taking the whole process together, that taxes must be, in effect, bounties to that portion of the community which receives more in disbursements than it pays in taxes, while to the other which pays in taxes more than it receives in disbursements they are taxes in reality—burdens instead of bounties. This consequence is unavoidable. It results from the nature of the process, be the taxes ever so equally laid. . . .
>
> The necessary result, then, of the unequal fiscal action of the government is to divide the community into two great classes: one consisting of those who, in reality, pay the taxes and, of course, bear exclusively the burden of supporting the government; and the other, of those who are recipients of their proceeds through disbursements, and who are, in fact, supported by the government; or in fewer words, to divide it into *tax-payers* and *tax-consumers*.[1]

Most Americans would rather adopt a vague attitude of resigned acceptance toward taxation than to engage in Calhoun's severe reasoning and thus face the unfashionable conclusions such reasoning suggests. The prevailing attitude is expressed in the adage "Taxes are the price we pay for civilization." Exactly in what sense this is true is a matter usually left undefined. It may mean the more taxes we pay, the more civilization we get. Or it may mean merely that one must accept the bad with the good, in the same sense that one might say, "Mosquitoes are the price we pay for summer evenings."

In any case, there can be little doubt that few understand taxes for what they are. Equally to the point, few understand how high taxes are. The average person knows as much about what he loses to taxes as he does about the location of the nearest Lagrange point in space. This is remarkable, because not one in one hundred knows what a Lagrange point is, let alone where the nearest one is located, whereas everyone has heard of taxes. Yet the astronomical costs which taxes impose are almost as obscure as the more exotic points of astronomy.

The popular illusion that taxes are lower than they are testifies not only to the reluctance of the public to think clearly about the burdens of politics, but also to the skill of those politicians who disguise the tax burden. Indeed, they have succeeded only too well. A close reading of the *Congressional Record* or the published deliberations of the tax-writing committees indicates that some members of Congress are as confused as the public over the true extent and distribution of taxes. This is undoubtedly because the political logic of levying taxes is to disguise the burden as fully as possible. The inevitable results of such logic are extremely complicated tax laws and revenue collection on as many over-lapping bases as possible. This reduces the political costs of increasing taxes. It also makes for such sweeping confusion that the congressmen themselves cannot comprehend what they are doing. As an example, consider that Congress accidentally repealed the corporate income tax a few years ago. Six months passed before anyone, from staff lawyers who wrote the legislation, to the congressmen who voted for it, to the president who signed it, knew the difference. Not many taxpayers did, either, which was why, in the end, the technical repeal of the tax did not dampen collections. Everyone realized that it wasn't the spirit of the Tax Squeeze that had been amended, but merely a few legalistic phrases in a body of federal tax laws and regulations which now fill at least thirty feet of shelf space.

The plain citizen who tries to figure out what all this taxing minutiae means, let alone what it costs him, is starting from a position of extreme disadvantage. As already indicated, he is disinclined to discover more bad news; he has an "ignorance-is-bliss" attitude. So any who would ask exactly what the tax man is doing to him must be prepared to reckon with a loss of political innocence. But beyond that, the tendency to focus upon the categories of tax lore as defined by the tax collectors and politicians is also misleading. And as long as one accepts their definitions, he is unlikely to see exactly what taxation is costing him.

Consider, for example, the concept of "income." If you agree to a definition which limits your income to the money which actually reaches you, then you must clearly be blind to much of your loss—the money that the tax man kept you from ever seeing at all. And this, as we shall see, is only one sense in which the conventional view is faulty.

85

With this preface, consider that the real tax burden has now mounted to about $10,000 per family. That is big money, even as measured in today's depreciating currency.

First, you pay federal income taxes. These amounted in 1978 to $1,602 for the average family with income of $16,009 and no itemized deductions. The aggravation involved in paying this tax makes it the most memorable of all; it is the one which first pops to mind when you think about taxes. Yet it is a tax which we have persistently misunderstood.

Witness the debates over the income tax when it was first proposed. Its advocates were either laboring under a total misapprehension of the nature of their proposal, or they were guilty of advertising frauds which should have curled the hair of Lydia Pinkham. The income tax was introduced on the basis that it would *permanently reduce* tax collection in America. What is more, the income tax was to have greatly *simplified* taxes. Professor Amasa Walker told Congress that the overriding benefit of the income tax was that "it is 'clear and plain' to the contributor and every other person." That may have been true in 1913, but today, anyone who claims that our tax codes are "clear and plain" has probably not read passages such as this;

> If the facts necessary to determine the basis (unadjusted) of adjusted basis property immediately before the death of the decedent are unknown to the person acquiring such property from the decedent, such basis shall be treated as being the fair market value of such property as of the date at which such property was acquired by the decedent. . . .

The person who can understand this passage is probably qualified to decipher the original draft of the Book of the Dead. At any rate, it is clear from the accounting of the IRS itself that most taxpayers do not understand. According to an official summary reported in IRS Document 6230, TCMP Phase III, Cycle 3: "Almost half of all returns filed are in error. . . ." Today our misunderstanding of the income tax is no longer complicated by thinking that the tax is "clear and plain."

The greatest current misconception about the income tax is the belief that the "next guy" is getting away with murder, and that there are wide loopholes which could be closed to ease the burden on "the little man." But like the nephews and nieces of an apparently rich relative, we are waiting for nothing. The windfall of lower taxes which we expect at the expense of those more wealthy will never occur. The rich as a group are a depleted resource. Any tightening of loopholes would primarily have the effect of increasing taxes upon the middle class, which now pays most of the burden.

As of 1975, the top 50 percent of income earners paid 92.9 percent of the total tax bill. These were people with adjusted gross incomes of $8,931 or higher. The highest 10 percent, with incomes of $23,420 or more as of 1975, paid 48.7 percent of the total tax take. And those in the highest one percent of income, with $59,338 or more, paid 18.7 percent of all federal income taxes. The Internal Revenue Service listed 1,149 Americans with incomes of $1 million or more in 1975. While it was widely reported that thirteen of those individuals paid no income tax, the other 1,136 paid an average tax of $1,011,000. If every cent earned by these individuals and every other person with an income over $50,000 were taxed away, the revenue could finance the federal government for only two weeks.

Contrary to popular impression, loopholes have not spared higher-income persons as a group from paying an increasingly large portion of the rising tax burden. In 1970, the highest 25 percent of taxpayers anted up 68.3 percent of the total bill. By 1975 they were paying 72 percent. As of 1977, those with incomes of $17,000 or more earned 55.5 percent of the total income and paid 74.3 percent of the income tax.

The "loopholes" which exist reduce the burdens on certain kinds of income only. Most of the money shielded from taxation belongs to the middle class and the poor rather than the rich. As Paul Craig Roberts has pointed out, "Seventy percent of the reductions provided by loopholes go to taxpayers who are not in the upper brackets." This was confirmed in a study undertaken by the Congressional Research Service of the Library of Congress: "The characterization of tax reform as a soak-the-rich endeavor is inaccurate. . . . The loophole closing variety of tax reform usually represents an attempt to achieve a more comprehensive tax base by eliminating certain exclusions, exemptions, deductions, or credits." In other words, the move to close "loopholes" is largely an effort to squeeze more resource out of the average person.

Tax reforms now being proposed include ending the deduction of interest on consumer debt and home mortgages, striking the property-tax deduction, taxing fringe benefits and medical care; there are even some pioneering new principles of confiscation, like taxation of enjoyment in your work and the rental value of your home. Senator Orrin G. Hatch of the Joint Economic Committee discovered that the taxing of fringe benefits alone would "mean an increase in taxes of $240 on the average taxpayer." That was the cost of closing only one loophole. When the wider range of deductions and exclusions is considered, proposed tax reforms would squeeze three dollars from the middle class for every additional dollar that can be wrung out of the rich.

President Carter's plan to tax the "three-martini lunch" is partially an attack upon fringe benefits. It is more than that, however. It is a fiscal assault upon the pleasure principle. It is the tax collector saying you must be miserable in your work. If you are not, it does not matter whether travel or entertainment expenses you incur are good for your company's profits. They must be taxed because, in the words of President Carter, this kind of expenditure "must produce personal enjoyment in order to have its intended effect." That is a new and potentially far-reaching principle of taxation. It holds that the key to whether business spending is deductible is not whether it serves to maximize net income, but whether the persons participating enjoy what they are doing. On that basis, bosses with handsome secretaries may someday be asked to pay an income-tax surcharge, just as tax reformers are now moving to tax the three-martini lunch. (In fact, the three-martini lunch almost never consists of even a single martini. Cocktails of any description are ordered by diners on only 8 percent of lunches. The average cost of these expense-account meals in 1978 was $6.69—so it is hardly high living at The Four Seasons, which would be subject to higher taxation if this reform were to succeed.)

Another indication of how remorseless the income-tax squeeze may become can be drawn from the demand now circulating in Washington that homeowners be taxed on the annual rental value of their properties. This is called "taxing imputed rent." The argument behind it is that the owner of a home, by living in his dwelling, obtains the benefit of shelter for which he would otherwise have to pay rent. Figure out how much you could earn by renting your house. That is the amount by which the reformers would raise your income, in all probability boosting you into a higher tax bracket without your having seen one additional cent in revenue. As Paul Craig Roberts wrote in *Harper's* magazine, this new principle of taxation opens tremendous new opportunities for increasing the burdens on the middle class:

> [It] can be applied to home vegetable gardens and to the services of housewives. Cooking services, sexual services, cleaning services, child-bearing services, and laundry services are also income in kind. The

imputed value of a housewife who is good at all of these tasks would exceed the salaries and wages of many husbands. The government could then take your house and make you hire out your wife to cover the unpaid taxes you couldn't pay.[2]

These kinds of extensions of the income-tax squeeze may seem like something of a joke, but don't think for a moment that such exaggerated or preposterous tax claims cannot be put into effect. The politicians, as in the past, will suggest that the new taxing principles are meant to ensnare the rich—the claim under which the income tax was first introduced.

Since 1913, when the first rates were established, America's population has grown about 120 percent, but the number of persons filing income-tax returns has increased by almost 24,000 percent. The individual in the lowest brackets today is taxed at twice the rate that millionaires paid in the beginning. The indisputable long-term process then has been to lay every dollar at the disposal of tax collectors, a principle which has been explicitly incorporated into the federal-government budget analyses with the introduction of "tax-expenditure accounting." Practically every dollar spared from taxation is theoretically treated as a government "expenditure." In other words, whatever money you don't pay in taxes is considered a subsidy to you by the government. Legislative attempts have already been promoted by Senator John Glenn and others to automatically terminate the "subsidies" to you after a five-year period. If the imputed rental value of your home is counted as untaxed income by the policy wizards in Washington, then the prospect is not as remote as it seems that further tax reform could impose even more preposterous burdens on you.

The evolution of income taxation during the past dozen years has already gone far toward that end. While many people believe that Congress has frequently lowered taxes, the opposite is true. Inflation is ratcheting people into ever-higher tax brackets, and the federal-income-tax take from the average family has been greatly enlarged. As inflation empties the dollar of value, you need more dollars to retain the same purchasing power. Even when you get a raise under conditions of inflation, your actual spending power could stay the same or go down. Yet you must pay higher and higher taxes, just as if your increased income represented a real gain in purchasing power. James Lynn, former director of the Office of Management and Budget, described the situation this way: "To pay for its current and newly proposed spending, the federal government has programmed a series of regular tax increases that each year will add from $350 to $450 to the average family's income-tax bill. These increases will continue indefinitely."[3]

Put simply, each 10-percent increase in your income has generated a 16.5 percent increase in your tax burden. A continuation of the same trends until the turn of the century would increase the federal income tax on a 1977 income of $17,763 from $2,167 to $6,289 in real terms. That would represent almost a tripling of the federal-income-tax take. Over that period, the taxpayer would lose $43,916 (in constant dollars), just because of the tax effects of inflation. This, it should be added, assumes that inflation until the end of the century will continue at the same average rate prevailing since 1970—6.3 percent. Since this assumption seems at present to be about as optimistic as the hope that the Romanovs will be restored to power in Russia, an even greater taxflation impact seems inevitable.

The faster the dollar loses value, the more rapidly the middle class will be pushed up the progressive tax ladder and the higher will be the marginal tax rates on each additional dollar of income. If Congress follows usual procedures to adjust for this inflationary impact, it will lower the rates in the lower brackets; this can be done very cheaply, since persons in those lower brackets ante up less than 7 percent of the total income tax anyway. So even a 25-percent reduction for the taxpayers earning about $10,000 or less would result in a slighter revenue loss to the politicians than a 6.5 percent reduction for the upper 25 percent—the middle class, which pays 75 percent of all income taxes. What this means is simply that increased inflation is bound to continue raising your tax burden.

Inflation not only means higher taxes on your income; it means higher taxes on your assets as well. Federal capital-gains taxation has amounted to nothing less than capital punishment. Because inflation means that each dollar is worth less, it takes more dollars to buy the same capital asset which sold for fewer dollars years ago. This does not necessarily mean, however, that the owner has achieved an increase in purchasing power. He may actually have lost, yet he must pay taxes on his loss. Dr. Martin Feldstein, professor of economics at Harvard and president of the National Bureau of Economic Research, studied the actual gains transactions reported on 1973 tax returns. He found that:

> In 1973 individuals paid capital gains taxes on more than $4.5 billion of nominal capital gains on corporate stock. If the costs of these shares

are adjusted for the increases in the consumer price level since they were purchased, the $4.5 billion nominal gain becomes a real capital loss of nearly $1 billion.[4]

With effective capital-gains rates ranging beyond 100 percent, it has become exceedingly difficult for the average individual to increase or even maintain his net wealth. Under conditions which have prevailed since 1969, your assets would have to double in six years, triple in ten years, and quintuple in sixteen years for you just to stay even. The 1978 tax law improved those odds, but only slightly. A continuation of inflation at a 7-percent rate would still keep the effective level of capital-gains taxation at higher than 100 percent for assets which exactly stayed even with inflation over the holding period of 7.2 years (which the Treasury Department has determined is the average holding period for stocks). Like Alice, we must go faster and faster to stay in the same place.

In addition to federal income and capital-gains taxes, the average person must also pay state income taxes and (in some instances) city income taxes. These collections have risen from an insignificant sum twenty years ago to $31 billion by 1977. This amounts to a burden of about $585 per family. These state and local income-tax collections have been soaring with inflation just as have federal taxes. But unlike the situation at the federal level, personal income taxes account for only a small percentage of the total local tax burden. In 1977, only 16.6 percent of state- and local-government tax revenues were collected from direct income levies. More than twice that amount came from property taxes, which in 1977 raked in $64 billion. That is more than $1,200 for each and every family living in the United States.

General-sales-tax revenues also take a real chunk out of your spending power. As of March 1978 the U.S. Department of Commerce put annual sales-tax receipts at almost $39 billion—about $735 per family.

This by no means exhausts the list of taxes that you pay. Consider the following:

· Combined federal and state gasoline taxes can mount to 13¢ per gallon or more.

· Federal excise taxes also apply to such products as oil and automobile tires.

· Every time you make a telephone call a federal tax is part of the price you pay.

- There are entertainment taxes levied on going to the movies, and sometimes for dining in restaurants.

- Federal and state taxes upon liquor can reach $15 per gallon.

- There is a $9 federal levy on every barrel of beer. State and local governments typically slap on several additional dollars of beer tax.

- Taxes are imposed upon tobacco products, which yield about $70 in revenue from each family in the United States.

- In most states you must pay a substantial levy to drive an automobile. In addition to your driver's license, you must normally pay a yearly tax fee. Beyond that, eight states and the District of Columbia subject automobiles to additional yearly taxes.

- Other miscellaneous levies imposed by the local and state governments alone raked in $19 billion in 1977, or about $358 per family. These include gift taxes, death taxes, severance taxes, and many other kinds of impost which it is our misfortune to pay in more ways than we know.

Thus far we have confined ourselves to the more or less obvious aspects of the Tax Squeeze. But what of the costs to which the government will not admit? Take, for example, corporate income taxes. Do you bear part of the corporate tax burden as a consumer and citizen? Many would say "no." The corporate controller pays the tax without any help from you. Unless you are a stockholder, so the reasoning goes, the taxes imposed upon corporations do not matter as far as you are concerned. If the corporate tax burden averages, as it now does, $950 per family, this is merely $950 less income for stockholders—$950 in revenues which the government can rake in without necessarily having its prongs in your pockets.

The trouble with such an argument is that it assumes that everyone in society is explicitly independent. It assumes that your good fortune or impoverishment is of no account to your neighbors unless they are somehow entitled to a share in your purse. The idea is that one must receive a gift of cold cash before an accumulation of capital by someone else becomes a matter to cheer about.

But the issue is rather more complicated on several counts. In the first instance, accumulation of productive capital is beneficial to almost everyone. This is so for the reasons outlined in our discussion of progress in Chapter 2. The greater the amount of capital available, the higher the standard of living will be. Put simply, there is a "free-ride" effect which an increase in productive capacity provides simply by increasing the number of opportune uses for the average person's time. This, as we have seen, is the process that raises the pay of butlers, even as their physical labor declines.

Thinking of the benefits of capital accumulation in terms of butlers' wages helps us notice an exception to the rule that everyone benefits from progress. An increase in the total available supply of productive capital may not benefit someone who already has a substantial amount of capital of the productive, static, or transcendental variety. The additional wealth coming into existence, while it benefits both the owner of the new wealth and the ordinary citizen, may have an adverse impact upon personal finances of individuals who already have staked out substantial claims to wealth. The reason is simple. New wealth is disruptive. It means that the holder of the old wealth must henceforth pay more to his butler. Not only that, increased capital may often reduce the value of previous investments. When increasing the capital accumulation enabled Sir Henry Bessemer to introduce a new and better process for the manufacture of steel, this increased the wealth of everyone—*except* the people who had great stakes in the old ways of doing things. Those who owned pig-iron factories and mills producing steel by the puddling or blistering processes experienced losses. The value of their productive capital fell with the innovation which a generally increasing supply of productive capital made possible.

Even when new investment is not explicitly directed toward the achievement of some technological breakthrough, when it does no more than bring into being a new competitive facility, this alone works to increase competition and thus reduce the incomes from the current configurations of capital.

At the same time, an increase in real productive wealth has a negative impact upon most static capital investments. Static capital is most valuable when productivity and production are declining. When productive capital is being consumed, and inflation is raging out of control as we use up resources faster than we produce them, then the greatest returns accrue to static capital investments, such as idle land or jewelry. For reasons that will become more clear later on, transcendental capitalists, such as leading politicians and high-level bureaucrats, may also find an increase in the total productive wealth of society detrimental to their selfish interests.

As poet Louis Simpson has shrewdly suggested, the deepest dream of governors is "bring evil on the land that I may have a task." This is not an imputation which is authorized only by poetic license. It is a plain truth that difficulties, disasters, and declining living standards create prosperity in government. This fact is so notorious in Washington as to be hardly debatable. Anyone who doubts that destruction, war, and economic calamity bring prosperity to government can simply check the record. Great spurts forward in government spending, which bring into being the higher salaries, and opportunities for career advancement on which politicians and bureaucrats thrive, always come about in conjunction with crises. In times of increasing prosperity, peace, and calm, politics is eclipsed, and the rewards to transcendental capitalists fall.

Seen this way, there is a sort of unholy community of interests among some of those with the greatest claims to wealth to discourage the accumulation of new productive capital, especially in new business enterprises. High corporate-income-tax rates have precisely this effect. By reducing the incentives to form new businesses and innovate, these high corporate taxes serve to reduce consumer living standards. In a passage which deserves wider attention, economist Colin Clark analyzed the matter this way:

> Many upholders of high taxation are sincere opponents of monopolies; but if taxation were lower and, especially if undistributed profits were exempt from taxation, many businesses would spring up which would compete actively with the old established monopolies. As a matter of fact, the present excessive rates of taxation are one of the principal reasons for monopolies now being so strong.[5]

The accumulation of taxes upon businesses does, therefore, squeeze the consumer. These taxes prevent wage rates from increasing. They stifle innovation. They reduce or eliminate the prospect of competition from new firms, thus maintaining artificially high prices which the consumer must pay. It is probable, therefore, that a reduction in corporate and other business taxes would have dramatic effects in reducing the squeeze on living costs. This is not simply because such a reduction would increase the profits of current corporations. More importantly, it would so multiply the rewards for accumulating new productive capital that many new businesses would come into being and the total wealth in society would increase.

After consideration, it should be clear that all taxes which are imposed under current conditions must bear upon the reductions in the quality of life. High corporate tax rates are part of the average person's burden.

Even monopolists do not benefit from high taxes in the long run. High taxes can have a beneficial impact upon their personal finances only so long as they are not raised higher than the level needed to forestall competition. When tax rates reach confiscatory stages, however, and little or no scope remains for productive capital accumulation, even within the existing corporate structures, then only transcendental capitalists profit. The managers and owners of established corporations suffer along with the rest of society.

This situation has prevailed for some time. Contrary to the general impression that corporations pay little or no taxes, the fact is that not once in the last ten years has the effective corporate tax rate been as low as it was in 1968, 52 percent. According to the Bureau of Economic Analysis, U.S. Department of Commerce, the effect of inflation has been to overstate corporate profits and thus increase the tax burden. The higher inflation goes, the higher the percentage of corporate tax, in spite of the loopholes. For 1974, when inflation as measured by the Consumer Price Index reached 12.2 percent, the effective corporate tax rate shot up to 102 percent. As Paul Craig Roberts explained:

> This is because inflation overstates profits by causing firms' books based on historical costs to understate the true cost of replacing the plant, equipment, and inventory used up in production. In this way inflation converts costs into taxable income, thereby increasing the effective tax rates on corporate profits.[6]

To better see how this works, consider what happened in Germany in the 1920's, when inflation reached such proportions that prices were increased, not only daily but hourly. The bag of flour which cost 100,000 marks when purchased by the supermarket may have finally sold for 3,000,000 marks. Yet this did not indicate a profit of 2,900,000 marks. To the contrary, it was a loss if the next bag of flour the grocer had to buy in order to replace his inventories and stay in business cost 5,000,000 marks. Any taxes the grocer paid on his nonexistent profit would have driven him even further toward bankruptcy. The same thing is happening in the United States today, but mercifully, on a more moderate scale.

The increasing burden of corporate and other business taxation squeezes down the value of productive capital. The corporations listed on the New York Stock Exchange have lost about half their value since 1968. Further increases in effective tax rates would tighten this squeeze and accelerate increases in the cost of living.

The total effect upon the consumer of the many taxes upon manufacturers and retailers is probably impossible to estimate. Howard Jarvis claims that a calculation by automotive economists imputed $4,500 of the cost of an $8,000 automobile to taxes. Even if this estimate is exaggerated tenfold—if the direct and indirect effects of taxation in raising the cost of an automobile amount to only $450 per vehicle—this would still comprise a considerable burden upon the average consumer. And this effect is certainly not confined only to automobiles. Every product and service one buys is subject to an almost unimaginable array of taxes. A study by the Tax Foundation, for example, found that taxes are levied 151 times in the production of a single loaf of bread. That makes the air in the typical white loaf a bargain by comparison.

Much more could be said about the degree to which taxes paid by others reduce your own quality of life—but the point should be clear by now: *The average family does not escape the burden which high corporate and other business taxes impose*. You are spared from the record-keeping obligations and the job of filling out the forms for these "hidden" taxes, but you are not free of their costs.

This catalog of underestimated tax burdens would not be complete without a look at a tax which is among the least understood and most burdensome: the payroll tax which supports Social Security. No other tax has risen so quickly in recent years. No other tax hits living standards with the same triple whammy as does the Social Security levy: it is simultaneously a direct tax upon income, a hidden burden supposedly paid by the employer, and a major factor shrinking productive capital investment.

Under the laws in effect on January 1, 1979, Social Security taxes could cost the working family as much as $1,403.77 in direct deductions, an equal amount in "employer contributions," and an even larger sum—up to $2,000—in lost income. The total of these costs means that Social Security taxes reduced the income of a middle-class family making $25,000 by almost $5,000 in 1979. This burden is now greater than even the income tax. It has increased by 100 percent in five years. It is scheduled to get even worse. Under the law in effect in January 1979, the worker's maximum Social Security tax was scheduled to climb to $3,046 by 1987. An additional $3,046 would be nipped from the worker indirectly in the "employer's contribution," and an even greater sum would be lost due to a decline in income.

Consider how this complicated burden began. When Social Security was instituted forty years ago, it involved very low taxes imposed upon a small percentage of the work force. The first persons to qualify for retirement benefits under the system had paid only a minimal sum of money over a short period of time. This was true of Ida M. Fuller from Ludlow, Vermont, Social Security's first recipient. She paid a maximum of $180 before her retirement. By living to a ripe old age, she got back many times what she lost.

As the years passed, however, new participants in the system have had to pay higher amounts over longer periods of their working lifetime. Today the maximum tax is 4,500 percent higher than the $60 a year Ida M. Fuller paid. This makes Social Security not only a greater burden but a more considerable factor in the preparation for retirement. Ida Fuller would have been one of the great seers of history to have guessed before the mid 1930's that she would be collecting Social Security in retirement. For most of the years of her working life, before the program began, she saved and made other provisions for her future. Today's Ida Fullers, wherever they are, live under different circumstances. Not only do high taxes and inflation increase the difficulty of saving, but the prospect of income from Social Security makes savings apparently less necessary. As of 1971, when Martin Feldstein studied the situation, the total value of anticipated Social Security benefits approximated $2 trillion. This represented about 60 percent of all other household assets combined. In other words, as of that date the total value of household savings accounts, insurance policies, stocks and bonds, the family car and home, the furniture, the Christmas plate, the potted palm, and all other tangible assets was not even twice anticipated Social Security income.

It would be extraordinary for members of the public to ignore so vast a potential asset as anticipated Social Security benefits. They do not. They treat Social Security—the transcendental capital of the middle class—almost as though it were money in the bank. This substantially reduces the apparent need on the part of the family to maintain its own savings. According to Feldstein, who studied the problem for the Social

Security Advisory Council, Social Security taxes in 1971 caused a decline in personal savings of $61 billion. Since by coincidence this was exactly equal to the actual recorded personal savings in 1971—$61 billion—a fair estimate is that Social Security slashes personal savings in half. Feldstein comments: "The implication that Social Security halves the rate of personal savings is startling but not unreasonable. For middle- and low-income families, Social Security is a complete substitute for a substantial rate of private savings."

Feldstein further calculates that by slashing personal savings, Social Security has reduced total private savings by 38 percent. This reduction in savings leads in the long run to a shrinkage of the productive capital stock by 38 percent. If not for Social Security, therefore, there would have been a 38-percent increase in capital stock, which Feldstein suggests would have led to an increase in the Gross National Product of 11 percent. For 1972 alone, this would have meant an increase in the total value of goods and services by $127 billion. What does this mean in terms of personal income? According to Feldstein: "If . . . [Social Security] taxes had been invested instead of just becoming transfer payments . . . wages would have increased almost 15 percent."

The fantastic growth of Social Security taxes and anticipated benefits through the decade of the seventies implies an even more adverse impact in reducing overall savings and thus slashing income. Even if this effect was no greater than that analyzed by Feldstein on the basis of the 1971 data, by 1979 the implied income loss for the average family would have grown to almost $2,500 per year.

In effect, Social Security converts a family's savings into transcendental capital. The tax moneys are immediately spent and converted into transcendental-capital claims, which in turn reduce living standards. The higher the Social Security taxes go, the greater the squeeze upon the average person.

Social Security is financed by the imposition of extraordinary taxes. This is true not only in the sense that the burden takes forms which are out of the ordinary, but also because Social Security taxes are among the few which are supposed to provide the taxpayer with some sort of monetary return. This makes it possible and even necessary to analyze the system not only in terms of what it rakes in, but also in terms of the probable yield. We have already entered into this discussion briefly in considering the good luck of Ida M. Fuller of Ludlow, Vermont, for whom no one could deny that Social Security was a good deal. In addition to notoriety, it brought her thirty-five years of compound profits from an investment of $180.

The similarity between lucky Ida Fuller's windfall as the first retiree on Social Security and the profits obtained by the early investors in a Ponzi scheme is too great to ignore. Preposterously high returns for the early investors are an essential characteristic of almost any swindle. Even where the practitioners are politicians rather than free-lance shysters, the favorable testimonial is necessary to gull and lure the larger mass of participants who must support the project if it is to reward its sponsors. This time-tested procedure was elevated to a kind of art by Charles Ponzi. Operating from a Boston office in 1920, Ponzi offered the public the chance to "make 50 percent in forty-five days." That is not a bad bargain, if you can get it. Ponzi's first takers really did. They got half the money invested by the next persons coming along. And so on. There never really was an investment. Ponzi just shuffled money from one person to another.

Although Ponzi's victims, like many of today's Social Security participants, were well pleased and cheered him when he appeared in the streets, some cynics turned up to point out that the whole thing was impossible. It was revealed that Ponzi had $4 million in assets against $7 million in liabilities. This gave him a considerably better ratio of assets to liabilities than today's Social Security system, which has only a few billion in cash on hand against liabilities of $10 trillion, 344 billion (present value as of October 1, 1978). Unfortunately for Ponzi, the judges of 1920 were unimpressed with his pioneering lunge into public finance. He went to jail.

The crucial difference between Ponzi's endeavors, which eventually carried him into a pauper's grave somewhere in South America, and the politicians' system of Social Security, which carries them to reelection, is the power of the tax collector. Most Ponzi schemes are doomed because of the natural limit to the number of suckers who will voluntarily turn up to keep the "chain" going. This is not a problem for the politicians. They can create the semblance of an infinite expansion of the chain by forcing everyone to be a sucker. By manhandling everyone into the system, no matter how pauperizing a bargain it becomes, they can maintain the flow of revenues—masking the progressive deterioration of the system. With this kind of backing, the politicians can indulge almost any financial fantasy they please. As long as they can continue to rope in additional participants or force everyone to bear the losses, the system can continue to operate. But no one should delude himself with the thought that the system works. Social Security works no better than Ponzi's original scheme. The individual Social Security participants—today's workers—are now suffering losses which would have made Charles Ponzi himself blush. The system has not collapsed merely because the public has an ill-founded confidence that politicians will be able to redeem losses currently being absorbed by imposing equal or even greater losses upon those now being born. This is the essence of the claim that Social Security represents "a compact between the generations."

Already the costs of Social Security to a person in his mid-twenties are so frightening as to accelerate the aging process. For someone who was earning the median 1977 income of $16,000, the 1977 Social Security tax was $1,937. At the same time, this individual went without $2,401—income he might have received but did not because Social Security reduced real savings and investment. That brought the total cost of Social Security for that single year to $4,338. But this is just the beginning. In the next year, 1978, the Social Security tax increased to $2,142. Assuming, to be on the conservative side, the same lost income of $2,401, that meant an average loss for 1978 of almost $380 per month. The new year of 1979 brought with it another 31 percent increase in Social Security taxes. Again assuming an income loss no greater than the year before, this meant a total for the year of $4,209. Under the law in effect in 1979, still another 13-percent Social Security tax increase was in store for 1980. That would expand the tax burden alone to $3,176 per year. Add to that the $2,400 of lost income, and the cost of Social Security for that year would be $5,577. The next year, 1981, was scheduled to bring another 24-percent increase in Social Security taxes, making the total yearly burden $6,351.

Even if there were no Social Security tax increases for thirty-five years thereafter, until today's young person would be expected to retire, a continuation of Social Security under the same terms would cost the typical young person of our example $734,885 (1977 dollars) in lost principal and interest by the age of sixty-five. Never have politicians in any country imposed so great a burden in exchange for so little. As Brookings Institution economist John Brittain says more diplomatically, "If more young people knew what Social Security meant to them, more would be upset."

This program which the Social Security Administration claims is meant to "ensure your financial independence" does precisely the opposite. It all but guarantees that a young person today will face poverty in retirement. He will lose almost three-quarters of a million dollars in capital—a sum greater than his expected lifetime earnings. When he is no longer in a position to earn an overtaxed income, he will not be able to fall back upon his own capital. He will be dependent in every sense of the word upon the politicians for whatever they dole out, from false teeth to the Thanksgiving Turkey.

Whatever Social Security benefits prove to be thirty-five years from now, it is a certainty that they will be lower than what the individual could have attained by controlling his own money. Of course, no one, not even Social Security's administrators, knows the precise terms of the benefits the program will pay in the future. No one can say what requirements may be imposed upon beneficiaries or what the minimum age of retirement might be—sixty-five or eighty-five. Courts have ruled that the government is under no obligation to ever pay anyone anything. It can change requirements for benefits whenever the politicians so please. While the suggestion of a retirement age of eighty-five is undoubtedly an exaggeration, it is by no means unlikely that the minimum age to receive payment may be increased. Witness the recent suggestion of the Social Security Advisory Council that the basic retirement age be increased to sixty-eight. If they chose to raise the age to seventy, there is nothing you could do about it. Your payments to Social Security, unlike payments for any kind of private investment or insurance plan, legally entitle you to nothing

Even under current conditions, large numbers of Social Security participants die without receiving anything. Then, unless he has slyly managed to accumulate capital in addition to the fortune snipped out of his paycheck by Social Security, he leaves the entire equivalent of his savings to the government. The money taken in Social Security taxes will not be part of his estate. If he has a widow, she may receive a pittance. And his estate will receive $300 to pay for a fraction of a casket. But the vast principal sum plus interest paid by those who have been part of the system all of their working lives reverts to the government. The effect is that of a 100-percent inheritance tax.

For blacks, the situation is even worse. The average black man can statistically expect to collect Social Security for an even shorter time than a white. The effect of the system as a whole is to shift capital out of the hands of the black minority and place it at the disposal of politicians and bureaucrats.

If, instead of being forced to contribute to Social Security, the recipients had been free to invest their funds in productive savings or investment plans, any unused dollars would be theirs to dispose of as they saw fit. They could will it to family or friends at death. Or endow a committee to save the woodchuck. Or, in instances where individuals found themselves dying of an incurable disease at age fifty, they could cash in the current value of their investments for one slam-bang trip around the world.

By whatever measure you care to take, Social Security is an incredibly poor bargain. Its disability features compare unfavorably with productive programs which could be obtained for $10 monthly, or less than 5 percent of 1979's maximum monthly Social Security tax. The private disability insurance automatically begins coverage after one month. It also provides compensation whether or not disabilities are expected to last longer than a year. By contrast, Social Security coverage begins after seven months of disability and can be obtained only for injuries and illnesses lasting longer than a year. This excludes more than 90 percent of all disabilities from Social Security coverage. So, in effect, you pay Social Security twenty times more to get ten times less.

Demographic factors dictate that the situation will worsen rather than improve. In 1947, twenty-two workers supported one Social Security recipient. By 1957, only six workers supported one recipient. The ratio had dropped in half, to only three workers supporting one recipient, in 1973. Since the birth rate has been declining since 1957, it is only a matter of time until the workers-to-recipients ratio drops to two to one and possibly even less. This means higher and higher taxes to support a lower effective level of benefits. The American Institute for Economic Research once estimated that a continuation of Social Security under current trends would eventually require payroll taxes confiscating 60 percent of income.[7] (This is in addition to federal, state, and local income taxes, property taxes, sales taxes, excise taxes, and all the other forms of plunder, petty and great.)

The only real beneficiaries of Social Security are politicians, bureaucrats, and other holders of transcendental capital. They all benefit in the first instance because Social Security tax receipts have greatly increased the revenue at their disposal. Moneys which are paid for Social Security are directed into the Treasury and immediately spent. If this income had been left in the productive sector, much of it would have been saved. Untold billions would have been invested in new capital plant and equipment to create new jobs and finance development of better products. That same money in the hands of government went to purchase portions of the Vietnam war, four new coats of paint for the interior of the GSA Building, $8 billion worth of gathering, sorting, and filing away of information on you and other private citizens, and more. Some of it went to pay for absolutely nothing at all. The Secretary of Health, Education and Welfare admitted that this agency lost up to $7.4 billion in one year alone. Authorities estimate that the total amount lost by the federal government through all agencies and programs now exceeds $50 billion a year. That sum amounts to about two-thirds of all tax receipts from Social Security in 1977.

Social Security tax rates have been kept high enough over the years to guarantee that there is almost always a surplus of revenues for the politicians to dispose of in other ways. By miraculous metamorphosis of political accounting, which transforms liabilities into assets, the politicians issue bonds to cover the amount spent. They then claim that this spending represents an "investment." The difficulty here is that the bonds do not represent assets to the taxpayer, but liabilities. They can only be redeemed when further taxes are levied at your expense. So the billions of dollars' worth of bonds are not assets you can count on to preserve you in your old age; they are in fact indications of a cumulative excess of nearly $40 billion in taxation.

There is more to the Tax Squeeze, of course. It would take many books to fully expose the inequities and the costs of the tax system which is currently squeezing America's middle class. This survey has not even touched upon estate taxation, which is a major means of liquidating productive capital. Indeed, there are many other forms of taxation which have not been analyzed here, such as airplane excise taxes, tariffs on imported goods, and federal taxes upon retailers—all of which have their own special effects. To go further at this point, however, should hardly be necessary. Even this brief tour of the evidence should convince anyone that the tax burden he pays is far greater than first appears.

The median family with an income of $16,009 in 1977 was weighed down with a tax burden approaching $10,000. State and local taxes alone amounted to $3,451. Federal income tax took another $1,602. Social Security cost the family at least another $4,338. What is more, people suffered from indirect taxation with higher prices on everything they bought. There are taxes on gasoline, taxes on alcohol, taxes on tobacco products, taxes on public-utility bills, and taxes imposed upon gifts as well as the final tax imposed on death.

You need not be a very sharp mathematician to see that the money stolen by such hefty taxation adds up. If you could take what is being lost at current tax rates and bank it with compound interest, you would be a millionaire in forty years. In fact, you would have almost $1,350,000. The figures are staggering, preposterous. The burden is so far out of proportion to what the average family has the ability to bear that things clearly cannot go on at this rate for another forty years. Between 1967 and 1978, while America's population was rising only by 10 percent, the cost of government increased by 212 percent. This is a major reason why the American standard of life is declining. John Marshall was not kidding when he wrote, "The power to tax is the power to destroy." Excessive taxation is playing a major role in the destruction of America's progressive way of life.

8
The Quality Squeeze

When the currency expands, the loaf contracts.
—*Democratic Party slogan from the
campaign of 1836*

Andrew Jackson once predicted that the quality of American life would be flatly ruined if the printing of paper money ever drove the price of bacon to four cents a pound. His timing may have been off, but he was dead right in principle: inflation can have a pervasive, destructive influence upon almost everything within the reach of social relations.

This is certainly the case today. The symptoms of inflation can be felt in every quarter. Products fail. Service personnel become ever more curt and incompetent. A call to the operator is answered with a recording: "Please hang up and try again later. Due to heavy calling we are able to complete only urgent calls." When you turn on the kitchen faucet you find that the city is filling your glass with khaki-colored drinking water. When you step into a new multibillion-dollar transportation system, such as Washington's Metro, your fare is devoured by a malfunctioning computer, the doors on the subway cars refuse to close, then refuse to open, and the train itself stalls between stations. . . .

Inflation has turned the odds against us. Like the player in the carnival game who reaches with a mechanical claw for the gold watch buried in a mound of baubles, we hope when we shop to come up with something worth what we risked in paying for it. As the decay of money engenders a decay of productivity, which is in turn compounded by wage and price controls, even the product we buy that does what it was meant to is likely to be made of inferior materials. The hamburger at the fast-food parlor is likely to contain more fat and a lower grade of beef. Oatmeal cookies may still taste good, but may include fewer raisins and less oatmeal. As we get poorer, even our junk food gets junkier. The glaze on doughnuts contains less sugar; the hole is bigger. A half-century after an American vice-president noticed that there was no longer a good five-cent cigar, there is no longer a good five-cent anything.

This sort of sentiment, of course, like that of the hillbilly ballad "All the Good Times Have Passed and Gone," is subject to the double imputation of being both an old timer's and an outsider's lament. As history has been eclipsed and we come to believe in nothing but ourselves, there has arisen an exaggerated tendency to view all unpleasant thoughts in psychological terms. So the possibility that the prosperity we have loved and wanted from life may indeed have "passed and gone" is hardly considered except under the suspicion that it represents the grousing of the maladjusted. What this misses is the substance of the complaint. It may make sense. And indeed, even if today's grumbling were no more than the current expression of a long-prevailing human weakness for whining, that would carry little import for understanding whether the material quality of today's life is in fact declining. There has always been much to whine about. The Code of Hammurabi, from 1750 B.C., reflects concern about the declining quality of alehouses and the pallid, understrength brew they served. If the ancient Babylonians could quite literally cry in their beer, and be accurate about it, so can we.

This is more emphatically so because most groundless grumbling about the quality of life, of the sort which marks many generational disputes, normally expresses a contempt for affluence, not a foreboding of poverty. Often this has its roots in resentment by the elderly of new material advantages. The introduction of many such advantages over the years, from the paid vacation to the padded chair, has occasioned envious reactions (among those born too early to fully enjoy them) to the effect that newfangled ways represent a deficit in the human condition, sure to be regretted in the end.

The difference between that kind of complaint and our present analysis is important and substantial. In directing attention to the ways in which inflation and regulation have combined to undermine the quality of goods and services, we are not seeing life's colors through a fading eye. We are merely directing attention to a phenomenon which has remained in the shadows because few have had an incentive to clarify it. Indeed, the whole weight of consumer advertising and political propaganda is directed to support the proposition that the quality of life's material endearments continues to improve. No manufacturer ever composed a jingle to make this sentiment memorable: "Buy Blue Pigmy brand peas, now packaged in the can with shorter shelf life." Nor has any politician staked his reelection campaign on this kind of accomplishment: "During my term of office, planks rotted out of half the benches in the city's parks." If we are to perceive such developments, we must do so on our own.

Nor can we rely very heavily upon statistics—there are too few to illuminate declines in quality. Mostly this stems from the sheer impossibility of quantifying the "quality" inherent in anything. But it is also true that most of the keepers of statistics have scant interest in illuminating those facets of life which are currently in decline. This is partly because—like many others—they are induced to a kind of judicial blindness by the strength of their conviction in "progress." As believers in the concept of a Gross National Product, they assume too readily that as long as their totals keep rising, there is no possibility of a real decline in the standard of life. But as Seymour Melman, professor of industrial engineering at Columbia, has pointed out, the orthodox economic measurements may mask rather than illuminate the productive health of the economy.

> Certain myths have prevented many Americans from even perceiving the evidence of industrial decay. We are told that, as long as the GNP rises, the nation is well off, regardless of the functional composition of what we produce. Actually one group of goods and services represents productive growth: these are things that are either part of the current level of living or that can be used for further production. A second class of products represents parasitic growth: goods and services that are not part of the level of living and cannot be used for further production.[1]

Most of the fantastic growth of government represents that parasitic growth to which Professor Melman refers: what we have earlier discussed as a growth of "transcendental capital."

While official channels remain largely silent about the squeeze on living standards, average people, instructed by the power of circumstances, are beginning to understand. A survey by R. H. Bruskin Associates estimated the way that people have perceived changes in the quality of a variety of goods during the "five or ten years" preceding 1976.

As reported in *Money*, some of the answers were: "Ten percent said cars were better made, 64 percent said they were worse; 16 percent said appliances were better, 45 percent said worse; 19 percent said clothing was better, 49 percent said worse; 9 percent said furniture was better, 52 percent said worse."[2]

People everywhere are regaling one another with stories of the incompetence and malfunction of systems. This has become such a pervasive undertone of social life that resentment of things which fail to work has become a major theme of our jokes and graffiti. You can confirm this for yourself by listening to the next comic you come upon. Whereas jokes during a period of rising affluence tend to focus upon the indiscretions of the *nouveau riche* (Morton the plumber takes his wife out for an expensive meal and orders fifty dollars' worth of salami and eggs), today's jokes highlight personal disappointment with the quality of products and services. Consider this comment by Mickey Marvin:

> In order to alleviate the traffic problem, New York City has to eliminate 75 percent of the cars on its roads. Actually, it's easy to do. All they need is my mechanic.[3]

How does one account for the decline in quality? On a superficial level that is easy. When the cost of craftsmanship or personal service rises above what the public will pay for, quality declines. As the accumulation of productive capital opened opportunities in the past, it has reduced the incentive for ordinary people to devote themselves to craft labor. This, as has already been discussed, increased living standards while making it more expensive to finance the provision of butlers and maids. This kind of decline is associated with industrial advancement, not decay. Nor is it a general decline in quality, merely a decline in the quality of items produced for limited consumption. Only when there is an overall depletion of capital and the income of the average person falls is there a general epidemic of shoddy goods, incompetence, and inadequate service such as is encountered today. In the last decade, *as inflation has reduced the value of the dollar, businesses have chosen to reduce quality rather than increase the money price of their product as much as would be necessary to offset the inflation.* Price controls and the threat of controls encourage this tendency.

Just as the public is misled by inflation into believing that it has more wealth to expend than is really the case, it can be bamboozled, at least temporarily, by almost imperceptible changes in the quality of goods it buys. Consider, for example, the subtle and gradual change in the composition of candy bars. Over the years, almost every candy marketed has undergone a cheapening of its ingredients or a series of gradual reductions in size. Some bars have been whipped so as to be more fluff and less candy. As air is one of the cheapest ingredients, the bars can appear to be the same even when they contain less substance. Others are cheapened by the substitution of new ingredients: artificial chocolate and extenders take the place of more expensive cocoa; almonds and walnuts are replaced with peanuts; the number of nuts is reduced.

This is a tendency which has carried over to mixed-nut snacks, which have been repackaged to include driblets of fried, spiced flour, concoctions which were almost unknown when the dollar was of solid value.

Even where the quality of ingredients has not been noticeably adulterated, there has been a movement to package smaller portions in the same wrapper. One candy company has reduced the size of its simple milk-chocolate bar fourteen times in the last two decades by dribs and drabs as small as one-sixteenth of an ounce.[4]

That such small changes can add up to a major difference in what the consumer pays for was evidenced by the announcement from the Hershey Company in November 1978, that it intended to directly raise prices on its products. This touched off an immediate and substantial jump in the price of cocoa on world commodity markets. The traders and experts had evidently realized that the likely alternative to a direct price increase was not continued marketing of the same product at the prevailing price but marketing of new bars containing less chocolate. The decision to raise prices was actually a decision to maintain quality.

This is not always the type of decision that people feel they can afford to make. Consider, for example, the decline in telephone service, which is important to the average American, who will spend a full year of his life dialing and talking on telephone instruments. In recent years, this commitment to yak has become less pleasant as we have been treated to more and more of the annoyances and breakdowns previously associated with the more primitive telephone service abroad. A frequent dialer finds increasing incidence of malfunction in reaching the proper number. There are numerous instances also of "crossed wires" over which we must listen to strangers exclaim, "Hi, George, how are you?" while trying to discern what our own friends have to say. More frequently than in the past, the system appears to be overloaded: one obtains a busy signal, not because the phone he wishes to reach is in use, but because all the circuits are occupied. These developments have coincided with a decline in personal service for dialers. Operators are now more difficult to reach: one sometimes has to let the phone ring thirty times before an operator will pick up. And the operators themselves seem less courteous and helpful than they once were. In many cities, directory assistance has practically been eliminated. And there are other malfunctions and annoyances associated with what Seymour Melman describes as "economizing by scanting on certain classes of repair and maintenance."[5]

The problem of declining quality is pervasive. Inflation increases a business's cost factors, but at the same time, that business is under political as well as consumer pressure to hold prices down. The result is likely to be a disguised price increase effected by a cheapening of what is produced. Shoes are made of lower quality leather and cheaper substitute materials. The soles are attached by gluing rather than stitching. Shirts are produced with fewer buttons. Not everyone will notice the difference. Beverages such as beer and soft drinks appear in smaller containers. And the brews themselves tend to be whipped out through a cheaper brewing process which incorporates less costly ingredients and artificial carbonation. The shelves of supermarkets are stacked with oddly shaped bottles and containers which have been pioneered to disguise reductions in portion size. They contain less of what you wish to use than the apparently smaller ones they replaced.

This coincides with a continuing decline in the quality of the food in the average consumer's shopping cart. While economy-induced reductions in sugar content of some processed foods may have spared the public a few cavities, most similar changes have led to acceptance of foods which only a few years ago would not have met the quality demands of the then richer public.

This is certainly true in terms of fresh meat. There has been a general downgrading of the quality of beef at supermarkets, so that today it is rare to see cuts of prime meat for sale, and most big-city supermarkets stock less of even the "choice" grade. Much of what is bought today is beef of the lower quality—so-called "lean" grade.

As inflation has squeezed the already narrow profit margins of the supermarkets, owners have economized in their produce departments as well. Since they can afford less of the spoilage that inevitably results from the marketing of certain kinds of fruits and vegetables, they have reduced or eliminated many, such as romaine lettuce, from their inventories and shifted away from the marketing of others in ripe condition.

This is why it is all but impossible to obtain a tomato in a supermarket which is anything but marginally more appetizing than a ball of plastic. Naturally ripened tomatoes are subject to rapid spoilage. But today's variety do not have this problem because they are scarcely infused with any of the qualities of life. "The average tomato," as Calvin Trillin notes, now "has more or less the same shelf life as a mop handle."[6]

The declining quality of meats and produce has been paralleled by a decline in the average quality of canned goods purchased by the consumer. Not only have certain regulations been eased to tolerate a larger residue of insects and rodent excrement in the canning process, but an increasing number of consumers are purchasing lower quality "generic" brands of fruits and vegetables. These generic brands, which are normally sold under labels of studiously plain design, now comprise up to one-quarter of the sales of items such as string beans. And even the higher grades of produce, which are sold under brand names and private labels, tend to be packaged in cans with a shorter shelf life. The extra quality inherent in more expensive packing methods can no longer be afforded by many consumers.

There is more to be told about the real or alleged deficiencies in the quality of the food in America's supermarkets, but the tale is too well known through the literature of the health-food movement to bear repetition here, except perhaps, to give one more surprising example: the quality of eggs has declined. A reduction in the quality of hen feed has resulted in eggs which are thinner-shelled and have less rich yolks.[7]

The institution of surreptitious price increases through practically imperceptible reductions in content must in the end be considered reductions in quality also. The consumer does not deal in precise weights and measures. On the contrary, a customer, just as the word implies, is one who is accustomed to purchasing many sorts of items under known terms and conditions. Not one person in 10,000 would notice, at first, if gallons of milk were only 99 percent full. If dairies were to short the customer by selling a fraction of a bottle at an unchanged price, the consumer would be deprived on that account. By the same token, if the cartons were rearranged to contain only eleven eggs, but appeared to hold twelve, the consumer would be well within his rights to be upset when it came time to eat the short omelet.

Less blatant changes than the swiping of one egg in a dozen may not be immediately perceived. When a paper company gradually and subtly reduced the number of sheets in a roll of toilet paper from 650 to 500 while at the same time snipping 20 sheets from the length of its roll of paper towels, the effect was a reduction in quality which the customer may have noticed without being able to pinpoint. It emerges in his general conviction that "they don't make things like they used to."

The evidence largely supports the conviction. As quality expert Joseph M. Kamen has written, even where controlled laboratory experiments show that people are unable to detect the minute individual shifts in quality occasioned in surreptitious price rises, they are able to notice the overall effect. In a study of minute changes in quality for the *Harvard Business Review*, Kamen reported that: ". . . over the years these sub-threshold alterations accumulated to a point where quality that was lower than the original standards was clearly apparent."[8]

The corruption of quality is almost an inevitable consequence of inflation when it reduces the real incomes of consumers. When people can no longer afford the product at its previous level of quality, firms have little choice but to cheapen what they sell. For one thing, no price can be increased less than a penny. On many consumer items, including some still found in grocery stores, the total purchase price is less than a dollar. This makes it all but impossible to avoid increasing the money price by at least one percent without repackaging. By contrast, the reduction of the size, or the marginal substitution of a lower-quality ingredient, can effect a hidden price increase of a much less dramatic nature. This is why, as Kamen observes:

> vending machine owners put slightly less beef in their sandwiches; . . . frozen pizza makers cut down the cheese and sausage content; producers of fishing reels reduce the number of ball bearings, then eliminate them altogether.[9]

With inflation-generated cost increases mounting, the savings which can be attained from even slight reductions in quality over an entire system can mount to a large sum of money. When Eastern Airlines decided in 1977 to withhold the cherries from cocktails which it sells its passengers, this alone saved more than $175,000, canceling out the effects of inflation in depreciating more than two million dollars' worth of revenue in the following year. While this may have been necessary to the airline, it was nonetheless a decline in quality for the passengers who enjoyed nibbling their spiked cherries.

Inflation-induced cost cutting has also resulted in steps by manufacturers to reduce the number of offerings to consumers. Whereas in the past there may have been four alternatives to choose from, today there may be only two or three. For example, the squeeze finds one of its more literal expressions in the changes which have recently been transforming the underwear industry. It was once possible for a man to choose from sizes 30, 32, 34, and 36, but now Fruit of the Loom, one of America's major undergarment producers, has begun marketing only two sizes in that range—30-32 and 34-36. This means that underwear may henceforth be available in a perfect fit for only half as many men, those sized 31 and 35. Most of the customers who could previously have been satisfied with the old sizes must now choose the better of two uncomfortable alternatives: drawers which are too tight or too baggy. That is the sort of bargain created by inflation.

Durable goods are subject to the same kinds of erosion of quality as are more frequently purchased items. But because they are in general more complex, there is a greater engineering leeway to disguise deteriorating quality and even to convert cost-saving changes into design advantages. It is probable, for example, that if the auto industry were called upon to build the same automobiles which were constructed ten or twenty years ago, a direct comparison between today's version and those of the past at today's prices would yield an unhappy judgment of current quality. It would be clear, for example, that the coachwork in current models is not as well finished as that of a generation ago. The various parts do not fit so closely together. The sheet metal is far more imperfectly finished. Chrome pieces are even likely to be coated plastic rather than solid metal. The interior is adorned with bare screws. In short, current models are more cheaply built than those of the past. David E. Cole, associate professor of auto engineering at the University of Michigan, a lively advocate of the value of today's auto products, admits that "the cost of keeping the fine detail would be unbelievable."[10] To produce yesterday's car today would cost at least double, and probably triple, what it did then. Randy Mason, of the Henry Ford Museum in Dearborn, Michigan, suggests that to duplicate the workmanship in a well-turned-out Buick of the past would take at least $38,000.[11] Most likely it would take more than that.

On the other hand, there is some comfort in the fact that today's vehicle is better designed. This means that even though it is more poorly built, the product which results can in many respects be favorably compared to past models. For example, new cars require decidedly less routine maintenance. Today's automobile does not demand a greasing every one thousand miles. Nor does the oil need changing so frequently as it once did. Improved ignition systems have dispensed with points.

Since they no longer exist, they do not have to be changed and puttered with.

Even many of the obviously cheapening changes in construction have been engineered to attain some benefits. The more crudely constructed dashboards, for example, which present the driver with a view of exposed screws and bolts, also allow easier access for the more expensive repairs that are required. The progressive replacement of metal, cloth, and wooden parts with plastic has probably effected some fuel economies, as well as improved serviceability. Sheet metal is now stamped out to a thinner gauge than ever before, lightening the load the engine must propel (but also, it must be said, making the vehicle more vulnerable to surface dents and hastening the onset of rusting). Handling capability has now arguably improved, especially inasmuch as today's cars are smaller and lighter than those they replaced.

An expert like David Cole concludes that in terms of the total package, a new car is a better bargain than it has ever been. In fact, Cole believes that much of the grumbling over the quality of today's cars is due to the fact that engineering improvements have spoiled owners, who have gotten out of the habit of visiting their garages ten times a year to meet the scheduled service intervals. As a result, when a car does break down now, it seems more annoying in a climate of higher expectations.

With that bow toward fairness, however, it is hard to deny that there has been a general erosion of quality, in spite of the best efforts of Detroit's engineers. In an environment of increasing regulation and high inflation, auto makers have been unable to significantly improve productivity over the last decade. *When costs rise, and real income declines, there is only one likely result: a decline in quality.*

New vehicles may require less service in terms of routine maintenance, but they also require more frequent, and more expensive, repairs. As an Aurora, Indiana, businessman told *The Christian Science Monitor,* "My 1957 Chevrolet was more dependable, in better condition, and safer to drive after 130,000 miles than my 1971 Impala custom coupe was the day I got it. My 1957 Chevrolet required no repairs except ordinary maintenance."[12] This kind of complaint hardly represents one man's bad luck. The *Harvard Business Review* reported on a telephone survey of 2,400 households which determined that even automobile owners who consider themselves satisfied with their cars had encountered broader and deeper problems with the quality than was the case with any other kind of purchase, whether frequently or infrequently made, and including even direct-mail goods.[13]

In any event, the public's impression that today's auto is inferior in terms of material and workmanship does no more than confirm judgments made in Detroit. When the Ford Motor Company reduced its warranty protection in August 1969 from five years (or 50,000 miles) down to only twelve months it told the world of its own predictions about the future quality of its products.

The decline in warranty coverage by the major auto manufacturers may also have involved a prediction on their part of the high inflation of the last decade. These companies have developed some of the most sophisticated cost accounting anywhere. They certainly realized that increasing monetary depreciation would not only eat into their returns from the sale of new vehicles but also drastically alter the economies of repair.

Any durable good like an automobile that is not scrapped when it fails (as is a pocket calculator) must be repaired from parts produced and inventoried somewhere. As inflation rises, it builds into the system an inevitable rise in repair costs.

In the first instance, auto makers, no less than people who make candy bars or fishing reels, are prone to do everything they can to avoid charging more for their product. This can involve, as has already been discussed, reduction in the size of the product, substitution of cheaper materials, and a decline in workmanship. Beyond this, however, the durable-goods manufacturer has an option which the confectioner does not: he can reduce the percentage of the total lifetime cost of the product that the consumer must initially pay. In other words, he makes the product more expensive to repair. Instead of setting a price to cover the expected repair costs under warranties such as those common before the 1970 models, the auto makers reduced the warranty coverage, thus effectively increasing their revenue from each car sold without increasing the initial price. As this tendency evolved, the cost of repairs rose out of all proportion to the increasing cost of a new car, so that by the advent of the 1979 models, the cost of repairs was three to four times as expensive as it had been when the long-term warranties were canceled. Since the auto makers no longer had to pay for many of the repairs, they reduced parts inventories. This raised the prices of the remaining parts and helped the companies compensate for the squeeze they felt on the returns from new-car sales. In effect, increased income from the sale of fewer parts helped the auto makers evade some of the costs of inflation.

Yet even if this were not their intention, inflation would still require that the cost of fixing an automobile, as represented by its disassembled repair parts, multiply rapidly. This is because it is practically impossible for anyone other than the original manufacturer to produce sheet-metal parts and major engine components such as blocks and transmissions. These parts are typically manufactured when the car is produced, and inventoried for later repair use. The cost of inventorying parts increases with higher interest rates. The prospective buyer must in effect take a loan on the part he wishes to obtain and pay the interest for all the time it has spent in the warehouse. High inflation drives interest rates up, thus driving up the cost to the consumer of major repair components. The minor parts, which are more often made by independent companies, are less subject to this tendency only inasmuch as they are less likely to be inventoried for so long.

No discussion of the declining quality of automobiles would be complete without a consideration of the radical reduction in the quality of driving surfaces. Just as one could not design a train while avoiding notice of the quality of the tracks and roadbed, so America's auto engineers must take the condition of highways and streets into account when they specify the handling requirements for new cars. A decade ago, America's roads were in good repair; today they are a shambles. Almost everywhere one drives, the paving is marred by sags, bumps, crumbling concrete, and gaping holes. These not only make for an uncomfortable ride and more difficult handling, they also damage the cars. That this damage can mount to considerable proportions is evidenced by the fact that in New York City alone there have been tens of thousands of lawsuits over property damage and personal injury occasioned by potholes in recent years. But the damage directly and explicitly attributable to impact of the car into a specific pothole—which throws the vehicle out of control or creates massive damage on the spot—is only a small fraction of the overall problem. Even the unmemorable potholes, ruts, and bumps do their work by shaking and rattling the vehicle, loosening nuts and bolts, creating squeaks, stressing the components, and jarring loose wiring and tubing which would remain intact under less traumatic conditions. Put simply, when roadbeds fall apart, so do cars.

In the nineteenth century the bicycle trust headed by Colonel Albert A. Pope and General Roy Stone really paved the way for the automobile by prevailing on governments to introduce asphalt roads suitable to a pneumatic-tired vehicle. Except for a brief interlude during the Depression, the quality of America's roadbeds has steadily increased until a few years ago. These improved roadbeds continuously eased the handling requirements for American cars. Steering on a vehicle that need not swerve frequently to avoid ruts and holes in the highways can be less than race-car-positive and still be satisfactory. Yet today's roads are beginning to present greater demands. The day of the good highway may be at least temporarily over—as was symbolically suggested by the collapse of portions of New York's West Side Highway.

The decline in the quality of the automobile is paralleled by a squeeze on the quality of many other high-ticket items. Appliances, for example, have been subject to declining workmanship, substitution of inferior materials, and a decline in service capabilities. The substitution of plastic for metal shelves in refrigerators, for example, introduced bending and breaking problems that were previously unknown. Cheaper plastic moldings and gaskets have also been subject to increasing complaint. As one typical householder found: "Three and one-half years ago, I purchased at great expense a refrigerator. . . . The gaskets around the door have steadily deteriorated and are now almost off. . . ."[14]

Other household items, such as furniture, have so steadily declined in quality that the shabby nature of many of today's products is almost self-evident. Solid wooden furniture has all but disappeared. Pieces that were once made of solid oak, walnut, or mahogany are now fabricated from pressed fiberboard with thin wooden veneers. Some are even veneered with plastic printed to affect the appearance of wood. Metal furniture parts are made of cheaper alloys, and the various pieces are more shoddily fit together than was the case in the past. Drawers are not snug and solid. The finely carved and wrought details which once marked the best of American furniture have slowly been reduced, even eliminated.

Widely purchased and expensive items such as mobile homes have also deteriorated in quality with inflation. They are increasingly plagued with faltering power systems, bad wiring, leaky sinks, and other irritations such as doors and walls that fall off. As one couple said: "Our kitchen sink had a leak in it the first day we moved in. . . . Our furniture is breaking up. After eight months of living here, it looks like we have lived here 80 years."[15] An independent study of the quality of mobile homes by the Center for Auto Safety concluded that they suffer from so general a decline in workmanship as to be "riddled with serious defects, such as unsafe wiring and leaky roofs," which result "in extreme vulnerability to destruction by fire or windstorm."

The family home, unlike the mobile home, is not vulnerable to being blown away. Yet it too has suffered noticeably from the decay in quality spread everywhere by inflation. Look through a new house today, and you see signs of inferior workmanship and a substitution of shoddy materials for those which were commonplace only a generation ago. And the parts that you cannot see are even more likely to have suffered a radical decline in quality. This is true from the top to the bottom. The roofs on new houses, for example, are no longer constructed of tongue-and-groove wooden planks, but thin-gauge plywood. The floors, except in the bathroom and the kitchen, may no longer even exist in the sense that they formerly did—as finished wood or tile surfaces which could outlast the carpet laid upon them. In many new homes, the carpets *are* the floors. Beneath them is nothing but padding and raw, unfinished plywood. The beams in the walls and the ceilings, which were once hardwood, such as oak, are now typically soft woods, like spruce and pine. Moldings around doors and windows are often no longer made of wood at all. They are cheap plastic. So are baseboards. Interior doors are made of plywood surrounding cardboard cores. Indeed, some are cardboard covered with plastic. Walls are made of plasterboard so thin and insubstantial that on a dare one could put his fist through to the other room.

Some of the changes in the technology of homebuilding are commendable. New plastic pipes, which replaced those made of copper or galvanized iron, are incomparably easier to install and are not subject to rust or corrosion. (If the new plumbing materials have any drawback, it may be their untested impact upon health.) Also on the positive side, today's house should be electrically superior to one of the past. It is now wired for 200 to 400 amps, effectively eliminating the prospect of overload due to heavy appliance use.

But whatever can be said of the technical advances in home construction, the evidence of quality decline in most new houses is too stark to be ignored. Carpentry work is sloppy. Inferior materials are employed at every feasible juncture. Walls are not always plumb. Doors are poorly hung. And there are many other defects turning up in a deluge of complaints by new home buyers, such as this one: "Water started pouring down the walls and through the electrical outlets. Walls cracked and buckled. The place became nearly uninhabitable."[16]

Although complaints are naturally enough directed against the builders and others who turn out increasingly troublesome products, a remarkable number of consumers turn to government for help. This involves a rather excruciating irony. Faced with industrial decay, shoddy goods produced through indifferent workmanship with increasingly inferior materials, we queue up at our mailboxes to post complaints, which are carried away under an expensive stamp by the U.S. Postal Service, an institution which is itself the target of about two million complaints each year. Postal employees are often discourteous. The service they provide is even poorer than it has ever been. Odds are that a letter or package mailed today will arrive more slowly than it would have a generation ago. A special-delivery letter has about a 25-percent chance of arriving a day or more later than the regular mail. A letter from mid-continent to the West Coast now frequently takes more time en route than the six-day delivery schedule established by the Pony Express in 1861. And the chances of any package arriving in damaged condition are rated at about 30 percent and may be even worse. Even though the Postal Service is handling only about half as many packages as it did in the 1960's, it is managing to crush, mangle, or destroy more of them. A spot check of the Chicago bulk-mail center by the General Accounting Office found *3.7 million* loose and untraceable mail items dumped out of boxes and packages, with the addresses shorn off, lying in various states of disrepair throughout the center. . . . It is upon this kind of service, then, that the dissatisfied shopper or still-hungry nibbler of a shrunken chocolate bar must depend to relay his complaint of declining quality to a government agency.

If the mail does arrive detailing the consumer's grievance, this is normally translated into a further breakdown of the system. As reported in *The Washington Star*: "Letters and phone calls from individuals and organizations across the country more often than not get snarled in a bureaucratic, paper-shuffling jam. Some end up in the trash can."[17] Analysis of complaint statistics shows that only about 37 percent of those who complain to government win satisfaction, as against more than 80 percent who are satisfied by returning merchandise directly to retailers. Said John Goodman after a study of government complaint-handling programs, "If we were using the business standard on government agencies, everybody would flunk."[18]

The reason that government cannot handle the flow of complaints about the effects of industrial decay is that the government itself is the chief transgressor upon productivity. The respected English journal *The Economist* estimates that the productivity of government spending in all Western countries has declined by not less than 100 percent in the last decade.[19]

This phenomenal decline in the return from vast government spending has much to do with the squeeze on the quality of many aspects of life. Our streets and roads are crumbling. Crime has increased dramatically. Court dockets are clogged. As we shall see in the next chapter, the huge government expenditure on education has been accompanied by a general decline in learning. Urban programs have consumed a fantastic fortune while making Jane Jacobs' comments from *The Death and Life of Great American Cities* even more applicable than ever:

> . . . look what we built with the first several billions: low-income projects that became worse centers of delinquency, vandalism and general social hopelessness than the slums they were supposed to replace . . . Civic centers that are avoided by everyone but bums . . . Commercial centers that are lackluster imitations . . . Promenades that go from no place to nowhere and have no promenaders. Expressways that eviscerate great cities. This is not the rebuilding of cities. This is the sacking of cities.[20]

Despite rampant government spending of our tax dollars, the quality of our daily lives is deteriorating.

The squeeze upon the quality of American life is real. It is created by the growth of transcendental capital and aggravated by inflation. The plunder of the productive sector has caused industrial decay and an inevitable decline in the quality of the products we use and the services upon which we depend. For once, it is true as alleged: "We don't make them like we used to."

9
The Underemployment Squeeze

The diploma gives society a phantom guarantee and its holders phantom rights. The holder of a diploma passes officially for possessing knowledge . . . comes to believe that society owes him something. Never has a convention been created which is more unfortunate for everyone—the state, the individual (and, in particular, culture).

—*Paul Valéry*

The decaying quality of American employment is by all odds one of the least understood aspects of the Squeeze. This is true for several reasons, one of the more prominent being that not all of the under-employed could plausibly be considered victims. Indeed, many may be quite pleased with the posts they fill, satisfied with their incomes, and convinced that they are doing something which contributes significantly to the public weal. The underemployment of their talents may represent far more a loss to the rest of society than it is for them. For others, the millions who cannot find jobs and millions more who are overqualified for the jobs they do hold, the Underemployment Squeeze is more painful and apparent. Yet in one case or the other, whether underemployment has yielded a high income, as it does for a GS-18 whose job has no productive significance, or has left a victim pounding the streets with no job at all, there is one common thread: most people's training and talents are being put to only a fraction of their possible use.

The growth of transcendental capital and the consequent decline of genuine production has left government employing more and more people. The results are typical symptoms of underdevelopment: less actual output per job, a decrease in relative wage rates, a decline of innovation, reliance upon increasingly antiquated tools, dependence upon foreign borrowing to finance both current consumption and further investment, and as we have seen, a breakdown of product and service quality.

America has large numbers of highly trained individuals for whom there are no opportunities to take full advantage of their education and skills. As Scott Burns says, "we created an entire class of educated professionals: a cadre of lawyers, accountants, engineers, managers, and technicians. But we neglected to build the industrial infrastructure for them to run."[1]

Like the Uruguayans who once employed 1,000 persons to run an airline with one functioning plane, we have devoted an ever greater portion of our national ingenuity to employ more persons to generate less tangible output. Whether these individuals are well- or ill-paid, they are paid for doing less. And as they do less, they consume productive capital rather than contribute to its accumulation, thus helping to guarantee that the entire population grows relatively poorer. The effects are already in evidence. The once high wages of American workers have declined relative to those paid abroad, so that as of 1978, American workers' compensation ranked only fifth among the ten richest industrial countries. Consider the numbers themselves, which here represent not income in dollars, but the foreign percentages of American pay[2]:

	1960	1970	1975	1978
United States	100	100	100	100
Canada	80	83	96	91
Sweden	45	71	113	120
West Germany	32	56	99	111
Belgium	31	50	105	120
Netherlands	25	51	104	116
France	31	42	72	84
Great Britain	31	35	51	51
Italy	24	42	73	75
Japan	10	24	48	68

What you see here is proof of the progressive underemployment of Americans. The Japanese, who in 1960 earned only 10 percent of the prevailing American wage, will by the time you read this be earning more than 70 percent. The Dutch, whose 1960 income was only one-quarter of that earned in America, now earn *16 percent more.* These changes, of course, reflect many factors. But primarily they are evidence of the fantastic growth and profitability of transcendental capital in the United States.[3] The creation of new, abstract forms of property in America has diverted our enterprise and attention toward gaining the higher rewards which can be obtained through politics. The growing reliance upon regulations, tariffs, and other subsidies has maintained profitability of established enterprises at the expense of innovation. Rather than increase productive capital investment to facilitate the marketing of newer, higher-quality goods, we have depended too much upon political gimmicks to stimulate demand for existing goods. The consequence, succinctly described by *Business Week*, has been the breakdown of U.S. innovation: "It used to be that companies would dream up products like Polaroid cameras, the Xerox machine, and the transistor. Today super-cautious management, a capital squeeze, and growing government regulation have stifled such inventiveness. The result: fewer jobs, less growth and a loss of foreign markets."[4]

The decay of American productivity is not merely a distant threat, it is a current fact. As of late 1978 just about two-thirds of the sixty-seven industries whose performances are monitored showed productivity declines. Some, such as mining, have declined steadily over the last decade. The effects of these developments are visible in the influx of foreign cars on the highways, the foreign televisions in our living rooms, and much else besides. Imports of capital equipment, such as power machinery, have increased more than twice as fast as exports. This shows up in our deficit in international trade, a fluctuating but large figure which should be counted, as Seymour Melman has said, among "the warning signs of a real industrial debacle."[5]

When we cannot sell enough to pay for the foreign products we buy, we must borrow the money somewhere, either by reducing our own savings or borrowing from foreign lenders. We have increasingly done both. Foreign central banks have purchased more than $120 billion of the massive federal budget deficits of recent years, thus helping to finance the current levels of American consumption. And additional hundreds of billions of foreign loans and investments have been needed to take up the slack in our productive capability and finance new investments.[6] New growth companies in the electronics field—one of the few sectors of the American economy to outperform the competition—have been forced to turn increasingly to foreign investment from Japan and Germany to obtain needed venture capital.

These are the external signs of industrial decay. They would appear to be too gross to be ignored, yet they have been ignored, and for a long time. This is partly because the mad scramble for transcendental-capital gains would be stalled by the mere notice of shortcomings in America's productive capabilities. It would have been too gauche for the vast ensemble of transcendental capitalists to have proceeded with the same alacrity to their abstract form of pillage if its effects on production had been fully known. So partly for that reason there has been very little effort expended to see just how severe the problem might be. New, reassuring theories have been invented to rationalize the decline of production. If more and more persons were doing less, we were told that this was a sign of progress—a shift to the service society. If foreigners developed new and better technologies and began to outdo us in world markets, this, too, was a matter for self-congratulation—it merely demonstrated the effectiveness of the Marshall Plan and our other efforts to regenerate Europe and our defeated World War II adversary, Japan. At every point, political efforts to mask the consumption of productive capital have created new bureaucratic enterprises, expanding the access to transcendental capital for millions and at the same time further tightening the squeeze upon production. Loss of millions of productive jobs has been masked by the creation of millions of new government posts, many of which have paid people to do little, but all of which are supported by well-advertised rationales and justifications. These obfuscatory campaigns generally have had the effect of engrossing the entire public-policy agenda—dominating the news and absorbing what attentions most people could devote to consideration of what was happening to their world.

The result has been to concentrate the profits of underemployment in an older generation which has already staked out its claim to transcendental capital while deflecting most of underemployment's hurt to the young. This can be seen readily by viewing the impact of education upon employment qualifications and opportunities.

Over the past several decades there have been enormous increases in government education expenditures—giving the United States the highest per-capita education expenditures in the world. During the 1970s government-subsidized two-year colleges were being opened on an almost weekly basis—at times faster even than newly franchised hamburger stands. When combined with the increased capacity of four-year colleges, especially those supported by state governments, the total effect of these developments was to open hundreds of thousands of new posts for the employment of teachers, administrators, and clerks. At the same time, the number of individuals continuing their educations was raised to 7,000,000.

Whatever else can be said of these developments, several things at least are certain. First, those who are now in college who would not have been otherwise are therefore not in the full-time job market. This means that in nine cases out of ten, their educations are being financed, not out of current income, but from savings. The money to finance tuition and living costs comes either from the accumulated proceeds of summer jobs and parents' savings, or the savings of others offered up by government in the form of subsidized tuition, subsidized loans, and outright grants. So the additional millions in the classrooms are kept there only because additional billions of capital are being diverted to their support. This money, of course, is not available to finance additional productive investments.

Another indisputable aspect of the rampant growth of education is that almost all the new jobs created are suitable only for highly educated persons. Other than a few janitors, all the administrators, the teachers, and even most of the clerical help have at least some college education. Many have graduate degrees. The full measure of the magnitude of our expenditures on education also must take the costs of educating these individuals into account. The multibillions which were spent in the past to educate teachers can be no more productive than are the teachers themselves. This is true for the same reason that one would not count the expenditures of billions to train an enthusiastic army of buggy-whip makers as anything but a loss unless those talents could be put to productive use.

One further aspect of the education explosion: the doubling, then tripling of education expenditures has coincided with a marked decline in the *quality* of that education. Almost one of every seven persons reaching the age of seventeen today can neither read nor write. Even universities which are meant to be centers for the study of letters spend vast sums entertaining students who barely know the alphabet. To Dr. Campbell Tatham, professor of English at the University of Wisconsin, "it seems pretty clear that the students can't write—or read—in some cases. Sometimes they are illiterate in writing and incoherent in talking. But those are not areas that I stress very much."[7] Professor Tatham conducts an English class in which students do not read books. They read the covers of record albums. If they have heard of Charles Brockden Brown, they probably think that he was Jackson Browne's younger brother.

This evidence, and more like it, supports an unhappy conclusion: the intellectual rigors of today's education cannot be very great. Reports abound of graduates of teachers colleges who cannot form simple sentences or "correctly add simple fractions, such as ⅓ plus ¼."[8] One wanders beyond the boundaries of normal hope to expect that such poorly instructed and obviously incapable teachers could themselves contribute any substantial instruction to the next generation.

Yet, in a perfect illustration of how the failure of the system feeds upon itself, the declining ability of the schools to encourage students to learn is broadly seen by the teachers themselves as a reason to employ even more highly educated teachers. A drive has been launched to expand education to early childhood and place day-care services in the public schools. As a supposed convenience to parents, the American Federation of Teachers has proposed that classes be extended to up to eleven hours a day for as many as 320 days a year. This would triple the time spent in public schools by the average child. The program would require the hiring of one "certified teacher and two paid assistants" for each five students. This would hike education costs by $40 billion while underemploying another 200,000 teachers. The advantage of these vastly increased expenditures allegedly lies with the pupils. It is proposed that they will be better able to read and write after spending thrice the time under custodial care in the classroom. But this is a manifest absurdity. The only advantage of such a program would be higher incomes and greater claims to transcendental capital for those teachers who would secure new posts. As Nicholas von Hoffman has observed:

> Teachers have shamed parents, made them feel guilty by telling them that if we don't lower the class size—i.e., spread the work around by paying the same number of people to do less of it—the kids won't learn to read. Under the slogan of nothing but the best for the kiddiepoos, it's that much of the best for the teachers.[9]

The remarkable success of the professional educators in increasing the subsidized demand for their services has been compounded by the imposition of bureaucratic rule-making for the purpose of expanding education's administrative apparatus. The greater the number of stupid procedures, the more intense the clerical effort required to fulfill them. This means that records which may literally be of no value to anyone at any point must nonetheless be gathered and filed away. Consider, for example, how regulations on hiring procedures affected Reed College in Oregon. HEW required that Reed advertise its faculty openings on a national basis, rather than depending upon perfectly sufficient inquiries through academic channels. Consequently, the number of applicants multiplied from about 500 to 6,000. The regulations required that accurate records be kept on each of the superfluous applicants. Among the mandated details was a formal assessment of each applicant's experience, qualifications, and physical attributes, as well as a statement of why Reed did *not* hire him. The clerical expenditure for this nonsense came to about $40,000. And that was just one of 10,000 instances in which the educational bureaucracy in America has become a sink for time and talent.

Usually, these exercises in expanding trivial tasks are not beneficial to anyone other than the parties to whom they provide a paycheck. The clerks who fill out, stack, and file away the millions of superfluous records of one sort or another may have useful daydreams while they work. If so, their time is not totally wasted, as it otherwise appears to be. It is certain that the students at Reed College, for example, whose education was the ostensible object of the efforts cited above, will never derive much benefit from those clerks' time and effort.

The growth of educational expenditures in America may be best understood as a selfish indulgence of the educators. They used the expenditures as an excuse to derive income for themselves. In the process, they created at least two burdens upon the future. In the first place, they consumed vast amounts of capital, while wasting much of whatever productive contribution they might otherwise have made. In the second place, they have dispatched much of American youth on a false start. To the many other influences which suggest that education is the stepping-stone to success, the teachers have added their own relentless incantations: "Get more education. It will make you rich." The consequence has been to produce a whole generation of hectored children, like those of John Hardy, the vehicle merchant of *Winesburg, Ohio*:

> Hardy . . . like thousands of other men of his times, was an enthusiast on the subject of education. He had made his own way in the world

without learning got from books, but he was convinced that had he but known books things would have gone better with him. To everyone who came into his shop he talked of the matter, and in his own household he drove his family distracted by his constant harping on the subject.

He had two daughters and one son, John Hardy, and more than once the daughters threatened to leave school altogether. As a matter of principle they did just enough work in their classes to avoid punishment. "I hate books . . ." Harriet the younger of the two girls declared passionately.[10]

As Sherwood Anderson astutely suggested, one can convey a conviction that education is important even while instilling a hatred of books. That is indeed what we have done. The result is that the primary residue of years spent in educational institutions may be the conviction that the diploma is the key to success. Students who can barely read or who spend their time in college English classes evaluating album covers emerge with little learning, but the conviction that such an experience has somehow fitted them to earn a great income in an interesting, rewarding job. They feel that their diploma is their entitlement. They expect an almost automatic victory over life's uncertainties because they have been educated and education is the ticket to life's good things. The diploma is like a driver's license: 'one cannot mix in traffic without it. And so, having done as they were told and obtained the requisite piece of paper, America's young, educated majority come face to face with this fact: the jobs they seek do not exist.

According to Professors Richard Freeman and J. Herbert Holloman, the percentage of college graduates taking jobs unrelated to their majors has increased dramatically since the early sixties. In the seventies, fully one-third of the men and two-thirds of the women have had to accept employment outside their area of study. This was up from about 10 percent for men and 13 percent for women a few years earlier. The proportion of blue-collar workers with a year or more of college has doubled since 1966. According to Institute for Social Research Surveys, these overqualified workers are far more dissatisfied and restless in their work than are older, less-educated workers.

There are likely to be still more dissatisfied workers in the future when the scintillating jobs which they have been taught they deserve fail to materialize.

The number of young people reaching age twenty-one in 1979 is almost 85 percent greater than it was in 1960. And the percentage of these individuals seeking employment is greater still. Because of social changes which make it less likely for women to stay in the home, and because accelerating living costs make it less possible for a family to support the familiar American style of life on one income, millions of people will be looking for well-paid jobs which do not now exist. In fact, an average of almost 30,000 jobs a week will have to be created by 1985 just to accommodate the new members of the work force. This is in *addition* to the increase in employment opportunities that will be required to replace current jobs that are bound to go out of existence. *U.S. News & World Report* estimates that about another 30,000 of these will be needed annually, bringing the total requirement for new employment to about 60,000 a week.[11]

For these posts to actually be created is by no means impossible. However, under current conditions the odds against it are only slightly better than the chance of finding a diamond in a Cracker Jack box. For the past decade, the economy has averaged no better than 35,000 new jobs created each week. And that has been almost miraculous considering the burdens which have been placed upon productive capital by the multiplication of transcendental-capital claims. With productivity declining along with our relative position in the world economy, it seems all but impossible for these employment needs to be met.

It now requires an average of about $50,000 in capital to support the employment of one individual in production. In some industries, such as petroleum, the capital costs are quadruple that. Since we have been borrowing from abroad to maintain even the current level of consumption, there is no obvious source of the additional savings needed to bring these new jobs into being.

Those who will suffer most will be the young. Many of them will have come along too late to stake out a claim on any kind of rewarding employment. They will be educated to expect something beyond most of their capabilities to attain. As Professors Freeman and Holloman write: "By all relevant measures, the economic status of college graduates is deteriorating, with employment prospects for the young declining exceptionally sharply."[12]

Ironically, a substantial contributing factor to the erosion of the prospects for the young is the very expansion of the educational system in which they spent their childhoods. The many billions in capital devoured to erect school buildings, until they were as numerous as gas stations, and the billions more which went to pay salaries of unneeded teachers and even less-needed administrative personnel, the still more billions wasted on gimmicks and trifles—all these expenditures made it less likely that a graduate at the end of a long educational odyssey would emerge into a world in which he could find something to do. Put simply, *expenditures in the name of education have reduced rather than increased productive prospects in American life.*

Contrary to the common assumption, there is scarcely any established relationship between higher education expenditures and economic growth. In fact, the extraordinary demands of education on the American economy, which extend far beyond the proportionate outlays in countries such as France, Germany, and Japan, amount to a major burden on Americans which people in those faster-growing economies do not have to bear. Even if it were true, as it seems not to be, that the level of civilization in a country is raised by having each and every individual exposed to all the instruction he could possibly absorb, that is no proof that it would be to anyone's material advantage. Indeed, if the thesis that more schooling is always an economic benefit were even plausible, there would be a clamor to extend education to age fifty. There is no such demand, simply because it is clear to most people that they are better off taking life's instruction as an herbalist, an outdoor sign painter, or an inventory clerk in a bargain basement than they would be sitting in a classroom.

If education beyond a certain point really were productive—that is, if it substantially multiplied one's income—then those who could afford it would always be in the company of an entourage of private tutors. But they usually are not. First, because most genuine education is a personal enterprise, and for that reason, beyond a certain point additional instruction becomes more a consumer good, a service one chooses because he enjoys it, just as some enjoy wrestling or tennis. The second point is that one is educated when he is young because that is the only time he can afford it. As he grows older, the value of his time increases, so it costs him more to sit in a classroom. Since the return from almost any workaday endeavor is much greater than the income derived from additional increments of education, one would be surprised to find persons other than the young in schools.

Implicit in these observations is the idea that formal education does not necessarily have a direct impact on cognitive ability. This is indeed what recent studies by sociologists and psychologists show. Their attempts to isolate the factors which do point toward the likelihood of earning higher incomes have focused recently upon native intelligence and home background. The case that these are the underlying source of the basic advantages which additional education was meant to open to everyone has been very forcefully argued by Professor Christopher Jencks in his book *Inequality: A Reassessment of the Effect of Family and Schooling in America.*[13]

An even more challenging analysis of the prevailing view that education is a source of economic advancement is made by Caroline Bird in *The Case Against College*. Although she is herself a college instructor, she denies that colleges can take much credit for the learning experience of students, which she attributes more to their association with friends, family, and activities on the job. In an interesting pencil exercise, Bird produced this assessment of the economic value of a college education: "If a male Princeton-bound high school graduate of 1972 had put the $34,181 his diploma would have eventually cost him into his savings bank at 7.5 percent interest compounded daily, he would have at the retirement age of 64 a total of $1,129,200." This, she concludes, "would be $528,200 more than the earnings of a male college graduate and more than five times as much as the $199,000 extra he could expect to earn between 22 and 64 because he was a college . . . graduate."[14]

Whether and to what extent educational expenditures should be considered in the light of economic analysis is an interesting problem. Without doubt, there are pleasures in learning which cannot be computed in a strict economic calculus. These may indeed be among life's chief pleasures. And they need not be diminished as we grow older. The pleasures we derive from learning are less subject to the physical limitations which interrupt the passion for football or swimming sprints. And notwithstanding all that has been done by television to open the illiterate imagination, those who can read have much broader horizons than those who cannot. All this said, however, the pleasures of education alone cannot justify education expenditure on the current level. Indeed, few attempts have been made to justify such spending on the grounds that it engenders a pleasurable appreciation for the humane studies. It is by no means established, in fact, that the current education establishment is not counterproductive on even that score. Statistics show continuing declines in the mastery of even the more rudimentary aspects of learning. With many now in college and many more who have graduated who can scarcely read, write, and cipher, it does not seem plausible to defend the current expenditures on the basis that they broaden and elevate understanding.

On the contrary, the results of our current educational endeavors were never intended to be the training of worthy successors to Aristotle and Shakespeare. (Shakespeare, it should be noted, was largely self-taught. Some Shakespearean scholars, such as A. L. Rowse, have argued that his lack of university training may have been an artistic asset rather than a liability.) Education has persistently been advertised as guaranteed access to the ensemble of goods and services expected as part of the American way of life. Education is imagined to be an economic investment. This is why the discussion of education always comes around to a consideration of job prospects. Indeed, teachers and the education lobbies themselves have almost nothing else on their minds. Their schemes for further educational spending are not intended to improve the capacity of rude minds to contemplate the mysteries of life so much as they are designed to solve the mystery of how their own purses will be filled. To the extent that there has been any public philosophy on the matter, that is the sum and substance of it. We seek education, not because we wish to be wise, but because we wish to be rich.

Unfortunately, as we have seen, things don't work out that way. We rely upon teachers and schoolrooms to create human-capital investments, but wind up merely consuming capital while losing track of our sums. We not only spend far more on education than can possibly be construed as an investment for economic growth,[15] we also certify teachers who cannot add fractions, and we tolerate politicians who either cannot or dare not keep their budgets in balance.

Before concluding this consideration of the role of education in promoting the Underemployment Squeeze, it is worth backtracking a bit to explain in another way why we have placed so much of the blame on educational expenditures when many other sorts of spending and regulation have also contributed to the decay of productivity. Seymour Melman, for example, has made a case that America's underdevelopment crisis can be traced to excessive military expenditures, which have diverted talent and resources away from solving the challenges of consumer research. He estimates that the total effect of military spending since World War II has been to radically reduce the annual output of the American economy.[16] In some measure, he may be correct. If we had devoted resources to our military establishment as stingily as did Japan and Germany, even while shoveling money into education as rapidly as we have, it may well be that we should now be more prosperous. Indeed, this is practically a certainty. The percentage of our total resources devoted not merely to waste by the military, but other nonproductive overhead expenses, has outmatched the superfluous costs of education.

This admitted, there is still reason to direct a formidable portion of the indictment for underemployment toward the educational establishment. And it is not merely due to the gross material impact of the waste educational expenditures have engendered; the effects of our passion for education are much more profound, even as they are more elusive. *The role which education has come to serve is symptomatic of both the causes and the consequences of underemployment.*

In a certain measure, the hot pursuit of education is an attempt to evade the uncertainties of the future. This perhaps reflects our uneasy adjustment to an ever-more-complicated life, one which is organized to require greater and greater mastery of information which is in principle unattainable. While we can and do know much about our individual spheres of existence, and we can through special alertness and study often increase this stock of useful perceptions, we can no more know all that the current organization of life requires than we could run sprints all our waking hours. We can run for a few seconds after the bus, but we cannot do without the bus altogether. By the same token, the little specialized knowledge that we can master is only a small portion of the particulars of time and place which inform the evolution of commerce and history. We do not know what we really need to know. It is inconceivable, even in principle, that an individual starting off to the grocery store over a familiar path to buy a familiar product on a bright day in midsummer would know how to time his departure so as to avoid being in the intersection at the very moment a truck runs out of control. One can look both ways, but he cannot foresee. Nor can he systematically predict what he needs to know to be a "success." Just as it is impossible to bring all the factors which bear upon creativity within the ambit of calculation, so the factors which bear upon our success in our economic life cannot be clearly calculated from the dogmas of experts. Even apparently stupid people, operating on hunches, intuitions, and particular knowledge which only they were positioned to know, have made vast fortunes, while those who minded their books—not out of their love of books, but out of a love of money—found nothing there to finance the purchase of the "big white house on the hill."

It is this which stirs resentment against the incalculable. It somehow seems wrong, it almost seems to be cheating, if one person standing in a place we could never be, talking to someone we could never know, just happens to have an idea which becomes the zip-lock bag. That bag may keep our leftovers fresh, keep our milk from tasting of fish, and make us absolutely better off, but it is beyond the limits of calculation for us to know how we too could have attained such a success.

Our institutions have a way of reflecting our fears and desires, even when they are incommensurate and incoherent. We want progress. We want riches and prosperity. We want these things so much that we cannot tolerate their realization being a matter beyond the limits of our calculation. And this is one major reason why we have steadily and assiduously sought to downplay the role of the entrepreneur. His success, more than anyone else's, is dependent upon accurate foresight. The entrepreneur realizes possibilities others overlook. He takes risks others avoid. He is mostly wrong, for which he pays the loss. His success at coordinating productive activity in the face of an uncertain and unknowable future not only facilitates the overall accumulation of capital but also brings material success to him. The knowledge upon which his success is based is nothing you can look up in the library—it eludes all attempts to treat it as a "datum."[17] We cannot make production a matter of expertise, an exact science in which we are dealing with known quantities and absolutes. It is a matter, instead, of judgment, of hunches, built out of the interplay of hopes, expectations, and decidedly imperfect knowledge.

It is the denial of this elusive, incalculable, and almost absurd aspect of life which has its firmest expression in the recent American fervor for education. Such fervor is an expression of a desire to make success purely a matter of routine, to bring it within the grasp of technique. An individual sits for three hours a week for three months listening to lectures on "The History of the Yo-Yo Through the Ages." And he earns a credit. When he has spent enough time and has enough credits, he graduates. That what is learned through this activity is increasingly irrelevant to the obtaining of a degree is a predictable development. It merely represents an intensification of the desire to convert rewards into functions of a routine. If everyone who goes through the motions of sitting in the classroom for the requisite number of years is to obtain his degree, this is no more than he expects from the rest of life. It exemplifies the tendency to substitute attendance and the attainment of "qualifications" for productivity and accurate foresight as the basis of rewards. Most of the many millions whose talents are underemployed calculate on that basis. Time in school brings them a degree; time on the job brings them a paycheck, four weeks vacation, accumulating sick leave, and the prospect of retiring at 75 percent of full pay at age fifty-five.

It is easy to see how people lose sight of what is really produced under such circumstances. That is, indeed, half the point. The desire to assure one's future through education is partly a desire to avoid responsibility for meeting life's personal tests. How ironic then that these techniques of avoidance themselves are now proving futile. To qualify everyone for success, we emptied education of its content, and thus outwitted our purpose. We miscalculated in thinking that education could protect us from the incalculable and spent billions to discover that, as Caroline Bird puts it, "in strictly financial terms, college is the dumbest investment a young man can make."[18]

By promoting pupils without close regard for the quality of their work, we have dumped them into a world which is already beginning to suffer because too many adults are paid, including many of the teachers, without regard for the productivity of their work. The effect has been to accelerate the decay of genuine production, misdirect incredible amounts of human energy, and prevent the productive-capital infrastructure from developing sufficiently to put the talents of many people to use at all.

And this is a loss to everyone—a loss to those without work and a loss to others who can never enjoy the wasted talents of their neighbors. The GS-18, for example, whose ability and education brought him to the top of the government pay ladder, is in all probability using just a small fraction of his potential. He may measure his own productivity by the speed with which he clears his desk and the frequency with which he waters the plants in the office window, but these are measures of his personal satisfaction, not his contribution to society. There are persons in Washington who have quite literally spent years doing almost nothing. The Department of Agriculture devoted the better part of a decade trying to answer the metaphysical puzzle "What is a country ham?" At last count, their search for a definition, begun in 1971, had already engrossed more man-years than Dr. Johnson devoted to writing *A Dictionary of the English Language*. When the bureaucracy sought to set the specifications for a mousetrap, the official documents extended to 100,000 words, longer than Joseph Conrad's novel *Heart of Darkness*.

Such is underemployment. It wastes talent. It means two men standing at a construction site for each man working a shovel. It means firemen riding the rails when they have not been needed for fifty years. It means printers and typographers in big-city newspapers who contribute nothing to the final product—they turn up at work only to derive an income. It is all a terrible waste of human energy. Persons who are undoubtedly capable of great things are now doing little more than shuffling papers. As economist Jude Wanniski suggests, there are probably in Washington today individuals producing government films about the official way to brush your teeth who should be in Hollywood making the sequel to *Gone with the Wind*. Many of America's more competent and enterprising individuals have been carried by pursuit of their self-interest into roles as transcendental capitalists where their exertions often come to nothing. And this, indeed, is preferable to having them inflict additional harm beyond the mere costs of maintaining them in their posts. These costs go considerably beyond the payment of salaries. Think of the paper that the bureaucracy wastes. One hundred tons of wastepaper must be hauled away from federal-government offices at the end of each business day.

Some would defend these and other costs of maintaining the bureaucracy as the only means of providing employment for an otherwise "surplus" population. Indeed, many of the advocates of increased government employment in their bolder moments admit that most of the bureaucratic endeavors contribute little or nothing, except the excuse to provide a paycheck to millions of people. Consider this comment from *The Washington Post* by Fred Reed, who is a columnist for *The Federal Times*, the city of Washington's house organ for the bureaucracy. Says Reed, in a short history of employment in the United States:

> Private enterprise cannot readily be pressured into hiring people to do useless work, but government can be. The Executive Department became a vast WPA for the white-collar indigent, a Humphrey-Hawkins for GS-13s. . . . Bureaucrats are not primarily parasites who should make an honest living on the market. They are people for whom there is no work.[19]

While there is a refreshing honesty which shines through Reed's observations, he is nevertheless guilty of the kind of circular reasoning which characterizes most attempts to rationalize the vast underemployment of talent arising from the growth of government payrolls. On the one hand, it is not true that there is no work to be done. The only real limit to the application of human endeavor is the availability of tools to make that work possible. There are jobs today for persons building microwave ovens which would have been inconceivable a century ago, even had the design for microwave ovens been known. The capital infrastructure did not exist to make such production possible. The growth of wealth does not narrow the horizon of useful activity, but broadens it. In the earliest, rudest stages of human development, which are still observable among aborigines on several continents, the catalog of productive activities is starkly limited. Beyond the gathering of herbs and berries, hunting activities, and the prosecution of a few crude crafts, even the most enterprising bushman is stopped short by the limitations on his capital. There is very little he can do in the way of useful work as long as he lacks tools. And this is why primitive men normally spend less of their day in productive pursuit than men in a society where capital has been developed.

The impression that there is no work to do, then, is pure illusion. There will always be improvements to be made in the conditions of life, the more so when people are wealthy than when they are poor.

The fact is that most persons underemployed in bureaucracy choose to be there. As has already been indicated, the rewards from associating oneself with bureaucratic endeavors so far exceed the norm available in productive activity that many of society's more enterprising and calculating individuals have rushed to stake out transcendental-capital claims. The fact that these claims on production are normally open only to those with educational qualifications, to those who must put in time to meet requirements rather than achieve any conventionally productive output, only makes the process feed on itself. It points more people into the schools in anticipation of the higher rewards that can be captured only with the aid of the qualifications.

Analysis shows that for many other underemployed persons, such as welfare recipients or those who habitually spend much of their time collecting unemployment compensation, the costs of accepting productive work, if it could be found, are extremely high. Martin Anderson estimates that the combined effect of increased state and federal income taxes, Social Security taxes, and losses in welfare benefits take almost 75 percent of any earnings increase up to $8,300 for poor people who go to work.[20] It takes no great leap of the imagination to see why many persons are induced to keep their talent out of productive use when the rewards for doing so exceed what can be had by going to work (considering the cost of transportation and clothing for the job, and the nuisance of getting up in the morning). But beyond this, many persons are forced to remain unemployed because of bureaucratic barriers, such as minimum-wage laws. These have automatically disqualified many persons of low skill from employment. As economist Walter E. Williams points out:

> Low skills explain low wages but low skills cannot explain unemployment. In other words a person is qualified or unqualified only in a relative sense—relative to some wage. To speak of qualifications or skills in an absolute sense has little meaning. For example, a carpenter who is qualified and hence employable, at a wage of $4.00 per hour may be *unqualified*, and hence *un*employable, at a wage of $10.00 per hour. This idea applies to *anything*. A Sears suit is "unqualified" to sell for the same price as a tailored Pierre Cardin suit.[21]

All the many billions that have been wasted, along with the additional billions that might well have come into existence had the energies of some of America's more enterprising persons been devoted to production, would have prevented our current crisis of underdevelopment. But taxes and inflation have contributed to what has been well described as the "immolation of business capital."

While this has been harmful to most people, it is not strictly true that it has harmed everyone. In the short run at least, two distinct groups have benefited, whether consciously or not, by the factors comprising the underemployment squeeze. Owners of large amounts of productive fixed capital, while paying a heavy price in taxes to subsidize the underemployment of millions, have also been spared from threats to the value of their machinery. When large percentages of the population are contributing only marginally, or not at all, to productive activity, the obvious result is a slowdown or even a reversal of economic development. For those who have large amounts of capital invested in illiquid form, this slowdown in the accumulation of wealth helps spare them temporarily from domestic competition. Since fewer people have the money to go into business for themselves or finance new risk ventures to challenge existing modes of production, that activity never exists. This extends the value of old machinery. Just as antiquated equipment can be valuable in remote corners of the world long after it has fallen out of use in productive areas, so outdated equipment can retain its value in situations where competition (which would otherwise force owners to scrap such equipment) is significantly reduced. Stillborn competition, in effect, conveys to some the profits of underdevelopment.

But whatever these marginal effects of underemployment in subsidizing some owners of productive capital, they are multiplied tenfold in increasing the value of transcendental capital. As the withdrawal of the efforts of millions from productive endeavor greatly reduces overall wealth, this has the effect of lowering living standards in general and assuring a population of dependent citizens to provide political support for the continuation and expansion of bureaucracy.

The interpenetration of politics and economics has created monumental confusion between appearance and reality, between our traditional view of property relationships and the way those relationships actually function. The mixed economy has garbled the role of work, turning the creation of jobs from a cost of production into a kind of product. At the same time, the confusion has been compounded by the fact that some of our more lucrative posts pay people more to do less. We have created a precedent in which access to "new" property in the form of government payrolls has become a prime route to personal profit for millions. The first step on that route is to enter the educational system to attain the qualifications. With 44 percent of seventeen-year-olds as of 1978 aiming for careers in the professions, multitudes are sure to be disappointed. They dream of jobs that do not and cannot exist. This gross disparity between hopes and reality may impose only an indirect hurt upon the older generation of transcendental capitalists who have already secured their claims upon production. But it will impose a direct and frightful cost upon millions of the young. They will be left on the outside holding their diplomas, the political speeches on the injustice of unemployment still ringing in their ears.

10
The Health-Care Squeeze

A great many laws in a country, like many physicians, is a sign of malady.

—*Voltaire*

Health care now costs the average family more than $2,500 per year. This is up from $312 in 1950—an increase which shows no sign of abating. A continuation of current trends would put one dollar out of six in the coffers of doctors and hospitals by the turn of the century. That is big money. It would make the forced tribute paid to churches in the Dark Ages seem like a bargain. They exacted only one dollar in ten from their customers, and for that price offered the prospect of eternal life. For all we know, they may have delivered. It is at least imaginable that coins pressed into the priestly palm do their work. The donors may fly straight to heaven after the toil on this earth is over. Yet whatever can be said of that miracle of the cosmos, which as Pascal wagered would make a bargain of any expenditure, the money we spend on health care brings us less of a bargain every day. A review of the evidence shows that 1978's $1,602.13 hospital stay yields no better results than 1972's $788.51 hospital stay. In another four years, if the bounding costs have doubled again, the situation is not likely to have changed. The true miracle of modern medicine will remain as it is today: that so many will pay so much for so little.

There is no doubting that doctors and hospitals provide useful services. The sick and injured will always seek to have their fevers cured and their wounds mended. It is also true that doctors, as persons, are normally dedicated, likable characters who work hard to help their patients. Yet this alone does not account for the extraordinary incomes of today's health practitioners. Health-care costs now devour the fruits of five to six weeks' labor by each American family. This is well beyond what health services are worth. Doctors do not enjoy a median income approaching $70,000 solely by providing a service. They profit from monopolizing that service.

Doctors as a group have become transcendental capitalists, employing the rules made by government to create a claim upon the income of others. It is these rules, more than any other factor, that account for the skyrocketing costs of medicine. The rules separate the patient from control over his own hurt. This enables doctors, laboratory owners, and hospitals to turn the body's natural infirmities into monopoly profits. It leads to two kinds of frauds: deliberate frauds made possible by the fact that many patients no longer pay for their health services; and unconscious frauds, which are created by the operations of the entire system. There are documented cases of some unscrupulous doctors claiming income for home visits to every patient in a nursing home after simply walking through the facility. Dentists have been paid for drawing forty-one teeth from a single human head. Such abuse is symptomatic of a larger abuse —the general exploitation by the health establishment of the patient's hurt. Just as members of medieval guilds monopolized the supplies for their work (jewelers had exclusive access to gold), so the patient's illness has gradually become the doctor's resource. He and his associates use illness to their own advantage, preventing the patient from finding cheaper care, and thereby drawing a disproportionate share of resources into the maintenance of health services.

The fact that government regulations effectively make any medical problem the property of the doctor has helped disguise the questionable effectiveness of modern medicine. In most cases, extra money does not buy better health. The fact that the delivery of health services has been so effectively monopolized has led to the false assumption that when mortality rates improve, doctoring must be the proximate cause. This is another example of the kind of blind faith in progress which leads to convictions that do not stand up to analysis. The fact is that the refinement of the medical arts is only one factor—often a small one—in the general improvement in health since the Industrial Revolution.

Merchant bankers, inventors, entrepreneurs, and others in the forefront of capital accumulation have made a greater contribution to our national health than doctors. This is not as outrageous as it sounds. John Deere and John Lane, the perfecters of the steel plow, along with Obed Hussey and Cyrus Hall McCormick, inventors of the reaper, did more to improve health and reduce mortality rates than any 4,000 doctors who ever lived. The capital which they and others like them helped bring into being greatly improved the productivity of human labor. By enabling farmers to produce more food more quickly, they actually saved lives. The better-nourished bodies of millions were then better able to withstand pathogenic attacks.

It is not just the inventors and early distributors of farm equipment who should be credited with lifting life expectancies. Everyone who contributed to the development of productive wealth added eventually to the improvement in health. The persons who manufactured steel made the plow and reaper possible. So did the miners, the blacksmiths, the whole ensemble of productive occupations. They all played a part in creating what Walt Whitman called "the endless freight-train and the bulging storehouse."

A review of the actual records of life spans over the last few centuries gives little support to the thesis that medicine, rather than the improved quality of life, was responsible for reducing mortality rates. It is true that today's infant is expected to live longer than one born in the past. But almost all the increase is attributable to his greater chance of escaping childhood diseases. Most of the moderation in the deadliness of childhood afflictions had already taken place *before* medical science developed its preferred treatments. Ivan Illich, who studied the problem in cross-cultural research for his book *Medical Nemesis*, concluded.

> The combined death rate from scarlet fever, diphtheria, whooping cough, and measles among children up to fifteen shows that nearly 90 percent of the total decline in mortality between 1860 and 1965 had occurred before the introduction of antibiotics and widespread immunization.[1]

Some of the decline in childhood mortality was undoubtedly due to the evolution of a better balance in the parasitic relationship between micro-organisms and human beings. Those organisms which generated the most deadly infections tended to die out along with their hosts. This made an equally severe infection of later generations unlikely.

Moreover, much of the decline in the virulence of infectious disease in urban areas (that which is not attributable to the curtailing of chronic malnutrition) can be explained by nonmedical factors. The development of public sanitation and the improvement of water supplies contributed significantly to improved health. So did more effective means of indoor heating. As mentioned elsewhere in this volume, wine froze on the Sun King's table at Versailles in the seventeenth century. Today, even residents of slum dwellings are spared the prospect of perishing of cold. They also enjoy the more widespread use of soap, better personal hygiene, and more sanitary preparation of food than were normal in the past. All of these improvements are made possible by increased wealth.

There is additional evidence hidden away in the vital statistics to demonstrate that nonmedical factors have played the greatest role in expanding life expectancies. Dr. Johan Bjorksten worked with data from the U.S. Bureau of the Census and the Metropolitan Insurance Company to plot the life expectancy of a sixty-year-old man from 1789 until the present. His startling finding, as reported in *The Relevant Scientist*, is that there has been very little change. As Bjorksten explains, "A 60-year-old man now has, within 1.1 years, the same life expectancy as in 1789!"[2] Since those able to reach age sixty at that time were predominantly wealthy persons who were consistently well-nourished and otherwise enjoyed a superior material environment, the suggestion is reinforced that *access to capital rather than access to medicine is the primary factor in reducing mortality rates.*

During the early part of the nineteenth century the life expectancy of a sixty-year-old man gradually rose, reaching a peak around 1875 at pretty much the same average number of years of life remaining as today. For several decades thereafter, up until almost the 1920's, life expectancy at age sixty remained below what it had been in the eighteenth century. A large measure of this decline may be attributed to increased urbanization and, in a sense, to the fact that more of the nonrich had attained sufficient access to food to survive. The food-distribution systems developed more quickly than the complementary material improvements in housing, public sanitation, and purification of the water supply. As the rapidly expanding population, reinforced by waves of immigrants, created urban slums, relatively more of the aged were found living in less-wholesome conditions than had been the case earlier in the nineteenth century. To better appreciate how this affected health, consider a contemporary account of life in New York's slums:

> The Arch Block has always been subject to miasmatic odors from natural causes, but these have been multiplied and intensified by artificial means. The population is dense, and as little addicted to cleanliness as godliness. The streets, which until a short time ago were rudely paved with cobble-stones, are generally matted with the foulest garbage, thrown from the houses in defiance of law and decency. The sidewalks are strewn with the decaying refuse of green-grocers, and the arm of authority is so weak that even in the fetid days of mid-summer the attempts to remove this death-producing filth or to prevent its accumulation are few and feeble. In winter huge heaps of ashes are added to the piles of kitchen and grocer garbage, both intermingled with fouler filth, so that the roadways are passable only to horses and vehicles specially adapted to scaling an infinite variety of short ascents. . . . In summer these heaps disappear only because the heat spreads them more evenly and thickly over the roadways, while at the same time it liberates the noxious vapors the cold had imprisoned, adding them to the natural miasmas of the place; so that the atmosphere during the close sultriness of later summer would enliven the undertakers but for the fact that the inhabitants who breathe their last of it are as undesirable customers in death as in life.[5]

As conditions of sanitation and housing improved in the late nineteenth and early twentieth centuries, life expectancy in this crucial range turned up again, to dip again only during the 1930's. When the Great Depression reduced incomes, many people were required to skimp on food and cut back on coal allowances to heat their homes in winter. Such economies, notwithstanding what doctors could do, reduced vitality and thus made individuals more vulnerable to normal human ailments.

These changes in mortality rates were marginal. What is crucial here is not how much mortality rates have varied, but how little. The average number of years of life remaining for white men at age sixty has not varied up or down by more than three years since the Constitution was adopted. Such variation as has existed correlates not with the progress of the medical arts but with economic development and such nonmedical factors as the availability of proper nourishment, uncontaminated water, a comfortable home environment, and public sanitation. These are the factors which have primarily enhanced bodily resistance to traumata.

Diseases have historically waxed and waned long before medical

145

science achieved its current level of expertise. Doctors were mainly saw-bones, mystics, and barbers when leprosy began to dwindle. In the thirteenth century, almost every town supported its own leper hospital, with a total of about 19,000 leprosaria throughout Europe.[4] For whatever reasons, the incidence of leprosy declined markedly thereafter, becoming quite rare only a few centuries later except in isolated areas such as Scandinavia. This all evolved outside the control of physicians.

The prospects for longer life continue to be largely determined by factors other than medical care. Statistically, an individual has a much greater opportunity to enhance vitality and resulting life prospects on his own than can be obtained through any level of medication. A study begun in 1965 involving 7,000 people in Alameda County, California, verified that there is a distinct correlation between longevity and what is generally referred to as "clean living." Specifically, the study conducted by the Human Population Laboratory of the California Health Department isolated seven "golden rules" of behavior. They are "the things you learned in the fourth grade," said Dr. Lester Breslow, dean of the School of Public Health at UCLA and an author of the study. The seven rules are:

> Eat a regular breakfast every day.
> Don't smoke.
> Eat regularly and not between meals.
> Get eight hours of sleep.
> Keep a normal weight.
> Drink no more than one or two alcoholic beverages a day.
> Exercise regularly.

The study demonstrated that a forty-five-year-old man could expect thirty-three more years of life if he followed six of seven of the habits. His life expectancy would drop by five years if he observed only four or five. And if he observed three or fewer of the health rules, he could expect to die eleven years sooner, at the age of 66.6.

When this eleven-year increase in life expectancy for men who follow the seven health habits is considered in contrast to the increase in longevity over the last two centuries, one finds that the individual himself can exercise a greater influence over how long he lives than anything that can be done by his doctor. As Dr. Breslow comments: "The daily habits of people have a great deal more to do with what makes them sick and when they die than all of the influences of medicine."[5]

To recapitulate: The evidence indicates that improved nutrition and other nonmedical factors have helped more people survive childhood diseases. The evidence further shows that by following good health habits individuals can preserve their own vitality and thus postpone the morbid effects of the aging process. But no one has yet demonstrated any method to halt or reverse the chronic degenerative diseases of aging. Doctors today cannot cure ailments such as arteriosclerotic heart disease, malignant neoplasm, hypertension, senile diabetes, cirrhosis of the liver, and kidney failure, all of which are better understood as symptoms of aging rather than individual diseases which could plausibly be eradicated. Even if one could completely neutralize the symptoms of one of these disabilities, this would mean only minor gains in longevity. For example, a complete cure of cancer, according to National Cancer Institute data, would only boost average life expectancy by about two years.[6] But this medical miracle appears no nearer at hand than ever. And the procession of miracles which would be required to suppress each individual symptom of degenerative aging is difficult even to imagine. Certainly this kind of achievement is far beyond the current medical repertoire.

What does this all mean? Simply that *the popular impression that doctors have succeeded in making people live longer is virtually without foundation.* The best means of staying alive is to stay healthy—a condition which, it turns out, has far more to do with what one does for himself than what the doctor does. To the considerable extent that an individual's health is affected by changes outside himself, these too are largely beyond the doctor's control. Variations in economic productivity; the quality of nutrition, housing, and sanitation; as well as the conditions under which human beings interact—these are all variables with greater impact upon mortality rates than the availability and sagacity of doctors.

The foregoing discussion is not intended to imply that doctors and hospitals are irrelevant. This is clearly not so. Doctors at their best perform many valuable services. They mend wounds. They dispense antibiotics. And they are able to intervene successfully in cases of some acute injuries and afflictions to prevent death and provide the body's natural healing mechanism an opportunity to work. Moreover, good doctors, of whom there are many, reassure and encourage their patients. Even if this is no more than the role performed by a tribal shaman who encourages the sick to return to health through magic, it would be wrong to deny its importance.

It would also be naive to focus solely upon the physical conditions of health and deny the subjective conditions. So-called "psychosomatic" effects can play a major part in the mysteries of healing. In fact, studies suggest that powers of the mind over the body extend so far that placebos —medicines with no pharmacologically active ingredients—can actually touch off chemical changes similar to those caused by authentic therapeutic agents. The biochemistry of the brain is so complex that it can translate the will to heal into a direct physical response in the body.[7] The chances for such healing to work, however, seem to be directly dependent upon the patient's faith in the doctor. So in this respect, at least, our unrealistically high impression of the efficacy of current health care may be partially beneficial. The fact that we expect the doctor to cure us may stimulate the body's own healing powers.

That is one side of the story. But against the good which medicine does must be counted the hurt, and there is much of it. Not only have many persons been nursed back to health by medical practitioners, but a great number have been injured, maimed, and killed by doctors. In fact, iatrogenic disease, disease caused by physicians, is now a substantial health problem. Ivan Illich described it this way:

> The pain, dysfunction, disability and anguish resulting from technical medical intervention now rival the morbidity due to traffic and industrial accidents, even war-related activities, and make the impact of medicine one of the most rapidly spreading epidemics of our time.[8]

Doctors not only subject patients to medication which is sometimes addictive and has hurtful side effects; they also kill many patients outright. According to *U.S. News & World Report*, about 30,000 persons "die each year from adverse reactions to drugs."[9] Sheer blundering on the part of medical practitioners takes the lives of many others. United States Senate hearings in 1975 revealed that fully 25 percent of all medical-laboratory tests conducted in the United States are "substandard or wrong." This means, according to *The Reader's Digest*, that "millions of Americans may be risking unnecessary hospitalization, unneeded surgery or inappropriate, and occasionally fatal treatment."[10] Far from being a safe spot for recuperation, many hospitals are actually danger zones. In fact, as Illich points out, "the average frequency of reported accidents in hospitals was higher than in all industries but mines and high-rise construction."[11] One of every twelve persons who enter a hospital as a patient incurs some injury or disease which he did not have when he came in the door. Research hospitals are even more dangerous, injuring one in every five patients, and killing one of every thirty. If you went to the hospital to live for two years, it would probably kill you—no matter what your health when you entered.

These statistics leave out the injuries which are inflicted upon the millions of persons who unwittingly subject themselves to unnecessary treatment. Testimony before a House Investigations Subcommittee by Dr. Sidney Wolf of the Public Interest Health Research Group indicated that as many as 3.2 million Americans are subjected to needless surgery each year. This results not only in large amounts of pain but also in the deaths of as many as 16,000 patients.

These facts suggest that the tens of thousands of medical malpractice suits filed in the United States each year may, to a large extent, be justified. Even as our medical system helps some patients, it inflicts harm upon others. Authorities suggest that the number of malpractice claims is a small fraction of what it could be if more injuries were reported. In fact, as many as thirty-five patients have their recoveries retarded, are injured anew, or are even killed for every malpractice claim filed. Ironically, when a fair percentage of the doctors in Los Angeles County withheld their services to protest spiraling malpractice-insurance premiums in 1976, the population experienced what *The Washington Post* termed "a significant drop in its death rate."[12] Prospective patients who would have otherwise yielded their lives to doctors had no choice but to stay home. When the doctors' slowdown ended, mortality rates rose again.

The questionable benefits of modern medicine and the downright damage that it can cause would not be the basis of a financial empire grossing more than $150 billion if it were not for the doctors' and hospital owners' privileged position as transcendental capitalists. It is this privilege, conveyed by the rules surrounding health care, which is almost the sole source of medical profiteering.

A report by the President's Council on Wage and Price Stability has analyzed many aspects of the medical monopoly. It demonstrates what most people already know: that doctors are raking in more and more money. Since 1950, the growth in their income has been even greater than would appear from a study of the Consumer Price Index, which indicates that doctors' fees increased 43 percent faster than other prices. But this leaves out the fact that in 1950 charity care comprised a substantial part of the average doctor's practice. This meant that many patients paid discount prices, especially for surgery and other expensive procedures. However, as medical costs rose, most people acquired health insurance, which tended to pay physicians more than individuals had paid in the past for the same services. The net effect of the increased insurance coverage was to greatly reduce charity care and thus disguise 20 percent of the increase in physician's fees.

The growth of insurance to subsidize purchases of health services has had consequences which tend to increase the burden of medicine upon the average person. For one thing, since much of the doctor's income is collected from third parties, the patients themselves are exempted from many of the usual restraints on purchasing. The doctor tells the patient what tests he requires, what other specialists or medical services he needs, when and how often he should return, what drugs he needs, and even whether he should be hospitalized and risk surgery. When insurance programs, especially government payment plans, are absorbing the costs of these exercises, the patient is far less likely to question their usefulness.

An example of how this procedure works was obtained by investigators from the Senate Special Committee on Aging who were examined by U.S. Capitol physician Dr. Freeman Carey and "certified as healthy." They then visited medical centers to complain of a common cold. Since their bills were to be paid by Medicaid, they were given a royal treatment. Doctors at one center on the Lower East Side of New York X-rayed one investigator several times, took blood and urine samples, then wrote out four separate prescriptions for drugs to treat what a doctor said was "asthma." Another investigator, visiting the same clinic, was whisked through a variety of tests, spent three minutes with the doctor, and was informed that she suffered from chest spasms and an upper respiratory infection.[13]

In a case reported in *The Reader's Digest*, a New York City resident with five children thought one of her sons was ill. Since she could not afford a baby-sitter she was obliged to bring her entire brood with her to a neighborhood medical clinic. As described by reporters Dan Thomasson and Carl West, this is what happened:

> Five hours later, she and each of the children had been needlessly examined by every one of the clinic's medical practitioners, ranging from an eye, ear, nose and throat specialist to a podiatrist. Her protests had been met with a "What do you care? You don't pay for it."[14]

The point of this and similar scenarios is this: the greater the third-party involvement in the payment process, the smaller the consumer's incentive to resist higher medical costs.

As the numbers of people covered by some form of health insurance rose from 54 million in 1950 to about 170 million today, the possibility was created for physicians to automatically jack up their fees. Instead of being reimbursed according to a negotiated schedule of prices, physicians began to receive a "usual customary and reasonable fee." This typically means that the doctor is paid whatever sum he asks for so long as his bill is not among the highest 10 percent of bills for the same service in his area. The procedure gives doctors the ability to guarantee skyrocketing income simply by demanding ever-higher payments from third parties. Under this formula 90 percent of the bills will be paid, no matter how remote they are from the market price. This compensation formula, which was introduced by government to reimburse physicians for Medicaid and Medicare services, reverses the law of supply and demand. The greater the concentration of doctors in a given area, the higher they are likely to set their fees. So if you want to find a cheaper health care, your best bet is to go to an area of the country where there are fewer doctors.

Since specialists tend to gain a higher portion of their revenues from third-party payers, and the patients whose bills are paid by others are more lucrative in the first place, more and more doctors have been moving into specialized practice. Those who remain "family doctors," to whom the patient himself usually pays a greater share of the bill, end up with substantially lower incomes than physicians moving into specialties such as surgery, radiology, and pathology.

Evidence abounds that access to the more successful medical technologies could be dramatically cheapened by freeing them from monopoly control. The current system requires patients to pay the overhead costs of producing and maintaining a fabulous array of complex, costly and often unnecessary equipment. As Illich has demonstrated, the medical tools which are most useful are "usually very inexpensive and require a minimum of personal skills, materials and custodial service from hospitals."[15] These are mainly designed to help the body fight infectious diseases and mend wounds. In contrast, expensive medical gizmos which the monopolization of health services forces all consumers to pay for are oriented primarily toward the diagnosis and treatment of degenerative conditions. Whatever benefits they provide to the ill do not extend to any very statistically significant reduction in mortality rates. For example, when Jesse Bailey died on April 3, 1977, after thirty-one hours in a Connecticut hospital, his widow received a bill for $8,125.55. Bailey had suffered from massive heart and kidney failure and his bill reflected the phenomenal array of surgeons' and doctors' fees to hook him up to a variety of equipment, subject him to batteries of tests, and inject him with exotic medicines. He paid more than $250 for each additional hour of life. This is the sort of bargain for which monopoly medicine requires every citizen to pay.

Not only must the consumers of the simple, effective medical services bear the financial burden of costly and relatively ineffective technologies, they must also dig deeply into their pockets to pay dividends on the doctor's transcendental capital—his license to practice. Almost every patient pays more than he needs to because provision of health-support services is unnecessarily monopolized by physicians.

Anyone of fair intelligence and discernment, which is to say anyone who can read and is sufficiently in command of himself to drive through a city in a rush hour, could with a few months' training adequately compete with doctors in the provision of many medical services. Since nonprofessional health technicians could be brought into service quickly and inexpensively in almost any number needed, they could reintroduce price competition into medicine. Costs to the patient for access to effective medical technology could be slashed to a bare fraction of those current today.

Would not this result in a dramatic reduction in the quality of care? Are not the mysteries of healing too obscure and complicated to be grasped by ordinary individuals? These and other questions are poised to spring readily to mind, having been inculcated along with the false but widespread impression of the miraculous curative power of medicine. But the stated and implied professional critique of allowing ignorant hands to meddle in the doctor's monopoly yields readily to analysis.

Even if it were true that an individual required every bit as much training as full-fledged M.D.'s now obtain in order to treat each condition with which a doctor is confronted, it would not stand to common sense that one would have to be instructed in every single health problem in order to effectively treat a limited number of them. If a nonphysician set out to treat only ingrown toenails, or venereal disease, or some similarly limited category of malaise, he could obtain every bit as much specific instruction as a doctor encounters for those difficulties in just a few months. So the argument against allowing free competition for various specific problems of doctoring is beggared at the outset.

What is more, scrutiny of the actual operation of American medicine reveals that medical technicians have already been entrusted by doctors to assume many crucial responsibilities for the well-being of the patient. They simply have not been allowed, in most instances, to organize effective competition to the medical monopoly. For example, some of the most difficult of all medical problems, those which occur in medical emergencies, are initially treated by medics. They are usually first on the scene of accidents. It is usually they who make the decisive diagnosis and begin the treatment. Since there are now more than 16,000 civilian medics in the United States, it requires no great leap of the imagination to see that nondoctors can also do the tasks that doctors do.

In many cases, the doctor's main role in the treatment of the patient is merely to charge his monopoly price. A study conducted by Dr. Paul Feldstein, economist at the University of Michigan, demonstrated that in 48 percent of all anesthesia work in the United States, doctors did not actually administer the procedure. It was performed instead by a nurse or a medical technician, even though the anesthesiologists often charged a full fee of $100 for every anesthesia procedure. Since the typical nurse was paid only one-quarter of this amount, the doctors made off with hundreds of millions of dollars in profits solely because of their monopoly position.

And even more gorgeous proof of the ability of nondoctors to compete is provided by William MacKay, a high-school dropout and medical-supplies salesman who actually performed hundreds of operations, implanting artificial hips and knees in patients who thought they were under the care of surgeons. MacKay in no way deluded the patients. He did not pass himself off as a doctor when he was not. His case involves no forgery of qualifications. He was merely a salesman of medical equipment who was pressed into service in the operating room at the request of the surgeons. In fact, he claims that if he had not been willing to assist in operations, and even take over from the ostensible experts when they bungled the job, he would not have been able to hock his wares.

A study of MacKay's exploits is available to all who have the stomach to study them in *Salesman-Surgeon: The Incredible Story of an Amateur in the Operating Room*.[18] The book details how MacKay's role came to light as a result of a malpractice suit against a New York surgeon who broke a patient's leg in an operating session at which MacKay was effectively the senior physician. It was he who repaired the patient's bone and actually inserted the artificial hip joint. An investigation by a state's attorney in Long Island subsequently established that MacKay's activities were not uncommon. To the investigator, of course, MacKay's exploits were interesting as instances of a possible felonious activity— illegal surgery. But they should be more interesting as proof that the law errs in prohibiting patients from calling upon MacKay directly for their artificial hips. Even though he was a high-school dropout, MacKay's role in practice was to supervise the surgeons. It was he who told them how to use their fancy equipment properly. And when they failed, it was he who rushed in to repair the damage.

The evidence that nonphysicians can readily assume the delivery of medical care is wide indeed. Even Mao's Cultural Revolution which was a cloak for so much absurdity, did produce one intelligible advantage for the Chinese people—"the barefoot doctor." By turning medical technology over to the peasants, the Red Guards showed how easily mastered the mysteries of medicine really are. Their method of purging experts and inviting in enthusiastic but unlettered cadres to assume their functions failed in a thousand facets of Chinese life. The peasants did not have the sagacity to operate the factory system or increase the output of the collective farms. They could not educate librarians, nor even maintain a zoo. All of these things were too complicated to yield to the heave-ho method of the Red Guards. But their efforts to improve health succeeded, perhaps because health is not a commodity but a personal condition which can no more be communized than it can be bought from a Park Avenue physician. In any case, as Ivan Illich has noted, the barefoot doctors' contribution to improved primary care is beyond doubt:

> The achievements in the Chinese health sector during the late 60s have proved, perhaps definitely, a long-debated point: that almost all demonstratively effective health devices can be taken over within months and be used competently by millions of ordinary people.[17]

Medical care *can* be effectively and cheaply delivered.

In Chimaltenango, Guatemala, Dr. Carroll Berhorst is practicing a kind of medicine which the laws would not allow him to develop in Kansas. That is not because he is a psychic surgeon. He is not. Neither is he an acupuncturist, nor a prescriber of forbidden drugs. Dr. Carroll Berhorst is merely a small-town American doctor who recognizes the need to cheapen medical care. He has constructed a one-hundred-bed hospital in Chimaltenango, where he treats impoverished Mayan Indians. However, he makes no effort to minister to all the Mayan difficulties himself. He has established a remarkably effective paramedical training program which has tutored many Indians in methods of diagnosing and treating illnesses. His paramedics are now delivering reliable, effective, and amazingly cheap care to the residents of remote villages. In 90 percent of all medical difficulties they encounter, these healers are competent to make a diagnosis and administer treatment. Those cases which are too complicated to diagnose or beyond their skill, they refer to Dr. Berhorst at his clinic. He then proceeds with further treatment.

This exemplary and noble man has provided a model of what American health care could be. Rather than use his knowledge to shut off and exclude ordinary people from intimate participation in the act of healing, Dr. Berhorst has encouraged self-confidence and autonomy. He has worked to encourage belief among people that they can cope with their own hurts. He has demystified medicine and thus helped heal many thousands of people, people in more morbid circumstances than face the average American. As a group his patients are malnourished. Their sanitary conditions are of the most primitive. They are weak hosts to a rich variety of tropical microorganisms. Yet, in this difficult and unwholesome environment, Berhorst has taught them to care for themselves with the more effective of modern medical techniques. His services are not entirely free. The Indians, as poor as they are, pay when they can for the care they receive from the paramedics and Berhorst's clinic.

In this they have an advantage which the average American does not. They pay only for the medical service they receive. They do not pay dividends on transcendental capital. Dr. Berhorst has not used political power to create a property right in the Mayans' injury and disease. If he had approached the matter the way most doctors are dealing with the American public, he would have mystified the problems of health rather than made them simple. He would not have trained the Mayans or placed medicine's effective technology at their disposal so they could attain a high level of self-care. They probably would have been grateful anyway. They just would have been poorer and less healthy. Because Carroll Berhorst is a healer, not a manipulator of rules, his efforts have been first and last productive.

The tycoons of transcendental capital who dominate America's health care use their privileged access to technical health devices to squeeze the public. Patients and citizens are obliged to pay far more than necessary for what medical science can effectively accomplish. This bad bargain is compounded because the monopolization of health services requires everyone to subsidize costly and ineffective techniques. The medical profession truly has "expropriated" health, as Illich charges. In so doing, doctors and hospitals have befuddled the public. Like tribal medicine men they have cultivated the impression that they alone have the magic powers to heal. They have been carried straight to the bank on the shoulders of this delusion.

Doctors and hospitals today are squeezing the public: taking ten cents out of every dollar the average family earns. This not only makes them a threat to the economy. In the long run it makes them a threat to health. Their exactions are contributing to the lowering of living standards. Since it was precisely the increase in productive capacity which widened the prospects of living to old age by better nourishing larger portions of the public and thus increasing resistance to invading micro-organisms, a sufficient reversal of this process would occasion a national relapse. It is already probable that the unnecessarily high costs of medicine have contributed to the reduced vitality of some low-income patients by inducing them to skimp on food in order to afford medicine. This is especially dangerous for the elderly, for whom high-quality food may be in many cases as important a factor in preserving vitality as medicine. Yet stories of old people skipping meals, filling up on tea and crackers, and even eating pet foods are hardly without foundation. When this indirect damage to health is considered in light of the clear and indisputable damage—the tens of thousands of deaths, the hundreds of thousands of maimings, and the vast amounts of human energy lost because of inflictions imposed upon the population by monopoly medicine—there can be scant doubt that the effect of much of America's health system is counterproductive in the fullest meaning of the term.

The difference between medicine as a productive aid to healing and the current system of monopoly privilege is important and enormous. The one contributes to individual autonomy and enhances the quality of life of the average person. The other creates a transcendental-capital asset out of the pain of the ill and injured. Their dependency upon the medical establishment, induced by that establishment through its political power, has become the basis of a plundering of production which reduces the average person's quality of life.

If your metabolism is wavering under the pressures of the Squeeze, a visit to the doctor will not help.

11

The Housing Squeeze

Where we love is home,
Home that our feet may leave, but not
our hearts.

—*Oliver Wendell Holmes*

Before he dies, every man should build a house.

—*Plato*

In 1950, seven out of ten American families had sufficient income to purchase a medium-priced house. By November 1978, seven in ten did not.[1] Such is the effect of the Squeeze. Inflation, higher taxes, and misguided political planning have combined to dramatically reduce the prospects that the American people will be well-housed. Not only is construction of new dwellings falling short, but the Squeeze is making it more difficult for many to maintain what they already have. Caught by rising property taxes, higher utility bills, and mounting costs for maintenance materials and labor, many owners have had little choice but to allow their properties to deteriorate. When they cannot afford to repaint, the paint peels and fades; unprotected wood then rots. Soon a once sound structure is barely habitable.

The normal process of decay is accelerated by political efforts that have not only consumed the resources which in some instances would have been needed for maintenance but also created incentives for destruction. In many cities whole areas are decimated because the rewards for destruction so far overwhelm the profits from building and preserving as to sweep aside the civilized revulsion at wanton waste. Hundreds of thousands of housing units have vanished under the onslaught of vandalism organized on an economic basis. And many more homes never came into being because the profits for obliterating housing have been raised so high as to lift destruction to the highest pitch of efficiency: the condition in which housing is never produced at all. In a sense, the home is razed before it can be built.

Even as this artificial shortage, compounded by inflation, increases the price of the housing which remains, it makes it more difficult for many middle-income persons to capture the paper profits implied by the higher value of their properties. To sell his home, one must find another place to live. That is becoming increasingly difficult because resources needed to finance the costs of building and maintaining sufficient housing under current conditions are becoming more scarce. Neither builders nor buyers, landlords nor tenants, are as rich as they would need to be to absorb the compound costs which have been imposed upon housing by politics.

As an indication of how far the Housing Squeeze has gone, consider that Louise Vanderbilt has joined with a tenants' organization in a rent strike. The monthly charge on her two apartments in a Victorian mansion in Newport, Rhode Island, became too much to bear. After she refused to pay, the court ordered her evicted. When the Vanderbilts are being evicted in Newport, there can be little doubt that there has been a reversal of fortune in the prospects for American housing.

Back in the days when the first Vanderbilt heirs were busy spending their $100 million, almost everyone could look forward to being better housed than his parents were. To a much greater degree than is the case today, the factors which determined what kind of home an individual would settle into were his own responsibility. Anyone with even a minimal income could, if he so chose, obtain his own home. *The Ladies' Home Journal* once devoted an entire year to a series of articles which told "step by step, dollar by dollar . . . 'How We Saved for a Home.'" The series comprised 100 first-person accounts "by 100 people who saved for and now own their own homes on an average salary of $15 a week. None higher than $30. . . ."[2] Looking back over the houses that could be bought on an average salary of $780 per year is an arresting process, for more reasons than one. It emphasizes in another way how much the dollar has been emptied of value. It also shows how plausible it once was for almost anyone to live in his own home. And many of these were homes one would be proud of today. They were not merely the Philadelphia-style row houses built by the tens of thousands at the turn of the twentieth century to accommodate the families of skilled and unskilled laborers. Some of the structures which were fully paid for in five years on an income of less than $1,000 were truly imposing. Looking back at a house which was "paid for out of a salary of $16 per week, saving $8," you see today's $100,000 home: a 2½-story clapboard house with several Victorian bay windows, two porticoes, and a full stone basement. Such a house was actually purchased for $8 per week. Today you would be lucky to pay the property tax on the same building for *$8 per day*. Few now could save enough in five years to pay the full price for a house of almost any description, let alone one as spacious and well-built as those accessible to the ordinary middle-class wage earner at the turn of the century.

The point is not that everyone was in fact well-housed seventy-five years ago. What we are speaking of here is not what everyone did, but what almost anyone could have done. In the past the American who wanted his own home could control most of the factors needed to obtain one. The cost of living was low enough that anyone who cared to save could do so. Money that was put aside grew in value, rather than being steadily decimated by inflation. When the time came to actually build the house, it was a simple matter to locate the property, pick a currently stylish model, and have the house constructed as quickly as possible by skilled craftsmen using the most efficient building techniques then known. The would-be homeowner probably did not need to apply for a building permit. If he did, he was simply paying a nuisance tax, not encountering a bureaucratic obstacle to construction. He did not need to bribe zoning officials to include his home site in some master plan. Neither did he need to prepare an impact statement or hire a lawyer to argue his case through a long series of appeals. By and large, he needed only to concern himself with building the house to meet his own standards. He did not have to pay 5 to 10 percent more to finance the costs of union featherbedding incorporated into strict "building codes."

When an American at the turn of the century bought a house, it was cheap, because he paid only for the house. He was not helping to finance massive government budget deficits which today jack up interest rates and doubly inflate the price of a house. Because he could save himself, he did not have to pay high interest costs on the builder's construction loan and high interest on his mortgage loan. He did not have to pay, through property taxes and other means, for an array of bureaucrats who have since attached themselves to the construction process. The fee that he paid for a lot map was only a few cents, not the $1,011 which buyers were paying in an overbureaucratized community such as San Diego, California, in 1974. He did not need to pay directly and indirectly for the fees of lawyers and experts both in and out of bureaucracy, whose haggles now add delays and costs to almost every facet of the construction process.

Once upon a time, when an American bought a house, that was all he paid for—the house. Now he must support an army of supernumeraries, individuals whose efforts do not contribute to the productive process and who may indeed be committing their talents to thwart and undo the constructive work of others.

And that is why, simply put, it has become ever more expensive to own or rent housing—even as we have discovered improvements in production which should have made housing better and cheaper. Whereas lumber was once felled by hand, we now have portable power tools which enable fewer lumberjacks to harvest timber more quickly than ever before. We have developed new and better means of plumbing, including pipes which can be mass-produced and fitted in factories for installation in apartment buildings and even single-family developments. We have developed newer synthetic forms of tiles, and aluminum siding which almost never needs painting. We have greatly improved and automated the mass production of copper wiring, plugs, and switches; even bricks and block. From all that we know today, we should be able to build a house or an apartment which is better and cheaper than ever. Yet we cannot. The reason is not that raw materials are scarcer, that human labor is unavailable, or that the quality we demand is so much higher than what was known in the past that it cannot be duplicated except at many times the cost.

There is one overriding reason why we cannot build better, cheaper housing even as the technology which would allow us to do so improves. One thing has so changed for the worse as to outdo all the progress of home building since the turn of the century. That is politics. Politics imposes costs today which did not exist in the past. This cannot be emphasized too much. *It is politics rather than any cause in nature which is making the cost of housing prohibitive.* Inflation, taxation, and regulation are placing private homes beyond the reach of most first-time buyers and at the same time undermining the economy of rental properties.

Consider how inflation has reduced the prospect of finding good housing. In 1950 the average home sold for little more than $8,000. The average interest rate on mortgages was 4.5 percent. Since the average of all mortgages financed about 75 percent of the value, the average monthly interest charge to carry the mortgage was $22.50. Because the inflation rates remained low during the decade of the fifties there had been only a modest increase—to $11,500 in the median cost of a new home—by 1960. (That was largely attributable to the fact that the quality of the product improved: the 1960 home was bigger.) With interest rates then averaging 4.9 percent, a buyer in 1960 with a 75-percent mortgage paid $35.22 in monthly interest charges. But as the dollar was substantially emptied of value during the inflations of the Vietnam-war era, two things happened. The price of new and existing homes rose dramatically. And interest rates shot up. By 1972 new homes were selling for $38,300, with interest rates averaging about 7.3 percent. This meant that the family buying a house and taking a mortgage of 75 percent faced monthly interest payments of about $175.00. To this were added other fees and charges for obtaining a loan which had been negligible in the past but which grew as the inflation rate rose, partly to disguise higher interest rates. By 1972 the cost of these fees averaged .83 percent of the value of the mortgage, or a monthly equivalent of almost $20.00. By 1977, as inflation continued, the average price of a new home had been boosted to $53,400 and the explicit interest rate had risen to 8¾ percent. This brought the average monthly interest charge to $292.00. To this were added other fees and charges, which had skyrocketed to 1.3 percent of the mortgage, or the equivalent of $43.00 per month. By 1978 the cheapening of the dollar had raised the price of the average home to $63,000, with mortgage money at 11 percent. This brought the average monthly carrying charge for interest to $433.00 plus almost another $60.00 if the initial fees and charges are prorated on a monthly basis. In other words, by 1978 the average monthly interest charge for a home mortgage was more than twelve times what it had been in 1960 and eighteen times greater than it was in 1950. If the prorated cost of the initial fee is considered in addition, the 1978 interest cost was fourteen times what it had been in 1960 and more than twenty-one times what it was in 1950.

Clearly, incomes which have allegedly "kept pace with inflation" have not kept pace at all. Wages raised to match increases in general living costs cannot be indexed to keep abreast of the increased cost of home buying. This is because the cheapening of money effects a double multiplication of the mortgage cost. It raises both the base price and the interest rate. The result can be a geometric increase in the interest burden on the home buyer. If the sale price doubles and so does the interest rate, the monthly interest payments quadruple. A tripling of the base price and the interest rate results in a ninefold increase in borrowing costs. And so on. Thinking about this aspect of inflation brings us to the precipice of an arithmetic abyss. There is no need to leap now that we have gathered sight of the basic fact, which is almost nowhere understood—that incomes would have to be twelve to fourteen times higher than they were in 1960 in order for the average person to be equally able to afford the payments on a new house.

If people are continuing to buy houses, as they apparently are, it may be more because of a panic about inflation than because they can genuinely afford to do so. Seeing their wealth constantly eroded, and recognizing that real estate has been one of the few investments that actually keep pace with inflation, many families have plunged deeply into debt— too deeply, perhaps, for their investments to be rescued by anything short of runaway inflation. It is difficult to see how the inflation-induced demand for homes could avoid being curtailed by declining ability of average Americans to shoulder greater debts. At some stage, it seems likely that many home owners who bought at inflated prices may have to absorb losses. These too should be counted, if they occur, as part of the cost which inflation has imposed upon people in search of housing.

It is by no means the case, however, that the entire price increase for new homes is attributable to monetary depreciation. As already suggested, a large part of the substantial increase in housing costs can be laid to government regulations.

Consider, for example, the building codes. Depending upon the area of the country one chooses, such codes may add as much as 10 percent to construction costs. The codes are worse in highly politicized areas, such as New York City, where the power of building unions has effectively prohibited many means of automating construction. Plumbing, for instance, which can be efficiently assembled into "plumbing trees" off-site, then brought in and planted, must be laboriously hand-assembled in New York City. When builders have ignored regulations and employed the modern methods of assembly, building inspectors have forced them to rip out the efficiently installed pipes and put them back by the slower, more expensive method.

Such is the absurdity of building codes, which are really unnecessary in the first place. If the safety of construction were the only object, it could be more effectively obtained through flexible standards monitored, as they are in France, by the insurance companies. But the codes continue because they represent transcendental-capital assets not only to featherbedding union members but also to the inspectors themselves. Counterproductive codes provide the inspectors with a leverage to demand corrupt favors from builders. Stephen R. Seidel reports in his book *Housing Costs and Government Regulations* that a survey by a New York City undercover unit "found virtually 100 percent of the City employees with whom we had contact were directly involved in corrupt acts or had knowledge of their existence."[3] Graft was reportedly so pervasive as to enable the average inspector to more than double his city salary. Of course, this dividend to transcendental capital does not produce benefits for consumers—only costs.

Perhaps the most pernicious impact of the building and housing codes is a reduction in the supply of houses. This has its most direct effect upon the poor, who are forced to pay more under the guise of being protected from substandard facilities. When inspectors close down cheap and perhaps dilapidated dwellings, and prohibit the construction of new housing providing the quality which the poor can afford, they simply displace the problem by driving up costs to all housing consumers and probably, in the end, reducing the quality of the available properties. Instead of having new housing, especially rental units, constructed to meet the actual ability of the poor to pay, we get construction almost exclusively oriented toward higher-income buyers. This cuts the poor out.

Housing and building codes have very little to do with actually improving the quality of dwellings, but they do have a substantial impact in increasing the cost of *all* housing. If it were really true that one could raise standards by bureaucratic fiat rather than through economic development, it would be a simple matter to infinitely expand the quality of housing by constantly raising standards required in the housing and building codes to levels beyond those which are known in current construction. For example, dwellings could be declared substandard if they did not incorporate a home computer and in-wall sensors to control the thermostats by detecting the movement of family members from one room to the next. And it could be mandatory that all homes have solar panels on their roofs and that water be processed for reuse on the premises.

These and many more architectural fancies could be built into the codes. That they are not is an unspoken admission that the codes do not raise standards. Most people realize that the exigencies of finance make housing standards which they cannot afford entirely impractical. They become "practical" only when imposed upon the less affluent minority, who are thereby forced to pay more for housing or are unable to afford housing at all.

But it is not only the poor who are squeezed by unnecessary housing and building codes. These regulations are major contributors to the overall Housing Squeeze that is now being inflicted upon every American. These laws make improving one's own housing extremely difficult; the creation of transcendental capital makes home improvement unprofitable.

Not only do building and housing codes make housing more expensive and limit the supply of housing, but zoning and land-use planning have made matters worse by dramatically increasing the cost of land available for home sites. Economist Anthony Downs estimates that a combination of building codes and zoning in the suburbs makes the cost of a housing unit there 25 percent higher than necessary.[4]

As zoning and planning have been intensified, the cost of land available for homes has skyrocketed. A quarter-acre plot which could have been had for a few hundred dollars in 1950—considerably less than 10 percent of the selling price of a new home—had risen by 1970 to about $5,000. It then amounted to about 20 percent of the sale price of a new home. By 1975 the price of the land under the typical house had risen to $10,800, or more than 25 percent of the median sales price of houses. Because "no-growth" zoning and planning policies limit the supply of land available for housing, they dramatically increase the price for those parcels which are available. An informative example of this process at work was provided in San Diego, where politicians and bureaucrats joined in creating an artificial scarcity of land by making construction off limits on 30,000 acres in the city's suburbs. As a consequence, owners who had already obtained planning approval for developments reaped transcendental-capital windfall gains from the new regulations. Tiny 6,000-square-foot lots rose in value from $7,500 to $17,500. This is illustrative of the kind of cost increases which intensified zoning and planning augur for the future.

Just about the only places where housing is still available at a moderate price, which is to say 30 to 50 percent below the national average, are in areas in the South and West which to date have been spared the handiwork of zoners and planners. As state governments and localities in these areas act under the prodding of federal legislation and administrative directives to institute rigid land-use plans, they too will create artificial shortages of land for home building. This will tend to foreclose the attractiveness of development which has made growth in the South and West far greater than in the more politicized areas of the Northeast and Midwest.

In fact, the whole evolution of settlement patterns in America in recent decades can be explained in some measure by the desire to escape the costs of regulation. As early as 1950 Miles Colean noted that "less onerous regulation and lower building costs in the outlying communities in a metropolitan area contribute to the dispersal of population and business from the central areas and to the consequent loss of their property values."[5] As the suburbs become politicized, the growth was further dispersed into new areas in the West and South and in some cases the rural North. In almost every case, a crucial corollary to growth has been the weakness of political cartels. Where political establishments have not yet attained sufficient power to parcel out the potential transcendental-capital gains inherent in the tight regulations of construction and the bureaucratic control of land use, housing growth has been possible. One can expect that as the move to capture these potential transcendental-capital gains is intensified and becomes more successful in the still-uncartelized areas, there will be ever less scope for growth. Eventually, the ultimate *reductio ad absurdum* of planning is to make a plan so detailed and rigid as to create land prices so high that they rule out any profitable use. By designating, for example, only one spot in a development plan for a shopping center, the planners confer a monopoly upon the owner of that plot. Unless he personally seeks to proceed with the development, the resulting monopoly price may be so great as to prohibit anyone else from doing so. Of course, that may indeed be what zoning is all about.

America's first zoning laws were written in New York City and enacted at the behest of the rich and fabled Four Hundred as a means of protecting the property value of their mansions, which were then being threatened by economic competition. Land had become so valuable for use in manufacturing of garments and housing for the garment workers that the rich were steadily retreating up Manhattan Island. By instituting zoning codes, they sought to avoid the nuisance of moving their mansions yet again in order to escape living with the poor. By using their political power, they simply made it illegal for the land to be put to its most valuable use.[6] This kept the hoi polloi off the steps of the Astor, Stewart, and

Vanderbilt mansions—at least for a time. It also reduced the housing prospects for the poor.

Land-use-planning legislation continues to serve that same basic purpose today. By protecting one set of economic interests (usually that of the wealthy and powerful) from competition by new, emerging interests, planning legislation keeps outsiders from disrupting the status quo. As expert Bernard Siegan put it:

> Zoning allows existing residents of a community to greatly influence or even determine who can or who cannot move into that community.
>
> It likewise gives inordinate powers and privileges to existing residents over people outside the community who would benefit from the filtering effect created by new housing, as well as those within the housing market who would benefit from a greater supply of land and housing. Involved are restraints on mobility and opportunity and the creation of social and economic difficulties for many, particularly those of average or less incomes. One group, those who got there first, exercises considerable restraints over the production of housing beneficial to many other groups.[7]

This tension between the insiders who control and the outsiders who are seeking to obtain a better life for themselves is inherent in all the land-use-planning controversies of our time.

It really involves no more than an attempt to keep the shoe clerks off the tennis courts. In the good old days when the shoe clerks were too poor to play tennis, one did not need to stand in line to obtain a court on Sunday afternoon or any other day of the week. Persons who had become accustomed to using resources themselves without competition were undoubtedly able to enjoy what is known as the good life. They had no trouble obtaining a court and playing all day if they wished. And when the tennis was tiresome, these same good people could take a drive out to their country homes (no lines of traffic clogging the roads) and relax in bucolic splendor. They could buy a place in Vermont, for example, for a few dollars an acre and lie back as country gentry to watch the poor farmers scratch out livings in the summer. In the winter, the good people came to go skiing. But then the shoe clerks turned up. The union foremen and the managers of doughnut shops in Brooklyn decided that they, too, would like to have an affordable place in the country. So they started to sneak up to Vermont to buy cabins on half-acre lots. With demand for land rising dramatically, the native Vermont farmers, who had never made more than $10,000 a year in their lives, suddenly discovered the possibility of becoming millionaires simply by selling out. And why not? The property-tax structure was driving them to ruin anyway.

It was from that dynamic that a further intensification of the demand for "planning" emerged. It became a convenient means by which some individuals could expropriate property, in the economic sense, from those who owned it in the legal sense. The zoning and planning regulations became, in effect, transcendental-capital assets to those members of the community who profit by retarding economic growth.

Back in the days when the shoe clerks did not have enough money to buy summer homes in Vermont, no legislation was needed to keep them out. But as former Vermont Governor Thomas Salmon told the House of Representatives several years ago, income had risen so far as to make planning "necessary." As he put it, "the demand for land was simply extraordinary, with special emphasis on the second home syndrome. . . . Despite inflation, discretionary income is up."[8] So land-use planning was instituted explicitly to drive up the cost of land and thus help to "preserve irredeemable aesthetic values" which were lost every time a shoe clerk pitched his tent on a half-acre lot. The persons who already owned country homes in Vermont did not want Kew Gardens moved out to spoil the pastoral splendor of their country retreats.

It must be acknowledged that we all enjoy some of the benefits when land-use planning drives up the cost of development to prohibitive levels. We all want to preserve at least some of our countryside from the ravages of overdevelopment. And no doubt some means must be employed to preserve farms and greenbelts from the artificial pressures for development which are imposed under the current system of property taxation, which exacts a capital levy on the basis of the use to which the land might be employed. (This levy is, as Noel Perrin suggests, the equivalent to having the IRS assess a strikingly handsome woman with an income-tax bill of $40,000 on the basis that "if she became a prostitute in Baltimore, she could earn at least $90,000 a year."[9]) Undoubtedly a change in these tax pressures and the acceptance of protective covenants in land-sales contracts would be a more wholesome means than land planning for preserving open space.

Another means which is seldom considered would be the elimination of subsidies to development of out-of-the-way areas. Government taxes the people in already developed areas to subsidize the provision of the transportation and communication intrastructure in the boondocks. When such practices take place in underdeveloped countries they are the result of a conscious resolve to seek development of the remote areas. Here, the government makes it just as cheap to send a letter from Fifth Avenue to Little Diomede Island, Alaska, as it is from Fifth Avenue to Broadway. If this practice, along with the subsidized provision of air travel, highways, and the mandatory provision of utilities, such as telephone and electricity, were curtailed, much of the current pressures for development of remote areas would be alleviated.

But these are points which deserve attention on their own. What concerns us here is the considerable effect of the growth of transcendental capital in the form of planning regulations in restricting the supply of housing. If current trends are not interrupted by a collapse of the real-estate market, a continued tightening of planning restrictions would dramatically foreclose the possibilities for major new-home construction. As Gurney Breckenfeld wrote in *Fortune*, "Some developers argue seriously that, once present inventories of developed land in the United States are used, the main source of sites for homes will be scattered lots owned by individuals—a vision that implies a truly staggering increase in land prices."[10]

Even if the zoning and planning process were not tainted by the fact that its support springs from a desire to deny the future, and especially to deny outsiders their role in it, even if it did not secretly aim at the denial of opportunity in general, the zoning and planning philosophy would be seriously tainted in another way. It is beyond the realm of possibility for anyone today to be prophetic enough to actually foresee tomorrow's knowledge. It is pure hubris for an individual such as Minneapolis-St. Paul Metropolitan Council Director John Boland to imagine that a master plan could tell all about the future. Yet he has said that his plan will enable every owner to "know everything about his plot; developers will know if a certain plot of land will be used for a grade school in 1986."[11] Never has there been a more grandiloquent pronouncement of false expertise. Human society is not a stable state but a process of interactions. It is so far beyond the capability of any individual or team of individuals to competently lay the future under their own egotistical control that there is perhaps no more sure source of amusement than to read the plans and predictions of past experts. Almost without exception, they are woefully wrong-headed. David Mandel's comment on the long experience of planning in New York makes just this point:

> The draftsmen of the 1916 zoning code of New York City began their work in 1913 and it lasted without substantial revision until 1939. Like

all zoning plans it was drawn in the light of technology generally available some years earlier and it was addressed to problems set in motion decades or centuries earlier and then apparent. The decent motives of those draftsmen and their competence are unquestioned but their forward vision had to be small. Their image of the ideal city was heavily tinted by their memories of a more bucolic and less populous city of their youth. They were constrained to protect the future as a virtually straight-lined extension of the past. They simply could not (nor could anybody else) anticipate and plan for the tumultuous events of the next 23 years: United States entry into World War I, the virtual cessation of immigration after 1924, the Great Depression, the ubiquitous and ferocious automobile, air conditioning, the supermarket, penicillin.[12]

The attempts to override the absurdities which are inevitably inherent in zoning plans make almost any major construction an occasion for feasting by otherwise unproductive experts. Lawyers, especially, command large fees for handling zoning litigation and corraling credentialed planners whose testimony is needed to refute the errant contentions of other planners. In a certain sense, the very incompetence of planners for the jobs to which they aspire assures the profession's success. The planners are guaranteed work as certified experts testifying to the need for undoing one another's mistakes. This, of course, compounds the effects of zoning in raising building costs by introducing an artificial excess of litigation. The more court procedures and red tape required to build, the less the home buyers pay for actual housing. The consequence, as Martin Mayer puts it, is that "by the time the legal processing is through on a case-by-case basis a developer's costs have risen to the point where he can't afford to build moderately priced housing on that land anyway."[13]

These and dozens of other factors arising from the greed of transcendental capitalists in and out of government have been working to strangle the production of new single-family homes. Similar factors are contributing to the demise of rental housing in America. No survey of the Housing Squeeze could be complete without some explanation of how urban renewal, government housing programs, and legal actions to separate the economic ownership of rental property from the nominal ownership have all contributed to heightening the Housing Squeeze and the consequent raising of costs for everyone.

Over the years, as one housing program has been stacked upon another, supported by the public in the well-intentioned hope that these efforts might improve housing quality and lower costs, results have tended to be just the opposite of those expected. Hundreds of thousands of housing units have quite literally been destroyed. And incentives for further destruction have been so firmly incorporated into urban society that it may be only a matter of time until the whole economy of urban rental property collapses. The consequences, of course, would not stop short at the boundaries of cities. There would be a dramatic nationwide deterioration of value obtained for the housing dollar.

To the person who is uninitiated to the mysteries of urban housing, it would appear to be a simple matter for the government to improve housing facilities for the poor simply by pumping in vast sums of money to build public-housing projects or to subsidize access by the poor to housing built by others. In fact, nothing could be further from the truth. If the record is to be believed, it is not only unlikely but almost impossible for government housing programs to produce satisfactory results. The reasons are complicated, but foremost among them are four:

First, as has already been suggested, it is the very interventions of bureaucracy which are responsible, in large measure, for shutting off the capacity of the poor to gradually improve their own housing. Once forced into a state of dependency, the poor have scant occasion to develop the skills needed for responsible living. Since they are told over and over that they are not responsible and cannot be trusted to be so, they fulfill these low expectations, not incidentally because they are paid to do so.

Second, the political gestures at solving the housing crisis must fail because under current conditions it is scarcely in the interests of any of those profiting from the housing crisis to see it solved. Those who are most directly involved in the political process—the bureaucrats, planners, lawyers, subsidized contractors, building-trades unions, bankers, and the rest—are at least temporarily (and in the case of the bureaucrats, perhaps permanently) benefited when the housing crisis becomes more acute. This increases the subsidized demand for their services. The fewer people there are who are able to house themselves, the greater the political demand for the housing experts to step in to build more housing on a cost basis inflated far beyond what people could afford to pay themselves. This makes for greater artificial profit all around. For example, the total subsidies for New York City's Manhattan Plaza Apartment Building on West Forty-second Street are estimated by Martin Mayer to run at about $1,200 per month for just a two-bedroom apartment.[14] That is an amount which approaches being double the after-tax income of the average person in New York. Obviously, the failure of government housing has opened some remarkably profitable possibilities among its alleged solutions.

Third, it is important to remember that housing projects have a schizophrenic mandate from the public. As is quite clear in the case of zoning and planning laws, a key motive in the manipulation of housing is a desire on the part of those who are already well-housed to profit by denying that possibility to others. As long as the housing bubble remains intact, actions which tend to reduce the housing supply or make the construction of new housing more difficult will inexorably contribute to higher profit for those who already have homes.

Fourth, it is not to be forgotten that we have enshrined into law incentives for destruction. These run so broad and deep we are effectively paying people to forgo civilized values.

All of these tendencies have been at work in the government programs affecting housing over the last several decades. A detailed, blow-by-blow account of scandal and stupidity institutionalized in these efforts is a matter for several books. And, indeed, several have been written. Martin Mayer's *The Builders* is a recent comprehensive analysis which points to the fact that "our present and predictable future difficulties really are the government's fault."[15] The record of politicians in destroying housing is also well documented in Martin Anderson's *The Federal Bulldozer*. And the tendency by bureaucracy to discourage independent effort to revive housing is documented in rich detail in Albert Lee's neglected book *Slum Lord*. What emerges from these studies and others is a pattern of government actions which, combined with inflation and high taxes, brought the Housing Squeeze into being.

Urban renewal, for example, demolished at least 425,000 units of housing during the 1950's and 1960's. Almost all of these dwellings belonged to low-income persons. Only 125,000 units were constructed in their place, and most of these were rented or sold at prices far beyond what the poor could pay. Because new building for the poor outside the renewal areas had been effectively blocked, the increased demand for the remaining homes had two effects: it increased the costs of all housing and reduced quality. In some cities, displaced persons had to pay 35 to 40 percent more in order to find a roof over their heads. Real-estate expert Chester Hartman neatly summarized the situation created by urban renewal:

> Redevelopment projects are leaving 30, 40, and 50 percent of displacees in substandard conditions while destroying substantial numbers of decent

low-rent units. Overcrowding is being only marginally relieved, and in some cases exacerbated. General neighborhood conditions often have deteriorated or become less satisfactory, thus cancelling out any gains in individual housing conditions. . . . Further, once the overall stock of low-rent housing—decent or otherwise—diminishes, landlords tend to allow their properties to deteriorate and municipal services tend to decline. What may be rated as standard housing at the time the displacee moves in may be seriously substandard within a matter of two to three years.[16]

The effects imposed by urban renewal were duplicated by construction of the interstate-highway system. Partly because planners aimed at leveling what they considered unattractive areas, superhighways plowed right through the center of cities, knocking down the homes of the poor, rather than skirting the cities, which would have been a far more practical and less costly procedure for an interstate system.

Public housing was intended to be the solution to the difficulties faced by the poor in trying to keep a roof over their heads. A quick survey could point to no better indication of the *real* effect of public housing than the story of the giant Pruitt-Igoe complex in St. Louis. It originally consisted of thirty-three eleven-story buildings of a design which won an American Institute of Architects prize. Although it was meant to be home to 2,870 families, it was never fully occupied. Many of the early residents were welfare recipients and others who had not developed the skills needed for compact, urban living. In short order, vandals destroyed the elevators. Thieves in the halls preyed upon the elderly and anyone else who happened along. Because there was virtually no police protection for the poor residents who were compressed into circumstances which offered them less opportunity to avoid crime than they had known previously, the violence in the projects became notorious. Delivery men declined to provide service to the buildings because they realized that their lives were endangered. Soon, those who could leave did. And because no one had a very lively incentive to preserve the value of the project, it steadily fell before the onslaught of enterprising thieves. As soon as an apartment became vacant, scavengers would break open the walls and floors, rip out outlets, wiring, and light fixtures, remove plumbing and appliances, even the doors and windows. In short order, whatever was not stolen was destroyed. Attempts by the housing authorities to raise rents in order to improve maintenance and to weed out undesirable tenants were met by a rent strike which dragged on for nine months and finally ensured bankruptcy of the project. By 1970, twenty-seven of the original buildings had been closed. By 1973, three of the buildings had been deliberately dynamited by the housing authorities. By 1974, when the annual operating deficit had reached almost $10,000 for each remaining unit, the entire project was closed.

There, in microcosm, is much of the story of public housing. In 1968, another political housing program was launched. Known in the bureaucracy as Section 235, the program had the announced purpose of providing hundreds of thousands of homes on subsidized terms for low-income families. The means by which this was to be achieved was a government-insured mortgage. Poor people would borrow to buy their own homes, with government agreeing to pay off the note in event of default.

The program may have seemed wonderful upon superficial analysis, but it, too, created incentives to destroy housing. In fact, Section 235 amounted to little more than a federally-subsidized plan for blockbusting. The program rewarded mortgage lenders for selling properties to the least-qualified buyers who could be found. In many cases, bums were literally gathered off the street and presented with keys to a new home and mortgages guaranteed 100 percent by the Federal Housing Administration. If, as the lender hoped, the buyer defaulted on his payments at the end of twelve months, he could initiate foreclosure proceedings. After another fifteen months when the proceedings were completed, the Department of Housing and Urban Development paid off the lender in full. This normally resulted in a return of more than twice what the lender would have received if the mortgage had been held to maturity. It is not hard to see why more than 100,000 Section 235 homes were in default as of 1977.

Almost without exception, these homes were destroyed after foreclosure, partly because they were left abandoned for an average time of more than four years. That was the time required for a ten-step paperwork process by which HUD claims the title to its insured properties. Needless to say, the effect of these abandonments on the neighborhoods in which they occur is devastating. The late Chicago Mayor Richard Daley told the Senate Banking Committee in 1975 that the Section 235 program had precipitated widespread destruction. Said Daley, "Most cities in the United States have been left with thousands of abandoned and vandalized structures in what had been desirable neighborhoods."[17] Seeing homes on their block abandoned and boarded with plywood, alarmed owners responded to the sharp decline in property values by selling as quickly as possible—before the plywood was stolen. So Section 235 reduced the quality of housing, creating slums where none had previously existed.

Efforts to resist the artificial creation of slums, and even reclaim dilapidated buildings and put them to use, have often been attempted. Albert Lee's book *Slum Lord* is the story of the efforts of one man who for a long time was successful in an attempt to upgrade housing in Detroit's slums. Using his own money, he bought one dilapidated building after another and immediately set about rehabilitating them. The buildings were rewired, repaired, and painted. New plumbing fixtures were introduced, and maintenance was put on a steady basis. To see that the buildings were properly cared for, the owner lived in the same neighborhood and turned out for maintenance calls on a twenty-four-hour basis. To reduce infestation of the area by rats, the owner financed his own bounty program, rewarding the tenants for every rat they killed. As a result, the rat population dropped dramatically.

Through such efforts, this one man came close to beating the system. By screening the tenants carefully and evicting those who were destructive, he created an island of sound, safe housing in an area where none had existed. He did all this while charging a minimal rent, even while catering to many welfare recipients, who were admitted on the provision that he get a lien on their welfare checks and deduct the rent money before they spent it.

For every progressive step he took, however, there was a bureaucratic objection. He was constantly taken to court by young lawyers and Wayne State University students who incited the tenants to withhold rent payments. His costly efforts to keep his structures repaired were constantly frustrated by the tenants, who could increase their own income by sabotaging the toilets, kicking in the walls, and breaking out the lights and windows. Under the law, they were entitled to live in the dwellings without paying rent until the landlord was able to make repairs. So they engaged in a form of subsidized destruction. Nevertheless, even this did not bankrupt the landlord.

What eventually did defeat him was his opponents' success in prevailing on the Detroit City Council to enact a new ordinance making it illegal for a landlord to sequester the checks of welfare recipients. The result was that fewer and fewer rents were paid. Most of the welfare clients cashed their checks and spent all the money. Without income, the landlord had no choice but to close his buildings. One by one, the structures he purchased on credit passed back into dilapidation. Eventually the man declared himself bankrupt.

What is the legacy of this man's long and trying effort? Philosopher John Hospers commented: "A part of the city that he had rescued from the rats and the vermin thus returned once more to the condition of uninhabitability: the buildings are vandalized, the heat and light turned off, and the ruined hulks now stand in the darkness, empty, the tenants with no place to go, and no entrepreneur left who has any incentive to buck the impossible regulations. All this is done, of course, with the full approval of the city government, which brands the entrepreneur as a slum lord and requests new revenues from the state and federal government with which to 'improve the cities.' "[18]

Such are the destructive consequences of contemporary housing policy. Today most Americans have felt the damage only indirectly, in the form of higher prices and lower quality. Most of the hurt has been concentrated upon a small segment of the population, the poorest 10 percent, who are trapped in deteriorating slums under conditions which penalize efforts at improvement and in many cases provide direct incentives which promote further destruction.

If the trends of the last several decades continue, the middle-class family could suffer with the poor. With inflation geometrically raising the costs of borrowing to build and buy new housing; with zoning and land-use-planning legislation creating artificial shortages of land; with lawyer-created red tape delaying construction for months or years and imposing thousands of dollars of superfluous costs upon builders and buyers alike; with all this, the danger of a general housing disaster, especially in urban areas, is not far off. When government programs destroy housing and spread slums into previously stable communities—the way infected rats spread the plague—it is far from unreasonable to expect that many millions more Americans will soon be living in dilapidated housing. When rental housing becomes all but universally unprofitable, as it soon will under current trends, more and more communities will be exposed to the ultimate consequences of current policy.

Nowhere are these consequences better visible than in the South Bronx, an area of New York City whose population exceeds that of Minneapolis. No other community comes so close to vindicating Lord Macaulay's baleful prediction, made to a biographer of Thomas Jefferson in 1857, that American government would one day set in motion anti-civilizing forces: ". . . your republic will be fearfully plundered and laid waste by barbarians in the twentieth century as the Roman Empire was in the fifth, with this difference, that the Huns and Vandals who ravaged the Roman Empire came from without, and that your Huns and Vandals will have been engendered within your own country by your own institutions."

Decades of rent control laid the basis for this destruction in the South Bronx. By freezing rentals at a level below the cost of depreciation, they made the tenants, in effect, the economic owners of the buildings. Yet the tenants had no incentive to preserve the value of the structures, only to use it up. Because the nominal owners, most of them other middle-income residents of the area, could not afford to maintain the buildings, the structures were inexorably destroyed, slowly at first, then overnight as the area was increasingly engulfed by fires. The introduction of a huge complex of subsidized housing oriented toward persons of middle income drew tens of thousands of the more stable residents out of their older dwellings, thus eliminating whatever stability the neighborhoods had maintained. In a pattern which has frequently recurred, everyone who could get out, did. What was left behind was a population composed increasingly of welfare recipients and others unskilled in the finer points of urban living. At some point, the concentration of such persons became so great as to sweep away normal civilized restraints. Life in the South Bronx was a round of violence, vandalism, and destruction. Many declined to employ modern means for disposal of refuse. As *Fortune* wrote, "So many tenants began throwing their household refuse out the windows into alleys, backyards, and even onto sidewalks that a new coinage— 'airmail garbage'—was added to the symbolism of urban blight."[19]

Even many of those contributing to such conditions sought to escape them if they could. For welfare recipients, this was doubly difficult because they had to be placed on long waiting lists to secure better subsidized housing. When such housing was found, they could accept it only if they could afford to finance the move themselves. One exception to this rule was well known. A sign painted in bold block letters posted in every welfare office explained that any tenant burned out of his apartment automatically became eligible for an assistance grant ranging from $1,000 to $3,000 to pay for new clothes, furnishings, and the cost of moving. Furthermore, the burned-out family automatically leaped to the top of the queue of those waiting for new housing. That is one reason why 68,456 fires were set in the South Bronx in the first five years of the 1970's.

Not all the fires, of course, were set by welfare recipients eyeing the opportunity to move. Some were undoubtedly set by landlords hoping to minimize their losses by collecting at least a few dollars from the insurance company before their policies were canceled. Some fires were set by vandals and by organized street gangs, who tore through buildings ripping out any fixtures that could be carried away and sold. They then lit fires, partly to disguise their crimes, partly to join in the excitement of the neighborhood pastime, and perhaps also because fumes from the fires became one of the few expedients to disguise the otherwise pervasive odor of moldering garbage and dog filth.

The South Bronx became a laboratory test of what can happen when human energy and capability are largely smothered by an inverted system of incentives. When malicious energy is encouraged with material rewards, and the concentration of this effect can be made to work in a single locale, then as far as the area is concerned, civilization itself is at risk.

For most Americans, the Housing Squeeze is not yet that acute and will never be. But after a whole history of steady improvement in housing, we now face the prospect of degeneration. The growth of transcendental capital in its many forms—inflation, high taxes, government housing policies—all tend to contribute to the decay of housing, if not its actual immolation. If rental housing is rendered completely unprofitable, and if lawyers and planners continue to ratchet down their grip upon construction, then the day will soon come when only a small minority of the population will be able to afford new homes of the style to which most people aspire. It is not easy to imagine how the millions of disappointed Americans, especially young people who largely lack the equity to buy a home, will adjust.

In the days when you could buy a house for $780 per year, those who did not care about the domestic pleasures of home ownership or were unable to earn the necessary money could always become hobos. At one time, as many as a million persons made their homes on the open road, sleeping in boxcars and riding trains from one hobo camp to another, singing railroad songs and mowing lawns for pocket money. Today, even that option is unavailable. We can't become hobos because the politicians also have ruined the railroads.

12
The Legal Squeeze

It will be of little avail to the people that the laws are made
by men of their own choice if the laws be so voluminous
that they cannot be read, or so incoherent that they cannot
be understood, if they be repealed or revised before they
are promulgated, or undergo such incessant changes that
no man, who knows what the law is today, can guess what
it will be like tomorrow.

—*James Madison*

A lawyer is a person who profits by creating confusion. Or when that
is impossible, he profits by the confusion created by others. In either
case, confusion is his stock in trade. The greater the division between
form and substance, between legal technicality and the attainment of
justice, between gobbledygook and common intelligibility, the more the
lawyer profits. The wider the gap a lawyer can create between the person
who ostensibly owns property and he who claims its economic worth,
the more money winds up in his pocket.

The lawyer's lucrative monopoly gives him an incentive to create
obstacles to the smooth functioning of the life of ordinary people.
Through their dominance of politics, the bureaucracy, and their monopoly over litigation, lawyers have insinuated themselves into every
human relationship. Whatever you do, or fail to do, there is probably a
lawyer somewhere who can find a pretext to sue you for it.

Consider these actual examples of recent lawsuits:

- A twenty-four-year-old man in Colorado entered a $350,000 suit against his parents on grounds that they brought him up to be less than a fit human being.
- A man sued the National Park Service after he was struck by lightning while on park property because there was not a written notification of possible lightning danger at the scene of the accident. An $84,417 judgment was overturned in appeal.
- A woman in San Francisco successfully sued the city, receiving $50,000 after she claimed that a fall in a cable car turned her into a nymphomaniac.
- A prisoner who escaped from a Pennsylvania jail sued the county sheriff and two guards for $1 million, charging that they were responsible for allowing him to escape and should pay damages because he ended up with a heavier sentence after his recapture.
- In Oak Park, Illinois, a sixteen-year-old girl was robbed by three gunmen. She identified her assailants and assisted police in apprehending them. The robbers then turned around and sued the victim for "conspiring to violate their rights."
- A twenty-seven-year-old Westland, Michigan, man claimed that a rear-end auto collision turned him into a homosexual and was awarded $200,000 by a Wayne County Circuit Court.
- In Los Angeles, an actor sued a bar which served liquor to a motorist who later struck his motorcycle, severely injuring him and killing a woman passenger. He was awarded $1.9 million. He had previously sued the City of Los Angeles and obtained a settlement of $175,000 after he contended that the road where the accident happened narrowed without warning. The man who actually drove the car and inflicted the damage was dropped as a defendant in the suit when lawyers learned that he had no insurance and little money.
- Members of the Los Angeles City Council prepared to sue scientist James H. Whitcomb of Cal Tech when he predicted that a moderate-to-major earthquake was likely to strike the San Fernando Valley. Council members alleged that Dr. Whitcomb should be liable if his predictions reduced property values.
- An auto worker in Detroit sued Ford Motor Company for $600,000 on grounds that fellow workers made him the butt of Polish jokes.
- A girl in Connecticut who broke a finger while attempting to catch a pop fly in a school softball game sued the school and softball instructor, alleging that she was improperly coached.
- A man who ran over a rusty coat hanger in his own yard with a lawnmower won $775,000 by bringing suit against the lawnmower manufacturer.
- An owner of a trailer-truck, after helping to bring an accident upon him-

self by modifying the engine, nevertheless sued the manufacturer and received an award of $1,760,000.

- In California, a failed Romeo brought suit against a woman who had stood him up for a date, seeking compensation for the time and money spent sprucing himself up and driving to and from her home.
- A onetime executive of the Ford Motor Company sued his former employers on the ground that having too many responsibilities had made him an alcoholic.
- The heirs of a chain smoker sued a cigarette company on grounds that the company had been responsible for the dead woman's cancer.
- A former student at the University of Michigan sued the school for $853,000 in damages to compensate for "mental anguish" he claims he suffered after being awarded a D rather than an A in a German class.

This is a mere sampling of the ways that litigation, promoted by lawyers, has contributed to a scrambling of life's expectations. Lawyers and their works have confused the boundaries of every relationship: between husbands and wives, salesmen and purchasers, parents and children, manufacturers and consumers, friends and lovers, teachers and students. No claim today is too preposterous or contrary to an ordinary appreciation of the limits of relationships to be entertained. Persons who were never married can sue one another for divorce and win.

The very unpredictability of legal judgments brings lawyers the greatest scope for profits. Lawyers have assiduously sought to destroy the regularity of the rules, to bend them to private purposes, to create "new property" in the form of transcendental capital which makes the tangible, material world subordinate to a new economy of rules and regulations which is largely under lawyers' control.

Contrary to what a lawyer might pretend, these developments are not a species of progress. The individual is not better able to protect himself because he has a "property right" in his job or because he can find a lawyer to magically reinterpret any written or implied contract. The individual, for example, who goes to a commodity broker to speculate may feel that lawyers give him a chance to play it both ways. He can make an investment and take the profits if it works. If he fails, he can bring a suit against the broker, claiming that he was really no investor and he did not mean to take such a risk. People may pretend that this kind of evasion is progress. They fool themselves. Legalistic equivocating is a process for subverting the future. It is a guaranteed prescription for making human beings irresponsible in the truest sense of the word. When we are paid to shift responsibility for our decisions to factors outside ourselves, we undermine our own technical and moral competence. That is the indictment the lawyers bear.

Lawyers are the accomplices of incompetence, especially moral incompetence. They have done no less than cloud over the distinctions between right and wrong, making it all but impossible for an individual employing his unaided intelligence to judge whether many actions are within the law or without. A remorseless multiplication of legislation, regulations, and court degrees—much of which is contradictory—make the question of whose "rights" are honored in a given circumstance a contest between lawyers. It may be decided on no better grounds than who went to court first, or who first courted the bureaucracy. Under such conditions, *we no longer have a rule of law, but a rule of lawyers.*

Lawyers dominate all branches of government—from the county courthouses and city halls to the Congress itself. They normally comprise an absolute majority in the U.S. Senate and the House of Representatives. They write the laws which empower 20,000 lawyers in the federal bureaucracy to write even more regulations, which are all interpreted by lawyers who comprise 100 percent of the federal judiciary. The confluence of all these efforts creates a phenomenal conflict of interest. Because lawyers dominate government, and more lawyers dominate the key points of power among lobbyists, whatever problem arises almost automatically leads to a lawyer's solution. That is why it is no exaggeration to say, as attorney J. Harris Morgan did in a film shown to the American Bar Association groups, "It is the public policy of this country that you [attorneys] be prosperous."

This is why so many talented young people are going into law schools. One survey in the mid-seventies found that 20 percent of all young people who had made a career choice intended to be lawyers. Whether their heroes were Ralph Nader, presidents of big corporations, or the luminously successful politicians and bureaucrats, the students recognized that lawyers are the alpha and omega of American society. They also sensed that under current circumstances lawyers have succeeded in reversing the laws of supply and demand. The more lawyers there are, the more attractive it becomes to gain membership in the outrageously lucrative lawyers' guild.

No people has ever paid so much to its caste of lawyers as do Americans today. Never in history have so many lawyers arisen in a single population, creating so much red tape, introducing so much inflexibility into all aspects of human action and protracting so many simple operations for months, years, and even decades. There are more lawyers in

America today than in all the rest of the world combined. At least *four times* as many lawyers per capita are squeezing Americans as are practicing in Great Britain. Americans support *five times* as many lawyers per capita as do Germans, *ten times* as many as the French, and believe it or not, *twenty times* more lawyers than the Japanese *per capita*.

These statistics suggest another reason why America's economic growth is falling behind that of other countries. *There is an inverse relationship between the prosperity of lawyers and the development of productive capacity.* This is true partly because the *speed* with which actions are taken is a major determinant of their success in a complex, modern economy. The readiness of lawyers to proceed with litigation whenever a decision is made that implies losses for someone, means that many productive opportunities must be forgone. Many such opportunities are taken up too long after lawyers have dragged matters out. As Lawrence H. Silberman writes, "productivity depends quite clearly on the speed of response to changing market conditions. The legal process importantly delays both the making of decisions (the willingness to take risks) because it introduces external imponderables, and the carrying out of decisions already made. In truth litigation of all kinds is becoming a major structural impediment to our economy."[1]

For example, when a brewery with a plant in New York City attempted to cease operations, on grounds that it was losing money, and to shift its production to more modern facilities in another state, labor unions went to court claiming that the workers had a "property right" in their jobs. The court obliged the company to continue operations at a loss. Lawyers had helped create new transcendental-capital claims which made the union officials, in effect, the economic owners of the brewery. The courts enabled them to drain away the capital value of the company. Similar developments have occurred in America probably no fewer than 100,000 times in the last decade, as productive enterprises have been forced to suffer losses through litigation and bureaucratically imposed costs and delays.

Because a corporation is forbidden by law from representing itself in legal proceedings, lawyers as a group are able to levy their own private tax, in the form of legal fees which corporations are obliged to pay in order to defend themselves. The officers of a corporation cannot go to court on their own behalf—unless they are also attorneys. This means that a lawsuit or a hassle with a bureaucratic agency is often deadly to a small business. Legal fees can consume the whole value of the corporation—a development which is hardly as unlikely as it seems. There are

500,000 corporations in America with a net worth of less than $35,000 and another 500,000 whose net worth does not exceed $100,000. Legal costs and difficulties are a major factor in the high incidence of bankruptcy among firms in this range. Even when such costs are paid by legal insurance, they are by no means avoided, but merely spread out over a wider base of policy holders. Higher premium costs reduce profit margins and have lately become so great in many industries as to place legal insurance beyond the reach of small firms. The proprietors of these firms live in constant fear that lawyers will put them out of business. If they are sued on a liability matter, for example, or are forced into court on a legal difficulty with a government agency, they may be bankrupted by the cost of their own defense—even if they are fully vindicated.

A rule peculiar to American law holds that the innocent party is not automatically indemnified for his legal costs when a false action is brought against him. In practically every other country in the world, a person bringing a false or frivolous legal action must indemnify the party he sues for all legal costs if he fails in the action. This, of course, raises the costs of prospecting for riches through litigation. It substantially reduces the number of lawsuits. And since that substantially reduces the prosperity of lawyers, the American legal profession has designed rules of jurisprudence which are far more lucrative. Here, the innocent are vindicated through bankruptcy. If they hope to recover their legal costs, there is only one road open: they must enter another separate and costly lawsuit.

Every way you turn, the American people are being squeezed by lawyers. They use their monopoly powers to pull capital out of productive use. Activities which should be accessible to anyone with a high-school education, such as incorporating a business, making a deed, searching a title, buying a piece of property, writing a will, probating an estate, settling an uncontested divorce or doing 95 percent of the other tasks which lawyers have turned into complicated nightmares, are monopolized. These tasks have truly become the property of the legal profession.

The lawyer's transcendental capital, his license to practice, enables him in many cases to charge you one hundred times what his services are worth, and sometimes more than that. That estimate is not scooped out of the air. Actual cost comparisons for simple legal actions in America and abroad reveal that lawyers charge the American people far in excess of what similar services command elsewhere. If you want an uncontested divorce in England it is a matter of obtaining a form, filling it out, and having it properly witnessed and notarized. The whole cost is only a few dollars. In America, such a procedure is monopolized by lawyers who charge up to $750 or more. As of 1973, it was actually *100 times* more expensive to probate an estate in the United States than it was in England. More amazing is the fact that in spite of paying more, Americans get worse service. The average elapsed time between death and the final settlement of probate is *17* times longer in the United States than it is in England.[2] In other countries, such as West Germany, the typical estate is settled in a matter of weeks.

One does not need to comb the globe in search of proof that Americans pay outrageous sums to lawyers for procedures people could better do themselves. The evidence is right in the lawyer's office. Big books of standard legal documents are printed for each state providing all the "hereinafters" and the "wherefores" to properly effect almost any kind of legal business. All the lawyer has to do is to tell his secretary to type the appropriate names and dates into the blanks. The only talent one really needs to complete most of the legal operations is typing ability.

This is why lawyers are constantly struggling to prevent legal secretaries from breaking free of law firms and providing the public with the same services lawyers do at a tiny fraction of the cost. Several Florida typists in recent years have established thriving businesses providing the public with contracts, deeds, adoption papers, and uncontested-divorce settlements. This has meant savings of hundreds of thousands of dollars for ordinary people, and thereby the loss of hundreds of thousands in monopoly profits for attorneys. Of course, the lawyers have struck back, doing all they could to intimidate their competitors, even having them forcibly jailed for daring to violate the legal monopoly.

Consider the case of Marilyn Brumbaugh, who successfully handled about six hundred cases before the Florida bar moved to drive her out of business. She was whisked before a judge as part of an investigation into "the unauthorized practice of law." The judge himself cross-examined her, asking questions about her business, which she refused to answer, invoking the Fifth Amendment. The reason that she chose to remain silent is that she could not find out what her rights were in a hearing into the "unauthorized practice of law." No lawyer would tell her. As she puts it, "No one would represent me because they are all members of the same country club. No one wanted to defend me. They are all under the authority of the Florida bar."[3]

Brumbaugh further reports that the judge told her, "If you don't talk, I will put you in the county jail without bond." She declined to testify, still invoking her constitutional right to remain silent, and as a consequence was imprisoned for part of a day. The experience did not improve her opinion of lawyers. In any future case, she no longer wants one. She says, "Now that I know how crooked they are, I don't want a lawyer. I will defend myself. . . . I will argue my case before a jury. I claim that anyone can do what I am doing. The lawyers realize this. That is why I am such a threat."

Another threat is legal stenographer Rosemary Furman, who set out to help women with divorce problems issue injunctions against their husbands. Furman reports: "Hell, I'd been doing divorce papers for years and years for lawyers. Why shouldn't I do it for others?" She established a $50 fee for her service and immediately got a rush of business, handling as many as twenty divorce cases in a single week. When attorneys got wind of her activities, the Florida bar acted toward her just as it did toward Marilyn Brumbaugh. A court proceeding was initiated under the direction of the Florida Supreme Court, which assigns the state bar the task of investigating and trying its own charges against unauthorized practice of law. In effect, the lawyers are judge and jury in their own case.

Like Brumbaugh, Furman was at first unable to find a lawyer to handle her defense. Eventually, after some struggle, she did find a member of the bar to take the case. Whether the courts, and perhaps eventually the Supreme Court, will uphold the transcendental-capital claims of the attorneys—the rule which isolates them from free-market competition—is a matter to be seen. Whatever is decided, one thing at least is clear: lawyers will go to great lengths to preserve the monopoly powers through which they squeeze the public.

Just how far they will go is scarcely understood, because most of us are unable to withstand the kind of intimidation lawyers use against those who challenge their monopolistic grip on the general public. One person who was stubborn enough to take the full treatment is Norman F. Dacey. By standing up to bar associations for almost two decades, Dacey has provided America with an unmistakable record of the corruption and injustice that lie at the heart of the current operations of the legal profession.

Dacey's fight with lawyers began innocently back in the early 1960's. As an investment consultant and mutual-fund broker living in Connecticut, Dacey was constantly astounded by the high costs of probate, which not only diverted a major portion of any estate into the pockets of lawyers but also involved such frequent and protracted delays as to impose a hardship on heirs. Dacey began to collect a file of stories illustrating the abuses of probate. Among his collection of horror tales was this one described in the headlines of a Cincinnati paper: "ANOTHER ESTATE CASE UNCOVERED: IT ALL GOES TO FEES!" Somewhat less rapacious was the attorney whose work led to this Missouri story: "Fees eat up nearly half of an estate of $19,425." Dacey still tells the story of an unbelievable case from Salt Lake City in which a woman applied for welfare—five years after her father died leaving her $765,000. In all that time, the estate was still tangled up in legal delays.

Dacey's reading and experience in the investment field convinced him that his clients would be better off if they could avoid some of these abuses. In keeping with his conviction, Dacey told his clients how to avoid probate—by arranging trusts through their banks. He did not consider himself to be practicing law. In fact, he never charged for his probate advice. It was all covered by his normal investment-counseling fee, which was no more than the prevailing rate. Many of Dacey's clients followed his advice, to the acute disappointment of their attorneys, who thereby lost the opportunity to collect fat fees for shepherding their estates through probate.

Dacey realized that he was by no means a popular man among the members of the Connecticut legal profession. He did not realize how unpopular until he came home one evening and read an extraordinary headline in a local paper. He recounts: "My wife asked if I had seen the papers, and there on the front page was a story saying that the court had issued an injunction requiring me to stop the unauthorized practice of law. There had been no hearing. The first I ever heard of it was when I read it in the papers."

Dacey heard a lot more of it thereafter.

He went into court to have the injunction lifted. He told the court that with only a high-school education, he had had no intention of setting himself up to practice law, but was merely giving his clients the benefit of his best advice on matters of investment. Dacey recalls the hearing: "The Connecticut Bar Association subpoenaed my clients, who were asked to reveal their personal affairs. They all claimed they were happy with my services. The bar claimed that the 'public' had been injured. I asked them to name one person who had been injured. They couldn't. Finally, the attorney for the bar said, 'The bar has been injured.' "

The presiding judge apparently found that conclusive. He refused to lift the injunction. Dacey appealed to the Connecticut Supreme Court.

It, too, upheld the bar's monopoly, describing Dacey's activities as "sordid."

Most people would have given up at this point. Dacey could have turned to selling insurance or simply restricted his investment advice to ways of helping clients make money, forgetting about trying to help them keep it. But Dacey decided instead to strike back. He wrote a book—*How to Avoid Probate*—which spelled out his case against allowing a lawyer to settle your affairs. As he put it, "When they issued the injunction, I figured if I could not tell people how to avoid the abuses of probate—the delay, the expense, the publicity—I could write a book and they could read it." The first edition, which he printed at his own expense, sold out in sixteen days.

In January 1967, when about 600,000 copies of *How to Avoid Probate* had been sold, Dacey got another surprise. The New York County Lawyers' Association charged him with criminal contempt of court for having dared to write the book. Dacey, his new publisher, and two booksellers were accused of practicing law without a license. The case came to trial before Judge Charles Marks of the New York Supreme Court, who was a member of the New York County Lawyers' Association. Dacey requested that the judge disqualify himself since he was technically a party to the case. He also requested a jury trial. Both requests were ignored. Without the benefit of any further hearing, the judge found Dacey and the bookstore guilty and issued an injunction prohibiting the sale or distribution of *How to Avoid Probate*. Moreover, Dacey was sentenced to thirty days in jail.

He appealed the decision to the Appellate Division of the New York court system. His case was argued before five judges. Four were members of the New York County Lawyers' Association. The presiding judge, Justice Stevens, was not. The decision went four to one against Dacey. In his dissent, Judge Stevens affirmed Dacey's First Amendment right to publish information on how a person may handle probate problems on his own.

Dacey appealed once more, this time to the New York Court of Appeals. Seven judges heard the case. Luckily for Dacey, only one was a member of the New York County Lawyers' Association. He alone ruled against Dacey. The final verdict stood six to one in his favor. In all, thirteen judges heard the case brought by the New York County Lawyers' Association against Norman F. Dacey. Without exception, all of the judges who were technically parties to the suit found Dacey guilty.

The seven judges who were not members of the Association unanimously found him innocent.

Dacey was spared from having to serve time in a penitentiary. But the appeals he was obliged to undertake to vindicate himself left him $50,000 poorer. In retaliation, Dacey sued the New York County Lawyers' Association in a federal court on grounds that members of the Association conspired to deny him free speech. The case was assigned to Judge Inzer Wyatt, a member of the New York County Lawyers' Association. He ruled that the Association was *immune* from suit. Case dismissed.

There, in condensed form, is the story of Norman Dacey's trials and tribulations—the consequence of one man's attempt to tell people how to avoid unnecessary legal fees. The whole story is too complicated to unravel at this writing, partly because the story is not yet complete. More than twelve years later, Dacey is still battling uphill odds in an attempt to sue the Connecticut Bar Association for malicious libel. On June 16, 1974, a jury found the bar guilty and awarded Dacey $60,000 plus expenses. But the decision did not stick. It was appealed to judges who were all members of the Connecticut Bar Association. They voided the jury's findings and ordered a new trial—excluding much of the evidence which the jury had found convincing. Dacey protested, and his protests again were ignored. He pointed out that since the judges would have had to pay a portion of any judgment, they had a financial interest in ruling against him. He pointed to a law prohibiting judges from sitting on a case in which they have a financial interest. In response, the Board of Governors of the Connecticut Bar Association passed a resolution providing a remission of fees to any judge who heard *Dacey v. Connecticut Bar Association.*

Dacey will grow old trying to wrest justice out of lawyers. But he has done the public a service in battling as long and as stubbornly as he has. His experience demonstrates convincingly that attorneys, even those sitting on the bench, will defend each other and flaunt conflict of interest, even run roughshod over freedom of speech when they think their legal monopoly is being threatened.

The lawyers' monopoly, their transcendental capital, is the basis of their ability to charge high prices. Without the power to prohibit "the unauthorized practice of law," there would be no stopping anyone from setting himself up in competition for legal business. Just about anyone who can read and formulate a sentence has the competence to perform most lawyerly tasks. Even with education as it is today, enough potential competitors undoubtedly exist to take the profit out of legal intrigue and confusion. In other words, if it were not for the monopoly powers which the lawyers who dominate government have granted themselves, the cost of legal services would plunge. That would be unhappy news for the attorney seeking what the Illinois Bar Association has claimed is "his proper place at the top of the economic structure."

The costs of this dominion are enormous. As has already been indicated, they go beyond the direct fees which lawyers charge for their various real and alleged services. The tendency to avoid all risks in decision making—which has a petrifying effect on productive capabilities—is a consequence of legal empire building. So is the growth of what might be termed "credentialism," which is discussed elsewhere in this volume. Ordinary people have adopted the conviction that one's rewards should be determined more by his credentials and less by his productive achievements, and this is partly because lawyers made that principle a central tenet of all their work.

Lawyers share out their monopoly powers on a basis which is determined by credentials. Only law-school graduates can become lawyers. By the same token, lawyers seek to redistribute productive capital on a basis of adjudication. Their vision of a "beautiful" system—if it is not, as Bernard Shaw alleged, one of "cases which ruin all the parties to them"—would be a situation in which every nonlawyer would have to bring a suit once a year before a bureaucratic tribunal to determine his income. The logic of the legalistic allocation of rewards almost inevitably turns toward credentials—toward what one *is* rather than toward performance and what one *does* as the standard of judgment. Because one has obtained a credential in the form of a college degree, because one is a member of an accredited minority or a woman, or has some other attribute which pioneering lawyers have seized upon, one is deemed "entitled" to rewards. Consequently we witness the spectacle of individuals clogging the courts with actions seeking to establish their credentials as Chicanos, blacks, American Indians, or what-have-you, in order to obtain good jobs, and in some instances substantial cash awards. The "I am-really-a-Chicano" lawsuit represents the first step toward a legal certification of everyone's attributes. If they have not as yet, members of every minority will soon be hiring attorneys to demand their share of the claims to life's good things which are being parceled out in courts. Albanian-Americans, for example, may complain with logical force that they are a minority, although they are not as yet a certified minority. And what of orphans? And short people? And those who are fat, thin, diabetic, have harelips, or are vegetarians? Because every individual is different from all others—is, in fact, a minority of one—the number of potential lawsuits to establish credentials or entitlements is almost as large as the whole population. And, indeed, without even looking toward the matter's logical conclusion there are many ripe possibilities for litigation by disgruntled and empty-handed members of the putative majority. Witness the celebrated Allen Bakke case.

By segmenting the population into groups and granting the members of certain groups legal priority in access to all forms of capital, the lawyers have pitched ordinary people into adversary relationships. Eventually, the irreducible logical contradictions between the various claims to privileged status and the limited supply of good things toward which these claims are aimed, draws these adversary relationships into the courts or the bureaucracy. That, in turn, guarantees the prosperity of lots of lawyers.

A booming industry has been created in fabricating new legal theories to bring more of life under bureaucratic control. Lawyers have increasingly and successfully extended application of the "due-process" clause in the Constitution to protect transcendental-capital claims, which in turn have increasingly taken on the legal status of property. In 1970 the Supreme Court ruled in *Goldberg v. Kelley* that welfare recipients have what amounts to a property right in the programs which subsidize their incapacity. In legal terms, they literally "own" their benefits. They cannot be denied those benefits except upon completion of painstaking legal procedures involved in notification, hearing, and appeal. Later decisions have extended due-process provisions to protect other forms of new property. In a 1972 case of a political-science professor at a Texas college, the court ruled that the plaintiff had a "property interest" in his job. Since he "owned" the post he filled, he could not be dismissed in the absence of a quasi-judicial proceeding, even though he did not have tenure. In other words, the court ruled that firing a person, for whatever reason, could necessitate the hiring of several lawyers.

In 1974, in *Arnette v. Kennedy*, the courts completed this triumph of "due-process" imperialism by confirming that bureaucrats have property rights in federal jobs. By this stage, in fact, almost all forms of transcendental capital are protected by layers of red tape. A taxi driver's medallion, a doctor's license to practice, and even the monopolist's hegemony cannot be revoked without painstaking legal procedures—any part of which is subject to multiple appeals, all employing lawyers on both sides of the question. The logical consequence of this has yet to be seen. It may be, as Robert M. Kaus suggests, "the day the justices rule that a losing candidate for reelection can successfully sue to get back his office. After all, how could the courts allow him to be deprived of his valuable government job simply because of the view he expressed in a campaign?"[3]

If the growth of due-process litigation falls short of that extreme, it will be the only forbearance by lawyers who are otherwise doing all they can to entangle and confuse human action. Daily, lawyers contrive some expansion of their dominion, imposing new costs, making American institutions ever less flexible and responsive, and underscoring the aptness of Grant Gilmore's conclusion in *The Ages of American Law*: "The worse the society, the more law there will be. In Hell, there will be nothing but law, and due process will be meticulously observed."[4]

Some hint of the dimensions of America's legal problem can be gathered from the fact that more than 150,000 new laws are passed each year, primarily by lawyers who dominate Congress, state legislatures, and local councils. In addition to the laws, numberless bureaucratic edicts are issued. In fact, according to Senator Patrick Leahy, more pages of new federal regulations were issued from January 1977 to mid-1978 than all the laws passed by Congress since the eighteenth century. The sheer volume of these edicts has carried the legal system beyond the limits of comprehensibility.

Even if the laws were written so as to be understood, which is emphatically not the case, it would engross a citizen's every waking moment to keep abreast of all the laws and regulations which might apply to him. As Howard Dearborn said after spending $3,000 in legal fees to fight a $25 fine imposed by a government agency: "We got fined for not knowing even though they never told us in the first place. There are so many people passing laws these days you couldn't read them all in one lifetime." We have long since abandoned the principles of brevity and comprehensibility of law advocated by America's founders. Edward Billing, who drafted the Constitution and the first laws of New Jersey, urged, "Let the law be printed that everyone may know that law which he is subject to, to the intent that no man may be condemned by a law he neither knows or ever heard of or understands."[5]

Today's legal system operates on just the opposite principle. Because incomprehensibility is a source of profit to attorneys, they see to it that almost every law they draft and every brief they file is clouded in murk. If you, the party of the third part, notwithstanding any abilities you have to the contrary, are unable to decipher the meaning of laws or briefs drafted by one set of lawyers, hereinafter the party of the second part, you are obliged to hire another attorney or group of attorneys, the party of the first part, to decipher what the party of the second part rendered incomprehensible. Get it?

The growth of government, especially the proliferation of laws and regulations, is synonymous with the increased prosperity of lawyers. In ninety-nine cases out of one hundred, the new rules created through government are forms of transcendental capital—legal instruments which have capital value for some private persons but which are liabilities for others. This privatization of law helps lawyers single out clients. Individuals, businesses, labor unions, and other groups find their prosperity increasingly dependent upon the capital value of the rules rather than their productive abilities. They thus have increasingly large stakes in seeing that the rules which favor them are preserved. By the same token, when bureaucracy is given the power to destroy any business, individual, or institution, no matter how productive, those with interests to protect must also hire attorneys.

Those attorneys profit handsomely, perhaps without ever coming near a courtroom. As the *Wall Street Journal* described the situation, "their knack is navigating through the maze of the government bureaucracy. They counsel clients on the ins and outs of federal law, lobby and argue on Capitol Hill and deal with regulatory agencies."[6] The demand for such legal services is greatest, of course, in a period of chaos, when the efforts of bureaucracy are intensifying, when new laws are being written at a prodigious rate, and no one really knows quite what to expect. Every time a lawyer in Congress introduces a new piece of legislation, he helps to employ one or more new lobbyists. With the number of bills introduced now approaching one hundred times the number proposed in the first Congress, which met in 1789 and 1790, one need not look far for an explanation for the incredible prosperity of Washington lawyers. As of 1976 *The Washington Post* conservatively estimated that at least five hundred attorneys in Washington earned more than $100,000 a year. In the year before Joseph Califano became Secretary of Health, Education and Welfare, his annual earnings from Washington law practice exceeded $500,000. It is the lure of earnings like that which make it extremely rare for lawyers who are elected to Congress to ever return to their home districts after they retire. They and their staff attorneys who draft legislation stay behind in Washington as experts who collect high fees for unraveling the mysteries they created when writing the laws.

Just a single piece of legislative handiwork can be a multibillion-dollar windfall for attorneys. Consider the Regional Rail Reorganization Act of 1973. It has given rise to what may be the largest, longest, and undoubtedly the most expensive lawsuit in the history of the world. As of early 1979 the actual trial of the suit had not even begun and lawyers had already claimed an estimated $25 million in legal fees. To this cost add at least $12 million more for government expenses, including salaries for seventeen lawyers in the legal department of the U.S. Railway Association. So as of the end of 1978, the legal preliminaries had already consumed $37 million. It is expected that the case will take a full decade, including time for appeals, and eventually cost taxpayers as much as $13 *billion*. That is another example supporting what one leading attorney told *The Washington Post*: "Every time Congress begins to legislate in an area, it's a bonanza for lawyers."

Just about the only way one can escape legal problems these days is to die and pass them on to his heirs. And that is exactly what happens. Lawyers are like vultures preying over the dead. They turn probate proceedings into protracted pillagings. In *The American Way of Death*, Jessica Mitford documented the high cost of funerals. But undertakers are pikers compared to lawyers. Americans who die leaving an estate of $60,000 or more (which includes almost anyone who owns a home) can expect to have lawyers take an average of *five times* more than the undertaker.

The full costs of the Legal Squeeze upon the American public can scarcely be estimated because most of them are indirect. No one can measure the loss in value of new products which never came to market because lawyers helped stifle innovation. The regulations imposed by lawyers in bureaucracy, which help employ more lawyers outside bureaucracy, create costs which can only be borne by large businesses. They, in turn, are discouraged from introducing new products partly because these new products may have unforeseen liability difficulties. The probability of lawyers filing suit on the slightest hint of any kind of damage remotely associated with a product or service is so high that the risks of introducing new, untested innovations have increased enormously. This is especially true because courts have ruled that manufacturers are liable for injuries and damage caused by people working with products in modified condition. In other words, a producer may be found at fault and made to pay a costly judgment, not for producing a dangerous product, but for producing a product which could be modified to become dangerous or, even more remarkable, a product which could be dangerous if used by an incompetent. For example, a manufacturer of a paper-making machine was forced to pay $800,000 to a worker in Alabama who injured himself with a tool produced by that company fourteen years earlier. In the meantime, the man's employer had modified the tool several times, removing safety equipment. The courts found the manufacturer liable anyway. Is it any wonder, then, as one producer told *U.S. News & World Report*, that "Some manufacturers are now reluctant to bring out new products because they fear lawsuit"?[7]

The tendency of large corporations to grow by acquiring smaller ones rather than developing their own new products is strongly encouraged by this Legal Squeeze. The risks of taking over an already existing product are far fewer than those involved in trying something new, something which has not yet been exposed to and withstood the scrutiny of lawyers prospecting for liability litigation. So the big businesses buy up small ones, and this, as the system would have it, also employs lawyers to litigate antitrust cases.

No survey of the costs of the Legal Squeeze would be complete without reference to the growth of crime. More than 600 Americans are robbed, raped, mugged, or murdered every minute of every day. If the total costs of the property damage alone imposed upon Americans by criminals were equally distributed, it would be equivalent to an annual loss of almost $500 for each family.

Why did crime become so endemic? One reason is that crime is lucrative. As Thomas Plate convincingly demonstrated in his book *Crime Pays!*, criminals have a lively incentive to continue pillaging the American people. The rewards of crime are greater than the costs. Successful criminals gross $25,000 to $75,000 per year. This is due, at least in part, to lawyers who have pioneered new ways of keeping criminals out of jail. The probabilities of escaping unpunished from a crime are now substantially in the criminal's favor. According to the district attorney's office the odds of committing a felony and escaping without a prison sentence in some areas of New York City are better than 100 to 1.

Under such conditions, crime can be far more lucrative than the opportunities available to many persons in productive work. A criminal, for example, who collects $75,000 burglarizing hotels in New York may net eight to ten times as much as the average employee who works for the hotel. If he can stay out of prison for two or three years at a time, he clearly profits substantially, even if he is occasionally caught and convicted. For one thing, he has a good chance of avoiding jail on conviction. According to a study of sentence variations conducted by the Law Enforcement Assistance Administration, even adults convicted of felonies with weapons are often placed on probation or given suspended sentences. In fact, a study using data collected in the city of Washington found that 51.8 percent of those who used dangerous weapons in assaults received light sentences, and one-third of convicted burglars were not sent to jail at all. Not only have average sentences been declining, but the percentage of the sentence which is actually served is now well under 50 percent.

Lawyers have contributed in a number of ways to the erosion of the penalties for crime. Defense attorneys have consistently maneuvered to exonerate criminals on the basis of technicalities. More and more reasons have been found to make the outcome of a criminal trial turn upon factors other than the guilt or innocence of the defendant. The vilest murderers have been turned loose on the streets, not because there is any doubt as to their guilt, but because an obsession for procedural rituals that allegedly comprise "due process" dominates the judicial proceedings.

Consider the case of Robert Williams. On the night before Christmas 1968, Williams raped and suffocated a ten-year-old girl in Iowa. He was seen stuffing her body into an automobile, so a warrant was issued for his arrest. After an intensive manhunt, Williams surrendered to police in Davenport. As he was being driven by police detectives back to Des Moines, where the crime occurred, a police detective attempted to persuade Williams to reveal the location of the murdered girl's body. The detective said: "It's going to be dark early this evening. They are predicting several inches of snow for tonight, and I feel that you yourself are the only person that knows where this little girl's body is, that you yourself have only been there once and if you get a snow on top of it, you yourself may not be able to find it. And, since we will be going right past the area on the way to Des Moines, I feel that we could stop and locate the body, that the parents of this little girl should be entitled to a Christian burial for the little girl who was snatched away from them on Christmas Eve and murdered. . . ." The policeman concluded by saying, "I do not want you to answer me. I don't want to discuss it further."

Williams had been cautioned by three state officials and two lawyers that he had the right to remain silent. He did so for another hour of the drive and then asked if the little girl's shoes had been found. He next directed the driver of the car to turn into a gas station from which in short order he led the police to the girl's shoes and then to the blanket in which he had wrapped her body, and finally to the corpse itself.

Williams was convicted of the murder, of which he was undoubtedly guilty. But almost a decade later his case was still being actively adjudicated—in the Supreme Court, which eventually overturned his conviction on grounds that the interrogation in the police cruiser played unfairly upon the murderer's sympathy for the girl's parents and had been a "charade" used to "pry" a confession. No one denied that Williams had been informed of his right to remain silent on at least five separate occasions prior to his decision to tell the whole story. Yet in overturning his conviction, the court concluded that Williams had been "deprived" of his right to counsel. According to the court, because Williams did not have an attorney with him at all times to attest that his confession was not an unintentional abandonment of his rights to remain silent, none of the evidence produced by his confession could be used against him.

This is at heart a doctrine of irresponsibility, as was suggested in the dissent of Justice Byron White, who wrote: "Men usually intend to do what they do and there is nothing in the record to support the proposition that [Williams'] decision to talk was anything but an exercise of his own free will." Yet the current doctrine of criminal law amounts, in essence, to the supposition that no one who is not a defense attorney has free will. By implication, any criminal could exonerate himself from his crimes simply by blurting out a confession faster than officials could recite his rights to remain silent. Note that the undoubted consequence of this is to employ many more attorneys. The guilty can no longer confess on a free-lance basis. Only with the paid concurrence of lawyers do the confessions count.

The Williams case highlights another problem of the legal system that is worth our attention. Protracted maneuvering by lawyers—motions, countermotions, and appeals—dragged out the process of determining guilt for almost a decade after the crime that everyone knew Williams committed. Such delays clog court dockets, discouraging the prosecution of other cases as well. Lawyers now have so many means at their disposal to slow down proceedings, to delay and frustrate justice, that it becomes impossible to prosecute many guilty parties. For one thing, the time between apprehension and trial is so long that the accused must normally be set at large during the years which elapse between the commission of the crime and the point at which he is tried. For obvious reasons, this discourages victims and witnesses from cooperating in the prosecution. Says Robert Kaye, chief of the Florida State Attorney's Office Strike Force: "People are afraid. They ask themselves, 'Is the defendant going to get me when he gets out of jail?'" In many cases, the criminal has a strong incentive to encourage that suspicion, because without cooperation of key witnesses he cannot be prosecuted. He knows intimidation pays, so he does it successfully. In some locales, more than 50 percent of scheduled witnesses fail to appear. And those who do appear must often reappear again and again as defense attorneys maneuver to delay the trial. One determined witness, Patricia Finck, a supermarket cashier, had to return to a Philadelphia court *forty-six times* to provide the testimony to convict two holdup men. Most witnesses would have given up long before, which is exactly why many guilty parties are never sent to jail. In some cases, the witnesses actually spend more time in jail (placed there for their own protection) than the perpetrators of crimes. In other instances, the passage of time defeats prosecution because evidence is physically destroyed or misplaced and witnesses die. When lawyers delay justice, they deny justice.

Another means by which lawyers have helped to loose criminals upon America has been the perversion of the jury system. In case after case, criminals have had their convictions overturned on the grounds that the jurors may have known something about the case on which they sat.

There is no more telling example of the damage this principle has done to the pursuit of justice than the case of Elmer Wayne Henley, the self-confessed murderer. Henley apparently participated in the torture and strangulation of as many as twenty-seven teenage boys in Houston. The evidence against him was overwhelming. Yet an appeals court overturned his conviction on grounds that the trial judge had not extended sufficient consideration to the defense attorney's request to move the trial for a second time to another location. It had already been moved once from Houston, where the crimes occurred, to San Antonio.

While the immediate result of this kind of ruling is obvious—another expensive trial employing more attorneys—it is also an expression of an even more subtle and destructive tendency: the insistence upon jurors who know as little as possible of the matter which they are deciding. By current legal standards, the perfect juror would be a person who had just awakened from a deep coma. If he were utterly ignorant of all that had gone on about him he would have precisely the characteristics which attorneys now seek in jurors. They demand that a jury impaneled in a criminal trial, especially a trial of any note, be constituted of persons who are not alert to current events. The less they know of the circumstances in which the crime took place, the weaker their grasp of any technical details involved, the better. The jury before whom the lawyer wants to perform is one which is "ignorant" in the truest sense of the word. He wants people who are not knowledgeable participants in the search for justice, but more like an impressionable audience—persons with no basis for their decision but their evaluation of the performance of lawyers.

The current conception of the jury is almost the exact opposite of that which made jury trials such a valued part of the American heritage. Originally the juror was not someone who was *ignorant*, but someone who knew. He was someone who had not only heard of the crime, if a crime was involved, but was also acquainted with the victim and the defendant. The idea of changing the location of a trial in order to have it heard by jurors who had no knowledge of the crime's details would have seemed a startling injustice to eighteenth-century Americans. When they spoke of a defendant's right to a jury trial they spoke explicitly of a trial by a "jury of his vicinage." That is, the trial was to be conducted by the defendant's neighbors. That made for a profoundly popular institution because a jury of knowledgeable persons was competent to judge the law as well as facts.

Today's jury can judge little except lawyers. Its function has been devalued to something akin to that of an applause meter. The result has been to further subordinate the pursuit of justice to the interests of attorneys so that the system itself vindicates renowned trial lawyer Jerry Paul's unholy boast: "Given enough money I can buy justice. I can win any case in this country, given enough money. A jury is twelve people deciding who has the best lawyer."[8]

There is a symbiotic relationship between the legal profession and the criminal. Although most lawyers would deny it, the prosperity of lawyers as a group rises as crime rises. If the same criminal turns up in court five dozen times, that means ten dozen opportunities for the employment of attorneys. For this to happen, however, the costs of crime must be kept low. Crime must be lucrative as a profession. Lawyers, above all others, have had the ability to see that it is, to make the probable costs of criminal behavior so low as to clog the courts with criminals who thus become the steady customers of attorneys, showing up time and again to face one charge or another.

Of course, it is far easier to see that high crime rates benefit lawyers than it is to assess the process by which the legal monopoly has contributed to the proliferation of crime. The mere fact that lawyers benefit from crime proves nothing. Front-end mechanics benefit from potholes, yet the mechanics themselves do not break up the streets. The process of creating potholes is, however, an utterly different sort of thing from the process of altering the rules of evidence, changing the requirements for impaneling juries, excluding uncoerced confessions, and inviting perjured testimony, all of which have combined with other alleged reforms of the criminal-justice system to reduce the costs of crime. It is precisely the work of lawyers which has made the difference in making crime pay, and thus creating more criminals, who eventually increase the demand for legal services.

Indeed, the very point of many of the evolving changes in criminal law has been to mandate the greater employment of attorneys. The famous 1966 Supreme Court "Miranda" decision, for example, did not give accused persons the right to remain silent in the face of police charges. Americans have had that right at least since the first ten amendments to the Constitution were ratified. If natural-law theorists are to be believed, the protection against self-incrimination was established long before that. The Supreme Court did not enlarge upon the "unchangeable, unwritten laws of Heaven," to borrow Sophocles' words from *Antigone*. What the court effectively said was that no case can be resolved without the employment of an attorney. As a consequence, most police officers now carry what is known as a "Miranda card." It includes these words:

> You have the right to the presence of an attorney to assist you prior to questioning and to be with you during questioning if you so desire.
>
> If you cannot afford an attorney, you have the right to have an attorney appointed you prior to questioning. . . .

It is easy to see how this policy and the other steps which have followed it were imagined to be good and just, especially by the lawyers themselves. There is no doubt that police can be overzealous, prejudiced, and even brutal. This is especially true in the case of persons who seem too weak to impose political or legal costs in situations where their rights are violated. But this does not explain why almost every change in the procedures of criminal law in the last several decades has rebounded to the enrichment of lawyers. There is no logical reason why civil liberties for criminal suspects could not have been expanded in ways which did not expand employment opportunities for lawyers. Other kinds of protections could have been introduced.

The intensification of the legal procedures needed to try and convict a criminal coincided with a dramatic increase in the population of lawyers and especially of law students. As these students were as yet without an established practice, and were in fact basing their careers upon the hope that larger numbers of attorneys would find employment, they had a lively interest in supporting legal precedents which created more legal jobs. This is true, even for the students who intended to specialize in corporate law or estate planning or any of the other fifty-seven varieties of legal specialty which have arisen in America. No matter what form of law they intended to practice, they all had incentives, and still do, to see their classmates gainfully employed.

The self-interested sentiment of attorneys has a tendency to find its way into judicial rulings because of the peculiar way in which legal theory is developed. It is almost solely the province of law students, whose research is published in law reviews. The judges on the bench do not spin their novel new theories out of the air. They follow ideas pioneered in academic law journals, ideas which, as circumstances would have it, rebound to increase the employment opportunities of those who write the articles.

The symbiotic relationship between the lawyer and the criminal is only secondarily a problem of the lawyer's intentions. It is more a logical consequence of the existence of a monopoly bar. What America's thoughtful pioneers were fond of denouncing as an "exclusive advantage of commerce" gives the lawyers incentives to impose costs upon the public because in so doing they raise their own incomes. In essence, we are paying lawyers to create problems for everyone because they can "capitalize" on those problems and turn them into assets to themselves. Their license to practice law, their transcendental capital, makes that possible.

That the granting to lawyers of this "exclusive advantage of commerce" can have disastrous effects was well understood by America's first settlers. Many of the early colonists escaped from England to free themselves from the domination of lawyers, who then comprised the aristocratic elite. More than six hundred of England's noble families derived their titles and estates through legal practice in the seventeenth century alone. Then, as now, lawyers grew rich and powerful by creating legal confusion, encumbering commerce with costly litigation, and manipulating the government to their own advantage. Then, as now, the power of lawyers overcame all political divisions. Neither the Royalists nor the Parliamentarians could bring them under control. King James I said of lawyers, "they all be knaves." He proposed reforms, which went nowhere. Later in the century, when Cromwell took over, he proposed new reforms to simplify legal procedures and reduce costs. His proposals, too, were bogged down in a Parliament controlled by lawyers. On a visit to England as a young man, Peter the Great was so flabbergasted by the domination of English society by attorneys that he resolved as part of his reform effort to hang half of the lawyers in Russia. The colonists who set out for America carried with them some of the same bitter distrust of the legal profession, but they expressed it in a more humane way. The Massachusetts Body of Liberties, drawn in 1641, banned lawyers from the colony. So did the Fundamental Constitutions of Carolina, as drafted by John Locke. Attorneys were also barred in several of the other colonies and forbidden from serving in councils or the legislature. The results of this quarantine on legalism were widely approved. It was said of Pennsylvania: "They have no lawyers . . . 'tis a happy country."

Pennsylvania remained a "happy country" for a long time. As late as 1787, when the Constitutional Convention convened in Philadelphia, John Quincy Adams wrote in his diary, "The mere title of lawyer is sufficient to deprive a man of public confidence." Antilawyer attitudes continued to permeate America for generations thereafter. It was only after tireless public-relations efforts that by the mid-nineteenth century people gradually relaxed their opposition to the assumption of monopoly power of lawyers. As Maxwell Bloomfield recounts in his book *American Lawyers in a Changing Society 1776–1876*, lawyers went so far as to compose and print many novels designed explicitly to counter popular animosity toward the legal profession. In one book after another, lawyers emerged as folk heroes who succeeded through hard work and selfless dedication to the public good.[9] All of this must have had its impact, because as the nineteenth century wore on, lawyers succeeded in placing more and more restrictions upon their competition.

In the days when Abraham Lincoln first began his legal practice, there was no requirement that a lawyer go to law school or have any special education. All he needed was customers. Anyone who could boast of a "good moral character" and could help solve legal problems was free to do so, and make a modest living in the bargain. Few lawyers got rich in America's early days because the force of competition kept prices low. For example, when Lincoln probated an estate of $100,000, he charged $5.[10]

That was long ago. Our lawyer elite has long since succeeded in banning "the unauthorized practice of law." In the process, they have so firmly gripped America in a Legal Squeeze that even Warren Burger, chief justice of the Supreme Court, has warned: "Unless we derive substitutes for the courtroom processes, we may be on our way to a society overrun by hordes of lawyers, hungry as locusts. . . ."

13
The Bureaucratic Squeeze

Everything government touches turns to crap.
                                        —*Ringo Starr*

Since 1972 there have been more bureaucrats drawing salaries in America than all the people at work in "all the durable goods manufacturing industries, including such giants as autos, electronics, steel, and heavy machinery."[1] Each business day, the number of bureaucrats increases by about 1,300. And each new bureaucrat contributes an additional overhead cost to everything you buy: he makes your groceries more expensive—by imposing 4,100 regulations on a pound of plain hamburger; when you buy a new car you are paying more for the accumulated efforts of the bureaucrats than you are for all four wheels—General Motors alone must employ 23,000 persons simply to fill out government forms. If the estimates of experts are correct, then the total effect of all regulatory exactions is to impose an annual cost of more than $130 billion upon the economy. That is about $2,500 per family.

Wherever you turn, the bureaucrat is costing you money.

Not only does the bureaucrat contribute indirectly to high prices, he often insists that prices be raised. The Interstate Commerce Commission, for example, has long regulated the truck, train, and barge traffic in the United States with a view to keeping prices high. This

205

regulation has been so intense that as of 1971 Herbert Witten, a consultant to the Department of Transportation, estimated that there were in existence 43 trillion unindexed rates on file at the ICC. In other words, there were more than 200,000 regulations for each man, woman, and child then living in the United States. According to Witten, who personally measured the tariffs filed in ICC offices, the papers on which the regulations were written would pile up to a stack eight times as tall as the Washington Monument.

A glance into the files of an agency such as the ICC shows that it does not stop short at abusing your purse. It also abuses your language. Consider this single sentence from a route restriction designed to limit the free flow of goods:

> It has been held that carburetors, distributors, generators, electric motors, and similar commodities are not embraced in the description "machinery"; that electric regulators are not "machinery"; that the term "building materials" relates to materials intended to be used for the erection and repair of buildings and not for building operations in general, and that, as a consequence materials for the erection of a bridge are not included since a bridge is not a building; that the commodity description "food products" embraces only such products as are fit for human consumption and does not include canned food; that the word "canned" in the description "Canned goods" refers to the process of canning and not to the receptacle in which the goods are placed, which may be metal or glass; that "groceries" are defined as articles for human consumption which are customarily served as food, or which are used in the preparation of food, except "fresh meats" . . . that only rough or unfinished articles are embraced by the commodity descriptions "iron and steel articles"; that engines and machinery are not included in the term "iron and steel articles"; that the commodity description "paper and paper products" does not include newspapers, magazines, circulars, and other publications; that the commodity description "fruit and vegetable juices" does not include frozen juices; that gasoline is not a "liquid chemical"; and that the commodity description "glassware" does not include sheet glass or rough rolled glass or glass rods.[2]

Only bureaucracy could declare with a straight face that "gasoline" is not a "liquid chemical."

Bureaucrats give such absurdities the force of law. The Department of Agriculture requires that temperatures in packing houses be kept low. A packing house which violates the regulation is subject to severe penalties. The result of the low temperatures, however, is that water freezes on the floor. The Occupational Health and Safety Administration says that ice on the floor creates unsafe conditions and must be treated with salt. Packing houses that violate the regulation are also subject to severe penalties. The Environmental Protection Agency says that the salt on the floor contributes to pollution. Packing houses that allow salt on the floor are subject to still additional penalties.

That is the perfect train of bureaucratic development. One bureaucracy creates business for another, guaranteeing that an ordinary person can never get it right. But few of us have either the time or the inclination to so closely study the operations of bureaucracy as to see the institution as it really is. Most people do not realize that almost every agency, however lofty its purpose, not only contradicts what other agencies do but also contradicts in some substantial way what it is supposed to do. For example, the Occupational Safety and Health Administration ordered that trucks and other vehicles on construction sites be rigged with devices that emit a loud squawking sound when the vehicles back up. The agency followed this order with another, stipulating that workers wear earplugs to protect themselves from the resulting noise.

The very bureaucrats whose regulations are aimed at requiring people to be healthy and sane on the job have themselves been guilty of just about every feasible infraction of their own rules. A visit by Labor Department inspectors to OSHA's headquarters in Washington found the rear exit blocked by a huge roll of carpet. This was in spite of the fact that OSHA people know more about exits than anyone. As they say, an "exit is 'that portion of a means of egress which is separated from all other spaces of the building or structure by construction or equipment as required in this sub-part to provide a protected way of travel to the exit discharge.' " Inspectors found a ladder lying in the first-floor aisle. OSHA knows about ladders, too: "Ladders shall be designed and constructed to give a minimum slope of 3½ inches per foot of length of the front section, and minimum slope of 2 inches per foot of length of the back section, and except that special ladders designed for straight-in-wall work shall maintain at least 1½ inches back slope per foot of length." The inspectors inspecting OSHA found other difficulties as well. There was no emergency lighting system. OSHA employees were using fifty-four exposed electric outlets. And they were sipping coffee from twenty-four coffeemakers lacking safety trays as required by OSHA edicts. Soon after the visit, Samuel Sharkey, then the public-information director of OSHA, tripped over a typewriter cord in his office and broke his arm.

It is easy to see that bureaucracies, even expensive ones, do not always make problems better. Where the mind balks, however, is in grasping the fundamental fact that *bureaucracies often expend resources to make problems worse.* This is no accident. It arises from the basic nature of the bureaucratic institution.

One description of this phenomenon has been offered by the astute British observer Dr. Max Gammon in what he calls "The Theory of Bureaucratic Displacement." As Gammon puts it, in "bureaucratic systems . . . increase in expenditure will be met by fall in production. . . . Such systems will act rather like 'black holes' in the economic universe, simultaneously sucking in resources and shrinking in terms of 'emitted' production."[3]

The Occupational Safety and Health Administration is a perfect example of Gammon's bureaucratic "black hole." For all the money and energy expended by OSHA in its first five years of protecting American workers, an average of almost 300 persons died from injuries or job-related diseases each day. While OSHA was occupied preparing regulations which would have forced the King Ranch in Texas to install 5,625 toilets on its ranges to guarantee that a cowboy was never more than ten minutes' walk from hospitable plumbing, thousands of people died at their jobs. When the bureaucracy turned its attention to mine safety, it came up with a new definition of accident:

"(h) Accident" means,
(12) An event at a mine which causes death or bodily injury to an individual not at the mine at the time the event occurs.

The regulators also turned a stern eye to the affairs of an old Indian who had worked a one-man mine in Arizona for many years. A compliance officer required that the mine be closed because the old man lacked a regulation safety helmet, a safety belt, and a walkie-talkie. The miner denied that these were needed because in fifteen years in a flat horizontal shaft not even so much as a pebble had fallen from the ceiling. He didn't even need a safety belt because he could not fall any farther in the mine than he could in the bar on Saturday night, and it would not do him any good to have a walkie-talkie because if he were in the mine and something happened he would have no one with whom to talk. When the bureaucrats insisted, he bought a safety belt, a walkie-talkie, and a yellow miner's helmet with a light and had them mounted in a plastic case at the mine entrance.[4] What else was accomplished? With 3,500 new mine enforcement and safety bureaucrats on the job, severe injuries are actually on the increase.

The same phenomenon can be noted in many different programs. The hiring of more agriculture bureaucrats has coincided with lower incomes to farmers. As already noted, the vast increase in expenditure for educational bureaucrats has coincided with a dramatic increase in illiteracy. There is a simple reason for bureaucracy's sorry performance record: *bureaucrats as a group have as their primary objectives the furtherance of their own economic interests.* Even Karl Marx, whose writings have inspired (or perhaps justified) more bureaucratic empire-building than any person's in history, saw that bureaucrats do not attempt to do what is good for the public, but rather what is good for themselves:

> As far as the individual bureaucrat is concerned the end of the state becomes his private end: a pursuit of higher posts, the building of a career . . . a particular private aim opposed to the other private aims.[5]

Pure logic necessitates that the bureaucratic system as a whole will create crises in the areas of life where it dominates. This is because of the abstract nature of bureaucratic missions. Unlike the shoemaker, whose services come down to actually fitting paired shoes onto individual human feet, the bureaucrat in charge of the shoes has his fortune hitched to shoes in general. If a crisis arose to put a hole in every boot in America this would be the greatest boon that the shoe bureaucrat could imagine. It would concentrate public attention on shoes and set off a cry that "something should be done." When the bureaucratic mission is abstract and directed toward the entire public, the demand for the bureaucrat's services increases as the quality of those services declines. It follows that in most instances bureaucrats will derive higher income from botching things up than from actually solving problems.

Bureaucrats are creating crises in energy, housing, health care, education, the administration of justice, the transportation system—anywhere public opinion grants them a mandate to exert control over the productive sector.

This is not to say that no individual bureaucrats are well-intentioned and capable. But those who take their missions too seriously are misfits in their posts. Any actual progress toward eliminating the problems of the public points toward the elimination of the bureaucracy itself. That is just what the bureaucrats do not desire. And that is why it is only occasionally, by a kind of miracle, that someone comes along in the bureaucracy who is too naive or noble to fit into the system. He really does take his job according to its stated purposes and behaves as if he were motivated by a disinterested concern for the well-being of everyone. As overwhelming evidence demonstrates, however, such an individual is soon an outcast because he is rightly perceived as a danger to the system. When he is not fired outright, which is indeed rare, as only one bureaucrat out of 10,000 ever directly gets the ax, he is punished by being shunted and bypassed for promotion. If he did not know when he began, he eventually realizes that *the mission of a bureaucrat is not to protect the public; it is to foster the bureaucracy.*

Consider the case of Ernest Fitzgerald, which remains among the more instructive of many which illustrate the fate of those who oppose the bureaucratic system. Fitzgerald was a management-systems analyst who had risen to a position of responsibility in the Pentagon in 1968. Every evidence suggests that he was a thoroughly capable individual. He had a distinguished record in private life and no doubt might have gone on to great things had he been willing to devote his energies to justifying waste. But Fitzgerald believed that the task of the management expert should be to reduce the burdens on the taxpayers, not increase them. This view and the behavior that sprang from it began to make his superiors and associates uncomfortable. When Fitzgerald complained that officers and civilian Defense Department personnel were arranging for future employment with the same companies whose defense contracts they oversaw, the Pentagon insiders were appalled. Fitzgerald was fouling the nest. When he was called by Senator William Proxmire to testify about the shoddy construction of the Air Force's C-5 cargo plane, Fitzgerald admitted the truth. Lockheed was planning to bill the taxpayers for a $2 billion cost overrun.

In any productive enterprise, one who sought to save even a small fraction of $2 billion would be a hero. If he could save even $2 million or $200,000 he would be given a promotion and a testimonial dinner. That is the way it would be if saving money were in the interest of the people involved. This is not the case with bureaucracy.

When Fitzgerald tried to save the taxpayers' money, he became the enemy of bureaucracy. His honest appraisal of the procurement waste threatened to undermine the prosperity of all those who were profiting from cost overruns. And that was not to be tolerated. As soon as Fitzgerald's testimony was made public, Pentagon officials immediately concocted new and false figures about construction progress of the C-5 contract. These false figures were then given the widest possible circulation. Harold Brown, then Fitzgerald's superior as Secretary of the Air Force, reportedly ordered staff in his headquarters to withhold documentation of Fitzgerald's charges from Congress. Brown then devised a strategy on the three best ways of having Fitzgerald fired. He soon was.

But the matter did not end there. Fitzgerald was too obstinate to let it. With backing from Senator Proxmire, Fitzgerald went to court to vindicate himself. After years of delay and protracted litigation that led to $400,000 in legal fees, he won a desk in the Pentagon. But he now has nothing to do. The other bureaucrats and military officers with whom Fitzgerald had once worked, who played the system according to its rules, are now Fitzgerald's superiors. Harold Brown, who engaged in highly questionable activities in doctoring Fitzgerald's communications with Congress and helping to fire him, was installed by Jmmy Carter as Secretary of Defense.

Another individual who was not a payroller was Frank J. Keliher, a former Library of Congress clerk. As a librarian, Keliher had actually read the Federal Employee's Code of Ethics. There he came upon a passage which stated that his duty as a civil servant was to find and employ more efficient ways of doing government's work. Keliher took his duties to heart. He wrote a memo suggesting that one of the lengthy forms used in the Copyright Office duplicated other forms and could be scrapped. On another trip to the suggestion box, he demonstrated the obvious—that money could be saved if employees refrained from destroying rubber bands and paper clips after using them just once. Keliher also designed a more efficient way for the Library of Congress to collect and distribute its mail. For his pains he was banned from the mail room. Undaunted, he composed another memo pointing out an additional means of reducing waste. This time, his superiors ordered him to report to the staff psychiatrist, who soon determined that Keliher had written too many memos and was unfit for service. Keliher, who by this time had become disgusted, concluded that the verdict must be right. He quit his job to find employment someplace where the desire to save money was not considered madness.

John Coplin was yet another individual who behaved as civic books suggest bureaucrats should. Soon after joining the Department of Agriculture as a meat grader, he uncovered evidence of pervasive misgrading of meat in Chicago slaughterhouses. Coplin took his evidence to the FBI and worked behind the scenes on an investigation which resulted in the firing or resignation in the face of corruption charges of almost three-fourths of the meat graders in Chicago. That was an impressive beginning for Coplin's career. He had many other honors to follow. In fact, he proved to be so knowledgeable in his subject that major universities invited him to teach courses and he won many civic awards. What he did not win was success in bureaucracy. John Coplin set a record for the longest tenure in the Department of Agriculture without a promotion—twenty-six years.

Robert F. Sullivan was part of a team of criminal investigators employed by the General Services Administration. For years these investigators had heard rumors of widespread corruption in the GSA. In January 1975 Sullivan was assigned to investigation of alleged contract irregularities in New England. He interviewed another GSA employee, Robert J. Tucker. Tucker told Sullivan what all the world now knows— that bureaucrats in the Boston area had been using the contract-awarding procedures for their own gain. Tucker's charges were more than rumors. He had supporting documentation, which he had already delivered to the FBI. During the course of the investigation, Tucker's superiors in the bureaucracy discovered what he had done and fired him "for removing government files." Seeing what had happened to Tucker, Sullivan realized that he too would be putting his job on the line by honestly prosecuting his investigation. For six months he wrestled with the problem. Should he try to halt the waste, or cover it up? Eventually he decided to press forward. He reported to his superiors what they already knew, that corruption was rampant, and waited. Nothing happened. After failing to secure corrective action through official channels, Sullivan contacted the press, thinking that perhaps public knowledge of the scandal might produce some remedy. It did. Sullivan was fired. His letter of dismissal congratulated him for being "altruistic and well-intentioned."

There are many more scenarios which illustrate the dictum that what is good for the public is not good for the bureaucracy:

- Dr. J. Anthony Morris, the noted epidemiologist, who once worked for the National Institute of Health, was fired for pointing out that the bureaucracy's vaccine programs were unsafe and ineffective.
- William C. Bush, a former NASA scientist, was canned after he complained to his superiors, to congressmen, and even to the Civil Service Commission that his entire office should be abolished. He had six as-

sistants working for him in what he described as worthless jobs. He would have quit directly but he did not want someone else to take his place and thus have the jobs continue indefinitely. Bush's patriotic concern could not prevail over the interest of the bureaucracy.

- Sandra Kramer and Valerie Koster were nurses employed with the U.S. Indian Health Services at Shiprock, New Mexico. After complaining to the press and Congress about unsanitary conditions at the facility, they got their reward: notices of dismissal from government service.
- Ralph Applegate was hired by the Defense Construction Supply Center in Columbus, Ohio, to make price evaluations on the prices of small items. When he complained that his superiors insisted upon paying far in excess of the market price of the supplies they bought, he was fired.
- James Armet was suspended from work in the Social Security Administration when he complained about the waste of $750,000 of taxpayers' money for experimental "office landscaping."
- Demetrios Basdekas was shouldered out of the Nuclear Regulatory Commission when he raised questions about the safety factors in the government's plan to build a fast breeder reactor to produce deadly plutonium.

In none of these cases was the accuracy of the information brought forward by any of these rare individuals in question. They were not fired or punished for lying, and certainly not for incompetence, but rather for challenging and exposing the false pretenses of the bureaucracy.

There are more details to these stories, and many more stories like them. Anyone who cares to regale himself at greater length can turn to a publication of the Government Affairs Committee of the U.S. Senate, *The Whistle Blowers: A Report on Federal Employees Who Disclose Acts of Governmental Waste, Abuse, and Corruption.*[6] The report contains a wealth of additional evidence that the bureaucracy is operated for the benefit of the bureaucracy, and only incidentally for the benefit of anyone else.

The bureaucrat responds to the disguised economic imperatives of his job. As already suggested, those point away from the provision of good service to the public. This is not because bureaucrats are ill-tempered or malicious. It is the nature of the system in which their talents are misemployed that they should contribute as little as possible to the solution of any problem within their charge. To do otherwise means rocking the boat. The bureaucrat who does so is faced with high costs and low rewards. Anyone who thought otherwise while in the employ of the bureaucracy would be indulging the same sort of idiosyncratic fantasy that sometimes makes English lords call their dogs to a formal dinner at the table. It is a sort of indulgence that one pays for at his own cost. Understandably, few can afford to do so. "The first rule of the game," as John Gonzales, a veteran of both state and federal bureaucracies, has explained, is, "whatever you do, CYGM [cover your gluteus maximus]." That is an authentic bureaucratic circumlocution, but its meaning is clear, especially to the bureaucrats themselves. They know they can be fired for providing good service, for opposing the fictions that are the bases of their jobs. They have seen from their own experience that it is rare for one of their number to be dismissed for providing bad service or doing nothing whatever. According to an official report from the Office of Management and Budget, the dismissal of one government clerk "for being late or absent from work all the time" required the employment of dozens of clerks to compile eighty-five boxes of documentation which could be stacked into a tower two stories high.

President Carter's recent civil-service reform has changed very little. In the view of many, such as Ernest Fitzgerald, the changes will only facilitate a further reduction in the quality of bureaucratic performance. If that is possible, it is because some provisions of the law that once shielded whistle blowers have been removed. While President Carter insists that those who speak up against waste, corruption, and fraud in government will be protected under the new law, many bureaucrats see the matter differently. As Gonzales says:

> Most bureaucrats I know are all too aware that tax-saving A. Ernest Fitzgerald, who has been "protected" by both senators and the media, now has no real job and very real debts; they believe that the GSA whistle blowers who have been magnanimously reinstated by the Executive Branch "protectors" have no real future in government. They are marked as unwilling to play the game.[7]

The typical bureaucrat is primarily interested in three things: power, prestige, and money. These things are obtained when his agency gets bigger. That means that anything which can be done to make it bigger is beneficial to him, including going to almost any length to spend more money, even to consciously waste it. The more resources spent in one year, the higher the budget for the next. Since most bureaucrats' pay is roughly proportional to the amount of the funds they administer, higher budgets mean greater salaries and fringe benefits for those who work in the agency. As already suggested, the bureaucrat has an ability to create additional public demand for his services by deflecting the resources at his disposal away from applications that might actually solve problems. With any luck, he can even make the problems worse. That, in turn, rebounds to his benefit by giving his agency more to do and eventually giving him a raise.

What all this leads to is something that can be aptly imagined as an expropriation of the public good. In areas of the economy where the bureaucracy does not directly provide services, such as the manufacture of automobiles or the distilling of gasoline, government regulations have a tendency to increase costs for the consumer and reduce quality. Even when these regulations are sought by the producers themselves, as they were in the case of the railroads, they have a tendency over time to make production unprofitable. This eventually leads to the bureaucratic absorption of the service, as it has in the case of the railroads, which now are largely run by two bureaucratic fiefdoms, Amtrak and Conrail. In areas of the economy where the bureaucracy is already engaged in the direct provision of a service such as it is with education, the tendency is for the bureaucracy to obliterate its competition. The more completely it can supersede alternative institutions, the more it can monopolize the will to do good.

Consider how this has worked in the case of education. In few other areas has the bureaucracy moved with such alacrity to squeeze the life out of institutions which compete with it. As Senator Daniel Patrick Moynihan has astutely observed:

> As program has piled atop of program, and regulation on regulation, the federal government has systematically organized its activities in ways that contribute to the decay of non-public education. Most likely those responsible have not recognized this; they think themselves blind to the distinction between public and private. But of course they are not. They could not be. For governments inherently routinely, automatically favor creatures of governments. They know no other way.[8]

It is not merely a paranoid suspicion that bureaucracy is embarked upon the destruction of nonbureaucratic institutions. Cardinal John Krol charges that government regulatory agencies are subjecting church institutions to "acts of subversion," involving sometimes "terrorist tactics."[9] Even when nongovernment institutions are able to resist the bureaucratic drive for their destruction, they are forced to take on the characteristics of that bureaucracy in the very process of resisting. Increasingly,

215

as Reed College found, they must hire more clerks to shuffle more papers that are irrelevant to what the institution was meant to do. The result is a general enervation of productive institutions and another proof of C. Northcote Parkinson's dictum that "an official wants to multiply subordinates, not rivals."

That the tendency of bureaucracy to subordinate everything to itself is not a quirk of the personalities involved but is basic to the whole bureaucratic enterprise may be judged by the enduring accuracy of Alexis de Tocqueville's insights. Almost a century and a half ago he visited America and detected, even in the rudimentary bureaucratic establishment of the time, an enterprise bent upon becoming "the supreme power." He saw it penetrating into every aspect of life:

> It would be like the authority of a parent if, like that authority, its object was to prepare men for manhood; but it seeks, on the contrary, to keep them in perpetual childhood . . . after having thus successfully taken each member of the community in its powerful grasp and fashioned him at will. The supreme power then extends its arm over the whole community. It covers the surface of society with a network of small complicated rules, minute and uniform, through which the most original minds and the most energetic characters cannot penetrate, to rise above the crowd. The will of man is not shattered, but softened, bent, and guided; men are seldom forced by it to act, but they are constantly restrained from acting. Such a power does not destroy, but it prevents existence; it does not tyrannize, but it compresses, enervates, extinguishes, and stupefies a people until each nation is reduced to nothing better than a flock of timid and industrial animals of which the government is shepherd.[10]

There is only one flaw in de Tocqueville's analysis: he did not foresee that bureaucracy *does* destroy.

To the residents of Horicon, Wisconsin, this is past being a point of conjecture. They have seen firsthand how bureaucracy can destroy. It all but wiped out a small firm, Marlin Toy Products, Inc., which once employed eighty-five of this small town's residents. Among the few products produced by Marlin were toy plastic balls designed for infants and preschool children. The transparent spheres contained artificial butterflies and birds, as well as small pellets of colorful plastic. The rolling of the balls agitated the butterflies and pellets in ways that interest children.

After these products had been safely marketed for a whole decade without one reported injury, or even a complaint about the possibility of injury, the Food and Drug Administration abruptly announced that Marlin's toys were unsafe. The bureaucrats said that a child might eat the plastic pellets in the event that the spheres were crushed. This was a possibility that had already been considered by the Marlin designers, who had developed their toys with rigorous testing to assure their safety in use by small children. For reasons that are easily imagined, both Marlin's insurance company and a large department-store chain had also conducted extensive testing to satisfy themselves as to the safety of the products. Everyone concluded that the Marlin toys were safe. Yet when the bureaucrats decreed otherwise, the people at Marlin bowed immediately to their judgment. All the unsold toys were withdrawn from the market at a cost of almost $100,000. Marlin's engineers then sat down with the bureaucrats to work out an approved way of redesigning the toys. After an agreement was reached, Marlin sank just about everything it had into an attempt to make up for lost sales with an extra push during the 1973 holiday season. Just as hundreds of thousands of the new toys were stocked in stores and beginning to sell, another bureaucracy struck. In September 1973 the Consumer Product Safety Commission published a black list of toys whose sale was prohibited for the holidays. A list of "dangerous" items included Marlin's toys—which had just been redesigned to the specification of the FDA bureaucrats. What had happened? The company demanded to know what now was wrong with its product. A few months later, after all Marlin's Christmas orders had been canceled and the company had lost $1.2 million, the Commission issued a statement attributing the whole thing to "a printing error." Too bad.

Now many people in Horicon who once had jobs working for Marlin Toy Products, Inc., do not. Those people are queued up at bureaucracy's door to collect unemployment compensation and other bureaucratic favors which they did not need or want until the bureaucracy squeezed the life out of their employer.

That the bureaucracy profits from the harm it does is inherent in the logic of the system itself. However amiable individual bureaucrats may be, the long-term effects of their actions will always tend to promote the wealth and prosperity of the bureaucracy. Their motto may be CYGN (cover your gluteus maximus), but in the very caution that weds them to the system is an ingredient which helps them pioneer new ways to destroy alternative institutions and, even more assuredly, to destroy independence and self-sufficiency wherever they find it.

This is why bureaucracy devotes so much energy to ensnaring individuals into conditions of dependence. In the inner cities, bureaucrats not only keep up a barrage of advertising urging low-income persons to become clients of the bureaucracy, they actually go door to door seeking to take charge of other people's lives. With tax laws and regulations drastically increasing the costs of independence, millions respond in a predictable way—they remain dependent. That is exactly what the bureaucracy wants. Every dependent individual who attains self-realization is lost as a resource to the bureaucrats. That they do not want. They want more resources—more helpless, hopeless human beings whose dependence is translated into a demand to do good, a demand which bureaucracy seeks to prevent others from meeting.

There is no more telling example of the personal implications of these bureaucratic imperatives than the case of Mary Wimberley. She was born with congenital cataracts and is today totally blind. In spite of her handicap, Ms. Wimberley determined to open her four-bedroom home in Anaheim, California, to other handicapped individuals. Her boarders are without exception either sightless or brain-damaged persons who would otherwise be spending their days institutionalized. Having spent much of her own life in institutions, Mary Wimberley determined to help others find real homes. "Putting people in institutions is a waste of human life," she says. "In an institution you exist. In a home you live."

Mary Wimberley discovered that her desire to help her fellows was not sufficient in itself to enable her to proceed. She needed bureaucracy's permission. And the bureaucracy did not wish to give it. This is because even the small gesture of independence involved in having one blind woman and a handful of her handicapped friends strike loose was also a small blow at the bureaucracy itself. It was a gesture which pointed toward the elimination of bureaucratic functions, not their expansion. So Mary Wimberley had to fight for the right to open her home to handicapped boarders. After a long battle that brought national publicity to her cause, she finally triumphed. But only barely. As she put it, "There was so much red tape at times I felt maybe I'd better just give up."

Thankfully for Mary Wimberley and for her friends she did not give up. A public outcry finally enabled her to live as she wished in her own home over the opposition of bureaucracy. That is the kind of triumph that is increasingly rare. Most who still seek independence are not blind ladies of exemplary character, but ordinary, plain people whose plights bear no interest for the media and whose stories, if they were told, could scarcely gain attention in competition with a thousand conflicting claims to justice.

It is in this baleful light that we must see the predicament of the ordinary productive individual. Bureaucrats throttle his efforts day in and day out, reducing or eliminating the opportunities which his independence might provide both for himself and for others. The very tendency of the bureaucracy to subordinate leads logically to favoritism for the large over the small. The established business institution which is familiar and predictable is not only more easily controlled but can more easily survive control. Larger businesses can afford the economic costs of meeting regulations, as well as the political and legal costs of reaching for bureaucracy's favors.

With bureaucracy imposing as many as 7,000 mandatory reporting requirements upon all kinds of businesses, it can all but guarantee that small business will never emerge as effective competitors with the already dominant firms. By requiring the entrepreneur to spend his days filling out forms under the threat of imprisonment, the bureaucracy can absorb the entire profit margins of small businesses. Many of the thousands of forms run up to seventy pages in length and are so murky as to make IRS prose seem by comparison as lucid as Thomas Paine's *Common Sense*. Former Senator Thomas J. McIntyre described the consequences: "We are deliberately forcing small companies to either go out of business or merge with companies that have the manpower to comply with mandatory reporting requirements. And if the paperwork continues, we will destroy the American system of free enterprise."

Bureaucracy is designed to do just that. It pays lip service to the familiar American ideals of competition, independence, and enterprise. But these pronouncements are as empty as a lawyer's commitment to speed the completion of a probate proceeding. The bureaucracy wants to control and direct. It can do this best by fostering the emergence of highly regulated industries which coexist with as little competition as possible. In such a situation, the resulting commercial institutions are as much dependent for their continued existence upon the preservation of their transcendental capital, in the form of licenses, regulations, tariffs, and other barriers to open competition, as they are upon their productive capability. This, in turn, makes them politically dependent on the bureaucracy. The complicated tendencies of the system merge to favor the status-quo prosperity of a few big firms rather than the uncertainty arising from the competition of many little ones. Even in activities such as farming, where there are still many competitors, the bureaucracy operates price-fixing cartels which eradicate as much of the competition as possible—at the expense of the independent individual.

Such is the case of orange-grower Jacques Giddens. He has invested his life savings in a forty-acre California orange grove. Each year he grows enough oranges on his property to show a profit. Yet each year he loses money. Why? Because the bureaucracy insists that he throw away all of the oranges he grows on thirteen of his forty acres. Every week a bureaucracy known as the Navel Orange Administration Committee meets to restrain free trade in oranges. This bureaucracy sets quotas which determine how many oranges can be sold in what location for what price. This system has never allowed Giddens to sell more than 65 percent of the fresh fruit he grows. Bureaucrats will permit him to dump the rest of his oranges at by-product factories at $10 per ton. But since this is not enough to cover costs of picking and shipping a ton of oranges, it is cheaper to let them rot. Giddens' predicament is worsened by the fact that he cannot save costs by not planting on the acreage from which he cannot harvest. The way the bureaucracy works, that would reduce his quota, and he would lose even more money. Says Giddens: "The law is crazy. I am growing perfectly good food in a hungry world and throwing it away so some fat cats in Los Angeles can make housewives pay more for their oranges in the supermarket."

Giddens once became so appalled with the system that he consciously defied the bureaucracy by selling 3,441 cartons of oranges for $15,000. But the bureaucrats retaliated by obtaining a permanent federal injunction barring Giddens from ever again violating their quotas. If he does, he goes directly to jail.

Like so many others, Giddens is a victim. He has experienced the last irony among many in a bureaucratic system: his own helplessness and dissatisfaction further enhance the prosperity in bureaucracy. Not only do bureaucratic institutions grow as they aggravate problems and provide less in the way of service, but the bureaucracy's incompetence rewards the politicians as well. The more damage bureaucracy imposes upon the public, the more helpless the average individual becomes in the face of a giant, intractable system, the better for the politicians. Each cry for help is an asset to an incumbent's political career. As political analyst Charles Clapp writes:

> Denied a favorable ruling by the bureaucracy on a matter of direct concern to him, puzzled or irked by delays in obtaining a decision, confused by the administrative maze in which he is directed to proceed or ignorant of whom to write, a constituent may turn to his Congressman for help. These letters offer great potential for political benefit to the Congressman since they affect the constituent personally.[11]

Nothing is quite so endearing to a voter as personal intervention on his behalf by his congressman. The more problems the bureaucracy can impose on you, the greater the demand for the congressman's service and thus the more popular he becomes. As Morris T. Fiorina has noted, "Incumbent Congressmen can make themselves all but unbeatable simply by presiding over continued expansion of bureaucracy. The more decisions the bureaucracy has to make, the more opportunities there are for the Congressman to build up credit."[12]

That is how the system works. As Fiorina says, "all of Washington prospers" when the costs imposed by bureaucracy increase. The more meddlesome and counterproductive bureaucracy becomes, the greater the crowd that lines up outside bureaucracy's door. Every productive enterprise that bureaucracy bankrupts, every productive job that it destroys, puts another individual in a state of dependence upon its succor. The more the bureaucracy botches its missions, the more it subordinates or destroys alternative institutions, the greater the demand for its services. When bureaucracy takes over education, it prospers more by fostering illiteracy than by teaching people to read. The fewer there are who can understand its turgid, convoluted pronouncements, the greater the demand for remedial-reading programs. These, in turn, require remedial-reading-program consultants, who produce judgments such as this: "There is no realistically promises that addresses the needs identified in the proposed program." (An actual sample of the prose from an evaluation of a remedial-reading program.) The politicians who authorize and fund this nonsense are reelected in record numbers by a public exhausted to a point of gratitude for small favors.

We have created a system which we do not understand. We have turned self-interest against the public interest by giving millions of persons incentives to profit from imposing hurt on others. We gave these people the ultimate rhetorical power: a conceptual monopoly over the public good. They alone are exempted from tests of performance other than what they claimed to do. Yet it is not even true that bureaucrats are paid to talk. Talk is something that one *does*. Those who are paid to do it are generally fluent ,and entertaining. Bureaucracy is not. It operates upon a different principle: in its purest form, bureaucracy does not profit from what it *does*, but from its good intentions. The spirit of this difference was well captured by Tom Bethell in his essay "The Wealth of Washington." He wrote:

> Don't work for an oil company—you might get your hands dirty. Work for the Department of Energy and ponder energy "policy," this is much more prestigious. You are a nurse? The pay is low and you change bed pans. Better try and get on a health "task force" and write a memo on "Health Care Delivery Systems." You want to paint a picture? Hard work. Better go work for the National Endowment and talk about creative partnerships at a meeting. Your salary is assured.[13]

The bureaucracy which is supposed to be the embodiment of good intention and wisdom is often neither, and this is in part due to a general misapprehension among the public about how society functions. Support for bureaucracy arises from a bluff, commonsense approach to comprehending the larger world. This is reflected in the widespread notion that society operates in much the same way as a family. When the father wants his children to mow the lawn, he points toward the tool shed and then kindly or gruffly, as is his style, makes a suggestion: "Mow the lawn." Many people believe that the larger society yields to orders in a similar manner. People understand that individual household economies function by allocation of responsibility. So they assume that when the national lawn needs mowing, it is a simple matter to point toward a few million tool sheds and hope that all the mowers are fitted with catalytic converters and roll bars.

But general movements in society are not determined by commands. The empowering of bureaucracies to issue such commands leads to consequences that are often totally opposite to those the public intends by contributing its support to the bureaucracy's allegedly good purpose. It is not true that bureaucracy does good because it is supposed to do good. Indeed, bureaucracy must blunder and fail because its premise of benevolence is well out of accord with the self-interest of the bureaucrats themselves. Yet even if this were not so, many bureaucracies, with their heavily centralized control, would fail for the lack of knowledge necessary to accomplish their ends. To a large extent, a bureaucratic organization does represent, as many have charged, an institutionalization of ignorance. B. E. Kline and N. H. Martin put it this way:

> The chief characteristic of the command hierarchy . . . is not knowledge but ignorance. Consider that any one person can know only a fraction of what is going on around him. Much of what that person knows or believes will be false rather than true. . . . At any given time, vastly more is not known than is known, either by one person in a command chain or by all the organization. . . . It seems possible, then, that in organizing ourselves into a hierarchy of authority for the purpose of increasing efficiency, we may really be institutionalizing ignorance.[14]

Thus we have bureaucracies, which are meant to teach us to read, build a better bumper, stamp out poverty, and more. Yet they do none of these things. Bureaucracy hurts and hinders, costing the average family $2,500 per year. As the people are squeezed, the bureaucratic operatives grow rich. They impoverish the butcher, the brewer, and the baker, all in the name of benevolence. Never before could it be so truly said, as it can today, that the road to hell is paved with good intentions.

14
The Energy Squeeze

It is certain that despotism ruins individuals by preventing them from producing wealth, much more than by depriving them of wealth when they have produced; it dries up the source of riches. . . .

—*Alexis de Tocqueville*

"If it gets any worse, we'll be in the poorhouse," said a man to his wife.

"We're already in the poorhouse," came the reply.

The comments of these ordinary people, reported in *The Washington Post*, put the Energy Squeeze in proper perspective. The tales of people planning to "sweat in the summer and freeze in the winter" are tales of impoverishment and financial crisis, not of geology and physics. Inflation and taxes have made people poorer, to the extent that they can no longer afford the energy which politicians and bureaucrats have made more expensive.

The "energy crisis" is not a crisis of energy at all, but a crisis of inflation and political policy. At a time when proven oil reserves are greater than ever before, you and other consumers face imminent shortages of petroleum products, along with threats of rationing, mandatory business closings, and more. Washington bureaucrats are even threatening your freedom to drive your automobile when and where you please. Support is building in Congress for mandatory measures to enforce additional sacrifices upon the public and require you to "do your part" to solve a crisis that the politicians created in the first place.

225

No doubt many sincere persons believe that the world is actually "running out of energy." That is a myth that has recurred many times since the Industrial Revolution. It arises whenever technological change outdates previous energy sources or, as in the current case, when financial and political crises in government prohibit people from balancing energy supplies to demand.

In neither case is the world actually "running out of energy." That fear is based upon the same knucklehead physics as Chicken Little's alarm that the sky was falling. Because energy and matter are two configurations of the same thing, we can never run short of either—as long as the universe exists. The only challenge we face is an economic challenge: finding and applying the cheapest form of energy for a given purpose.

No matter what the politicians and inventory clerks say, the world is *not* running out of energy—except in a sense that they don't mean at all. To the degree that the sun is being exhausted, energy from this solar system is being scattered off into other portions of the universe. So in that sense, we may have an energy shortage in another *five billion* years.

Energy of stupendous power is being generated all around us—to such a degree that it is a challenge for the human mind to realize how plentiful energy is. In one day enough sunlight falls on California to power the entire world for a week. And direct sunlight is only one of many virtually untapped energy sources. If you think for a moment, you can enumerate many others. There is gravity. As long as the moon revolves around the earth and exerts a pull on the oceans, the tides will ebb and flow with phenomenal power. That power could be harnessed and utilized. There is also energy (indirect solar energy) in wind. There is geothermal energy deep in the earth. There is the prospect for controlled fusion power, which would literally allow man to use water as a fuel to unleash the same mighty forces that are at work in the sun, without dangers of radioactive waste.

The inventory of energy possibilities need hardly get this exotic. There are vast amounts of untapped chemical energy in oil, coal, natural gas, and other resources. Both methanol (wood alcohol) and ethanol (grain alcohol) can be used in internal-combustion engines. If it were cost-effective to do so, human waste, garbage, newspapers, or almost anything could be processed into chemical fuel.

We are no more suffering from a terminal "energy crisis" than we were in the 1840's and 1850's. Whale oil was becoming more expensive, and there was supposedly a shortage of wood, which was then used for making iron and for firing the boilers of steam-powered vessels of loco-motives. Was the world running out of energy? No. As soon as coal became economically feasible, it came into widespread use. Coal gas supplanted whale oil for use in lamps, and there was a rapid conversion from the use of wood and charcoal to that of coal in the industrial process. Barely had the coal conversion gotten under way when a new form of energy began to be developed—petroleum, which originally sold for twenty dollars a barrel at a time when a steak dinner in New York City cost fifty cents.

Barely had the first barrel of oil been produced when experts began to insist that we had only from five to ten years' supply of oil remaining. In 1866 the U.S. government first proposed production of synthetic fuels for the time when "crude oil production ended." In 1891 the U.S. Geological Survey once again warned that the world's supply of oil would be exhausted "within twenty years." Government experts dashed to Scotland to study a crash program for extracting shale oil. In 1946 another shortage was purported to be on the horizon. The public was warned to prepare for the final exhaustion of petroleum supplies. What happened? World War II price controls were lifted and energy again became abundant.

According to experts, we have had only a few years' supply of oil remaining for more than one hundred years. While we have been using more petroleum each year, proven reserves have not declined; they have expanded. Year in and year out, more oil has been discovered than has been consumed.

Yet even if this were not true, there would still be no danger of the world running out of energy. We must merely face the economic challenge of paying for what we use. That is part of what Emerson called "the absolute balance of Give and Take, the doctrine that everything has its price." The higher that price, the more energy is available and the less energy is needed.

Consider how this works in practice. There is no better example than the application of automatic damper controls for home furnaces. In the days when number-two heating oil cost ten cents a gallon, few people had reason to install the automatic damper controls. The cost of the controls far exceeded the value of any potential savings of fuel. Since it did not make sense to install the controls, no company could afford to make them and stay in business. As the price of heating oil rose, however, automatic damper controls became more efficient. Eventually, the cost of producing the controls became less than the cost of producing the oil or gas that they saved. Presto: higher prices created energy conservation.

The phenomenon works both ways. If the price of energy should fall, one would expect less conservation. Fewer energy-saving devices would be used. Designs of buildings, automobiles, motorboats, and appliances would reflect the lower value of energy by consuming more of it.

This is exactly why automobiles of the late 1960's and the 1970's got less mileage per gallon than those of a decade or more earlier. Until the last few years, the long-term trend for energy prices has been down. As gasoline prices fell in real terms, people had less reason to conserve gasoline. Similar considerations apply to other energy uses. Buildings constructed during the late 1960's, for example, consume more energy than comparable structures erected in earlier decades. As the price of energy fell in real terms, architects naturally paid less attention to the energy demands incorporated in their designs. Dr. Charles Lawrence, a New York public-utilities specialist, conducted a survey of energy consumption of eighty commercial office buildings built in New York City after World War II. He found that buildings in the same neighborhoods serving similar purposes had variations in energy consumption of as much as 7 to 1. The buildings constructed when the price of energy was lower consumed more energy.

The decision to consume or produce energy is determined by the price. Before the oil age—when petroleum was just a greasy substance that was hard to wash out of clothing—nobody had a very lively interest in it. In fact, it was worth less than water. Farmers dug their wells to find water for irrigation and for their animals. If they found oil they grumbled about their luck and dug somewhere else. Only as the price of oil rose did the oil become a resource.

The higher the price, the more energy resources there are. That is the common sense of energy production and conservation. Unhappily, we have an Energy Squeeze because government policies have not always been based upon common sense. To the contrary, the politicians and bureaucrats have created crises by imposing costs on the energy-consuming public without allowing higher prices to increase energy supplies. While hectoring consumers to save energy and not be "fuelish," the politicians have subsidized waste and made conservation uneconomical. While decrying "dependence on foreign oil," the government actually set up an elaborate system to subsidize the import of foreign oil. When the subsidies, combined with price controls, had the predictable effect of reducing domestic crude-oil production, this increased the power of the Organization of Petroleum Exporting Countries (OPEC). In effect, the American government gave the OPEC cartel control over a larger portion of the world's producible supplies, enabling the cartel to raise prices to higher levels. In ham-and-eggs language, American politicians have subsidized OPEC.

In fact, OPEC might never have existed if American politicians had not followed a policy of "drain America first." Prior to 1973, while foreign oil remained cheaper than mountain spring water, American oil producers were induced by government policy to drain away many oil fields that would not have been economical to tap at the world prices that then existed. Import controls imposed by Congress artificially raised the price of petroleum in the United States, thus increasing U.S. production. By reducing the competition from foreign oil producers, who were then selling cheaper oil, the politicians rigged the market so that their constituents would pay more for energy. The political campaign to raise the price of oil was also turned against the oil-recycling industry. Firms which had been successfully recycling dirty motor oil were subjected to increased taxes, with the result that most were forced out of business. This, too, pointed toward higher oil prices by reducing the supply of lower-priced recycled oil.

These policies of artificially raising the domestic oil price by bureaucratic regulation were abruptly changed in 1973. In their place, the politicians instituted a policy to subsidize the importation of foreign oil and artificially hold the domestic price down.

The flagrant absurdity of these contradictory policies can best be understood in light of changed world monetary conditions. In particular, the decline of the U.S. dollar brought about by the rising domestic inflation led to a series of political moves designed to disguise the increasing impoverishment of our economy.

To understand the situation, one has to glance back a few years to the period when Lyndon Johnson was printing money to pay for the Vietnam war and his Great Society programs. The funny money not only inflated the cost of living in America but also disrupted the international monetary structure. So much money was printed without backing that it was no longer possible to settle international debts with gold. On August 15, 1971, Richard Nixon officially announced to the world that the U.S. government was broke. He suspended further gold payments to foreign central banks and, in so doing, effectively removed the last barrier to the escalation of inflation and debt. The new system of "floating exchange rates" has not worked effectively. Competitive devaluations on the part of governments have been so frequent that the result is a race to see which country can make its currency worthless first.

Under such conditions—when funny money is disrupting international trade—the exchange system has no way of dealing with the increasing insolvency of almost all the world's countries. In the short run, the existence of these difficulties has given large banks an opportunity to maximize their earnings by lending tens of billions at high interest rates to the governments in the worst financial straits. The loans enabled them to finance their settlement of accounts.

The whole thing could be considered shrewd dealing—except for one obvious problem. Anyone can lend money to bankrupts at high interest rates. The trick is to be paid back. Big American banks, with Chase Manhattan in the lead, were owed more than $53 billion at the end of 1979. The seriousness of the situation is underscored by the fact that this sum is far more than the banks could lose and remain solvent. And the prospect for the future is not good. The current accounts of the non-oil-producing underdeveloped countries, which are the main debtors to the banks, were thrown even further out of balance by the 1979 oil price increase. These countries have not even finished repaying the debts they incurred after the major oil price increase of 1973. Now they must borrow more. Without a dramatic change in the flow of funds worldwide, the banks could collapse.

Already, some of the debts have had to be "rescheduled"—a polite way of saying that they are in default. For example, in 1978, interest and amortization on a quarter of a billion dollars owed by Peru was rolled over by a consortium of banks led by Manufacturers Hanover Trust.

Naturally enough, the banks are doing what they can to avoid their day of reckoning. They realize that billions of dollars would be freed, perhaps enough to pay them back, if the international price of oil fell in real terms. Because there is large untapped oil production capacity, a price fall is not impossible. Even with the disruption caused by the closing of Iran's oil fields in late 1978 and early 1979, so many new wells were brought into production in other areas of the world that total petroleum output actually increased by 5 percent. Since that time, Mexico has announced new oil finds which may eventually rival those of Saudi Arabia. Venezuela has actually closed down 20 percent of its capacity. China is now exporting oil. And there is greater production than ever among other countries that are not members of OPEC. With producible supplies increasing, a decline in world oil prices would almost be a certainty if

American imports of oil were dramatically reduced, as advocates of a strong energy program envision. Senator Jacob Javits put it this way: "There is an urgent need for a most drastic conservation policy in oil on the part of the United States—largest importer of oil—to materially reduce the imbalance in international payments resulting from these imports. The danger is so great that even gasoline rationing cannot be ruled out as a last resort."

Clearly, the basis of the Energy Squeeze is not oil but money. The Squeeze is the result of the financial and credit conditions that threaten the big banks with collapse.

The situation is further complicated by the fact that the inflationists want to reduce the cost of oil for the rest of the world, while raising it here at home. This attitude has been embodied in the recurring "energy programs" of the Nixon, Ford, and Carter administrations. Carter even sought to impose a new quota on oil imports, limiting the amount of cheap foreign oil that Americans can enjoy, while spending $100 billion to produce more expensive synthetic alternatives. The tax aspects of Carter's plan would discourage domestic production of ordinary petroleum while offering loan guarantees for synthetic development. This would help rescue the banks' foreign loans while providing them with guaranteed profits for further credit creation. The banks would lend billions to finance production of oil from shale rock at $50 per barrel so that you and other consumers can avoid paying that much for ordinary petroleum.

The political difficulties of promoting such policies are considerably eased because they create golden opportunities for an entire spectrum of special interests. Those who sell coal, those who want energy-research contracts, bureaucrats in the Department of Energy, those who want to breed plutonium, owners of shale deposits, and many, many others are standing in line for the transcendental-capital goodies that an "energy program" would distribute. The politicians have even come up with a scheme to spread the gains from the Energy Squeeze beyond the bureaucrats and subsidized corporations to great numbers of ordinary people. They want to impose gasoline rationing.

The most widely discussed rationing scheme, endorsed by Carter, would distribute coupons (one would undoubtedly have to stand in a long line to pick them up) for a maximum of three vehicles per family. Consumers would then be able to sell any unused coupons to owners of recreational vehicles, persons with large cars, those hoping to take a vacation, poor people who could not afford a newer, more gas-efficient vehicle, joy riders, etc. The coupons, in effect, would become transcendental-capital claims of ownership for each gallon of gas. They would enable anyone to profit from the sale of gasoline—*except the people who actually produce it.* Those who could get the rationing coupons but did not need them could squeeze out a little transcendental-capital gain at the expense of those who could not obtain the coupons but did need gas. This, presumably, would endear these small-time profiteers to the Department of Energy, its price controls, allocations, ceiling prices, entitlements, and the other instruments by which the profitable energy shortage was fashioned.

Gas-rationing plans represent only one element in the creation of transcendental capital of the Energy Squeeze. The "Windfall Profits" tax continues the government's tradition of subsidizing OPEC while capturing resources from production to be shared out by more than 20,000 well-paid bureaucrats, legions of favored professors, corporate boondogglers, and anyone with an inclination to hustle bureaucracy and the basic literacy to fill out a grant application.

This will make for lots of small and even large fortunes. What it will not do is facilitate the production of energy or lower its cost to consumers.

Bureaucracy will have triumphed. Its imperative to eradicate competition and convert productive capital to transcendental capital will have been exercised yet again. Even without the tax, the Department of Energy has been imposing unbearable costs upon small businesses and strangling independent producers with red tape. By way of illustration, consider this telling story from *The Washington Post*, which was printed under the headline: "OILMAN SAYS ENERGY DEPT. IS RUINING HIM, AND IT AGREES." This one report says so much about the causes and consequences of the Energy Squeeze that it merits being quoted at length:

> The Vice President of a Kansas oil company that operates 225 independent gasoline stations in 27 states came to Washington yesterday to proclaim that Energy Dept. price and allocation regulations are putting him out of business.
>
> The Dept. of Energy agreed.
>
> "I am in Washington because my company is being destroyed by the Department of Energy," said R. J. Gaffney, Vice President of Highway Oil, Inc. of Topeka.
>
> "He's right," said a top official in the Energy Dept., asking not to be identified because of his Agency's mounting image problem. "He has given an accurate description of what DOE regulations are doing to people in this industry."
>
> Gaffney charged that one of the problems with getting the Depart-

ment to grant relief is the 5,000 plus backlog . . . they are buried under. "DOE hasn't even looked at our papers."

Gaffney said that at DOE's encouraging, Highway Oil invested $300,000 in gasohol production facilities. "Now we need gasoline to make it work," he said, and DOE won't let him get it.

"That's true, too," said the DOE official. "The only answer is to get rid of these regulations. There is no way they can work. They don't protect consumers, and they never have."[1]

Such is President Carter's "moral equivalent of war." It is war not upon an enemy but against production. It is a war of some people against the livelihoods of others. It is some people turning the rules into transcendental capital—their private assets that enable them to benefit at the expense of other citizens by doing what they could not do on their own without committing a crime. The "moral equivalent of war" creates bureaucratic profits out of hurts. It makes for gasoline lines. It makes summer heat hotter and winter cold colder. It means a lower standard of living, bankrupt businesses, and unemployment. Carter could not have found a more descriptive phrase to capture the essence of the government's energy program. William James defined the "moral equivalent of war" as nonmartial suffering, something which involves "discomfort and annoyance, hunger and wet, pain and cold, squalor and filth."

Part III
BREAKING THE GRIP

For every man alone thinks he has got
to be a Phoenix.
> —*John Donne*

If we wish to remain human, there is
on y one way, the way into the open
society. We must go into the unknown,
the uncertain and insecure.
> —*Sir Karl Popper*

15
The Imperative for Reform

The guaranteed life turns out to be not only not free—it's not safe.

—*Maxwell Anderson*

One of my tasks in these final essays is to answer some of the questions that I begged earlier on. The bulk of this book has been devoted to developing a conceptual framework and an impression of where America's major hurt lies. I have mapped this as best I can. Now I must proceed to a more difficult task—suggesting what can be done under the circumstances. I admit that my solutions are less than wholly satisfactory. Partly this may be because certain of our difficulties have gone beyond being susceptible to a quick fix. Partly, too, there may be such things as insoluble problems arising out of the interactions of hundreds of millions and even billions of persons whose political and commercial contacts comprise today's society.

I have no way of knowing whether this is true. It is impossible for me to canvass all the ramifications of human action in a complex society. I could never know which of life's social and economic difficulties are portioned out as part of an irreducible core of human conflict and which are caused by the disorder of present circumstances. Being unable to speak intelligently in either case, I am nevertheless willing to believe

237

that our current difficulties are subject to resolution. This may be no more than a prejudice on my part. Yet the prejudice that life's quandaries can be solved is a good one; it is certainly better than the dismal postulate that they are in principle hopeless.

Resolving to believe this much is half the battle. If we are to have a hope of preserving the progressive, modern way of life, or at least that part which is best in it, we must make a commitment for a true solution. By this I mean a solution which sets right the functioning of the whole social order, not one which merely enables a few to prosper from the decay, as did the *Clarissimi* who picked the carcass of the Roman Empire and whose descendants became the lords, dukes, and earls of the Dark Ages. It is absurd to think of withdrawal to a castle on the hill as a solution in the modern context. Not everyone can afford his own castle. Even those who can should not expect to sit at a remove from their neighbors and prosper while the social order crumbles. "Misery loves company" has been one of the deepest truths of the human condition, even before the demand for material equality was raised to a moral status above at least five of the ten commandments. Most schemes for survival in retreat would create one hundred new peasants for each new lord and would fail on that basis alone.

Neither is it very helpful to think in terms of retiring to a self-sufficient poverty where we are peasants one and all. You will not do yourself any good, except perhaps in the morale-boosting sense, if you think you can survive isolated from the complex social structure, relying on some latter-day Mr. Antrobus to pull you through a coming Ice Age. Even if he could finally perfect a formula for grass soup which would not cause diarrhea, the hope of a forward-looking human being does not lie in a return to the foraging stage of society. As important as self-reliance is and as large a part as it must play in a general renaissance of American life, neither you nor anyone else can safely predicate your future upon self-reliance alone.

The source of all that is admirable in human beings is the fact that our self-interest is complex. It extends to a concern not only with what we *have*, but also with what we *are*. At the proper moments, it is possible for us to care passionately about the meaning of the whole human experiment. That is why the record of every civilization, from Sumer onward, is more than a collection of potsherds and warehouse receipts. Foremost among man's work has been evidence of a grasping for the infinite, a yearning to be important in the universe. The gods and heroes of our myths, our many religions, and even our science of astronomy, which aims to fathom the remotest secrets of the heavens, all point to the complexity of the human character. Our dreams for a better world and our philosophy, which inevitably turns back to a search for the good, are not mere tittle-tattle. They are a powerful motive force which can provide us with the impetus we may ultimately need to survive as civilized beings.

What this means is that we can reform our errors—at least some of them—if we have the will to do so. But this cannot merely be goodwill. Our effort must be based upon an informed determination. We would be ducking our responsibilities to pretend that any real solution can be brought about simply by our resolving to love our neighbors. If everyone on the street turned to the next person and gave him a hug it would change little, except to accelerate the spread of communicable diseases. Our affairs have become too complex to be reformed by goodwill alone. The Squeeze cannot be cured with a hug.

To understand this, we must develop a new public philosophy. It must be one that can accommodate the basic paradox of social life: altruistic endeavors must be organized to take into account the fact that individual human beings are basically self-centered.

The irremediable selfishness of our plans and intentions has led us to overestimate dramatically the degree to which they are conclusive in determining the kind of society we produce. This has been a major failure of our politics. Because at the selfish core of our being we posit, "I want to do good," that comes near to being all that matters. We do not stop to inquire after the actual consequences of laws, programs, and bureaucracies erected to clear the slums, cure cancer, or solve the "energy crisis." Figuring out what really comes of these grand gestures is no fun at all; it demands hard thought and study. That is why we generally avoid the task. Instead, we are preoccupied with the only portion of the altruistic endeavor that is easily accessible to ourselves—what we intend and desire. In effect, we assume a godlike posture, acting as if we could produce our intended effect with a mere "abracadabra." We say through our impractical political resolutions, "This must be, because I will it so."

We should do better to assume a more humble and thus more realistic attitude. Adam Ferguson, the discerning Scot philosopher, pointed the way with this comment:

> The artifices of the beaver, the ant and the bee, are ascribed to the wisdom of nature. Those of polished nations are ascribed to themselves, and are supposed to indicate a superior capacity to that of rude minds. The establishment of men, like those of every animal, are suggested by

nature and are the result of instinct, directed by the variety of situations in which mankind are placed. Those establishments arose from successive improvements that were made, without any sense of their general effect; and they bring human affairs to a state of complication, which the greatest reach of capacity with which the human nature was ever adorned could not have projected; nor even when the whole is carried into execution, can it be comprehended in its full extent.[1]

If this attitude were widely shared, we should turn out a far more wholesome society, one which would take account of our almost instinctive pursuit of self-interest, and thus ironically be spared many of the difficulties which arise from our selfish desires to plan and direct.

Our current society is organized only partially to take self-interest into account. We readily admit that the profit motive is the wellspring of productive activity. But the percentage of the population engaged in productive activity is declining. In increasing numbers, people are turning their pursuit of individual profit into a scramble for transcendental capital, the abstract form of property created through politics. It is in this sphere of life that the pursuit of self-interest is not harnessed to provide a free ride for the public at large. Indeed, a major part of our system is so organized that an individual can pursue actions that would be dictated by a disinterested concern for the well-being of all only by sacrificing his own material interests. Such, as we have seen, is the case with bureaucracy. Persons who are controlling hundreds of billions of dollars have incentives to waste resources, almost none to conserve them. They are induced, also, to create problems where none exist, "to bring evil on the land that I may have a task." Our politicians suffer from this same contradiction between their personal interests and their supposed functions. They are meant to act in everyone's behalf. Yet their chances of reelection are multiplied a thousandfold if they devote themselves instead to promoting special, private interests. Seen as a matter of pure, logical calculation, politicians have an incentive to expand the bureaucracy and enfeeble the public in order to increase the demand for their own services. The voters, also, are caught in a contradiction between their simple self-interest and their function in the system. They are supposed to control the politicians. Yet to become knowledgeable about what politicians are actually doing, the voters must invest more time and energy in research and deliberation than their probability of affecting the outcome could redeem. With odds of 10 million to 1 or worse that a single voter could tip the outcome of a national election, a strong rainstorm will induce millions to refrain from casting a ballot, implying that they value the operation on approximately the same order as an expedition to a fast-food parlor to purchase a double-patty burger and fries.

The previous chapters of this book testify to the many unhappy consequences of this situation. The crucial aspects of our system that are organized to function in disregard of the self-interest of the participants are subject to such chronic malfunction that they are bringing the entire society to the point of ruin. There is no plausible basis to expect that these difficulties are self-correcting. Indeed, all indicators seem to be pointing in the opposite direction.

It took a very long time for our democratic institutions to degenerate to their present condition. For many years our political culture was one of self-restraint. There were functions which the people as a whole did not believe the government should perform—even in principle. This principled opposition to political expansion held the growth of transcendental capital in check. But when the previous inhibitions were weakened, then cast aside, this opened the way for political claims upon resources to reach their present prodigal level. As previous discussion has indicated, the weakening of the productive sector, consequent to higher taxes and inflation, has further heightened the tendency to seek profits through politics. This tendency feeds upon itself. Thus it is imperative that we reform our establishments so they take a more realistic account of self-interest. Without such reform, they are destined to become rapidly more counterproductive.

Ordinary people cannot fully come to grips with the abstract relationships created by the confusion of rules and means which arises out of dominance of politics over society. In effect, the creation of "new property" has meant nothing less than the evolution of two separate worlds: one of material objects, another of abstract claims. Unfortunately, it is the abstract world in which economic costs and rewards are calculated. That is not the world which is accessible directly to our senses and which our language describes. Indeed, the very success of transcendental-capital accumulation depends upon the fact that it takes place through abstract relationships which are outside the normal vocabulary of understanding. Part of the difficulty in writing this book has been that we have no words in normal usage which accurately describe what is going on. As much I should have loved to follow the advice of the founder of the Grand Ole Opry, who told his musicians, "Keep it down to earth, boys," I have been obliged to grope for new expressions and new ways of defining the economic relationships that are really informing the evolution of society. To give one example, no one would mistake

241

a term such as "transcendental capital" for the gruff simplicity of bar talk. For this reason alone, it will be extremely difficult to ever make the private exploitation of the rules a matter of common intelligibility.

In effect, the transcendental capitalists use the individual's vocabulary and ordinary patterns of thought against him. They employ persuasive propaganda and every feasible abuse of language and logic to gull the public, to disguise the actual operations of the political economy. Such tricks work. A generation ago, they were seen as a prerequisite of political exploitation by George Orwell in his grim vision of 1984. Big Brother's Newspeak bamboozled the public by confiscating "good" words and applying them to something evil. War was to be "peace," hate to be "love." Through this kind of linguistic manipulation, Big Brother enfeebled the minds of his subjects.

Our exploitation is rather more subtle and less malicious, but it depends upon the same weakness for believing in the magic power of words. If we support "defense," we support expenditures in the name of defense, whether they enhance security or not. If we believe in "education," then we endorse programs which are said to educate, even if the graduates of those programs cannot read, write, add, or subtract. And so it goes. We support programs which in fact demolish housing because we support "housing" in theory. We are attached to the concept of "health," so we support systems which invoke that concept, whether they are productive or not. The term "justice" appeals, so the guild of lawyers exploits that appeal with monopoly powers to drain resources from the citizenry.

All this happens because it is difficult for human beings to distinguish between a facade and reality in anything which happens outside the limits of their personal senses. Politics has geometrically multiplied this natural liability by penetrating into almost every affair and by creating an abstract world of economic property different from the world of legal property.

The transcendental capitalists have raised everyday life to a level of complexity that is inherently exploitative. It disables increasing numbers from full competition for life's advantages. All but a small percentage of the best minds are incapable of dealing with the conceptual demands created by the existence of a realm of abstract economic property whose boundaries of ownership and control are unlike what we have traditionally known. In such circumstances, the competition among the more intelligent to profit from manipulating the rules drives the system toward an ever greater level of complexity. Eventually the whole enterprise turns mad. The constant changes of laws and regulations carry the system beyond anyone's ability to discern what the changes mean. We look into politics and see that our horizons are practically black. It is true, as poet Thomas Traherne warned long ago: "A world without objects is a sensible emptiness."

No one can see with certainty what the next six months, let alone the next six years, will bring. The future is out of control. And this is the ultimate irony. We have lost our grip on the future which we sought to make certain and predictable. Perhaps we always knew that we were being exploited by politics, but we submitted. It was part of the price we willingly paid to make life predictable. We hoped to conquer the future by adhering to routines; to make success a matter of time spent attaining qualifications and going through the motions in a job which was guaranteed to pay us regardless of our contribution. We allowed ourselves to be squeezed, and compromised. We even became the primary cheerleaders of our own undoing because we thought the political institutions erected at our cost would help us gain a certain future. We tolerated bureaucracy, became bureaucrats ourselves, because the bureaucratic method nourished our delusions of servitude. Bureaucracy produced a plan. It laid everything under "control," from the price of gasoline to how the Oak Ridge Tennessee High School basketball team's cheerleaders, "The Statcats," filed onto the team bus. This detailed direction of our lives was meant to shield us from risk.

All this was to bolster the illusion of certitude. But right on the face of it, the effort to substitute bureaucracy for risk-taking and individual initiative was bound to fail. If it were true that human beings have a sufficient knowledge to evade the future's risks, we would not need bureaucracy in the first place. In pure logic, no one would bother with the painstaking precautions if the future were knowable. It is not. This is precisely why many of our awkward attempts to fend off the unknown, to make the future secure, have rebounded against that very purpose. The plans of bureaucracies, even if they were not misdirected to meet the requirements of the bureaucrat's self-interest, would fail anyway because they rest upon a false and egotistical estimation of what is calculable in life.

Much that the planner pretends to know is in principle unknowable. This is what makes him such a public danger. By every reliable measure, his attempts to secure a risk-free future have succeeded in shortening the horizons of action. People are more uncertain and afraid of what the future may hold than they have been for decades. Businesses which once would have committed themselves to investments with a ten-year horizon are now afraid to make commitments that do not promise to pay out completely within three years. In many areas, even shorter time horizons are the rule. For example, there were almost forty million fewer cattle in America in January 1979 than five years earlier. In spite of higher beef prices, farmers would not rebuild their herds, precisely because they could not see far enough ahead to calculate their costs through the two and a half years it takes to bring cattle to market. With inflation and erratic political regulations juggling expectations, farmers turned to producing more pork and chicken because those animals had shorter marketing cycles—eleven months for swine and only six weeks for chicken.

In a sense, similar considerations apply to human beings. The ultimate index of confidence in the future—the fertility rate—has been in sharp decline.

Yet we do not need to seek very far for external evidence that the future is out of control. We can see that from a sensitive consideration of our attitudes and those of our neighbors. A sense of resentful disappointment and even fear is too much in the air to be missed. The whole edifice of false convictions and false hopes upon which our seeming prosperity has been based is coming to be suspected for what it is—false. That it could collapse at almost any time is a possibility which is not altogether beyond the consideration of even the highest leaders of government. Alfred Kahn, President Carter's onetime chief inflation fighter, demonstrated that by reintroducing the word "depression" into the lexicon of public discussion. The "long run" is no longer merely a remote fear at the back of our minds describing matters which we expect to plague our grandchildren long after we have died prosperous in our beds. The long run is here.

Whether our impoverishment will take the form of a depression, a hyperinflation, or whether our economy will continue to move sideways in a "stagflation," with the average individual squeezed between rising prices and fallingi ncome, is a matter beyond my knowing. But whatever is to happen, the imperative for reform will be very much the same.

16
What You Can Do

Truth is not only violated by falsehood; it may be equally outraged by silence.

—*Henri Frédéric Amiel*

It should be clear from what I have been saying throughout this book that I could elaborate a rather lengthy list of specific social, political, and economic reforms which could be embraced within my conviction that transcendental capital has grown too profitable while the rewards for productive activity have waned. But I am not going to detail a comprehensive catalog of every specific change that might be effected. The list would be superfluous. Furthermore, it would be just as foolish for me to attempt to specify in every detail how the operations of a more successful society would be conducted as it obviously has been for the politicians and bureaucrats currently in control. The difficulties of society are so complex that they do not yield readily to either good intentions or good counsel. Recognizing that, I should be violating the new spirit of responsibility which I firmly believe must be part of our reconstruction if I were to draw tight blueprints for Utopia. That is a task which has eluded greater talents than mine.

With that necessary preface, I am eager to join with others working for the kind of changes that do hold promise; that is to say, changes that would encourage society to evolve in productive directions without attempting to specify in advance exactly what forms each institution should hold.

I shall consider, in two parts, the enormous problem of what exactly these reforms are. In this chapter, I shall address the issue of what specific actions an individual can take within the existing structure of institutions. This will include further consideration of the attitude an individual might wish to assume to prepare himself and empower himself for the coming changes in American life. The second part of the discussion, in the next chapter, will aim at illuminating some principles that ought to be helpful in settling the bases upon which institutions function over the longer term.

TAKE RISKS

The basic organizing principle upon which the renaissance of American life depends is your willingness to embrace risk. To open the broad potential of the future you must embrace risk and uncertainty. Only by opening ourselves to new possibilities and new ideas, and giving scope to every improbable ambition, do we multiply the chance that we ourselves shall succeed.

The true source of human progress is not expertise but creativity. The expert is only an individual who has mastered in retrospect what someone in the past may have discovered all of a sudden through the indefinable circumstances that conspire to produce genius. Creativity cannot be controlled. We cannot bring forth more Edisons by drafting armies of scientists and pressing them to work in government laboratories outfitted to duplicate the conditions of altitude, barometric pressure, and open floor space under which Edison's most fertile insights were achieved. Neither can we assure the productivity of commercial and industrial ideas by preserving at all costs the establishments which were created in the past as the expressions of individual enterprise and foresight. Because Alexander Graham Bell invented the telephone is no sign that today's Bell System will necessarily produce the breakthroughs which are constantly needed to meet the challenges of the future.

Preserving the profitability of the known, established institutions through monopoly privileges, tariffs, subsidies, and regulations does not make tomorrow better. It creates a nation of anachronisms in which yesterday's modes of doing business are still artificially profitable. It creates a situation where risk aversion is rewarded and risk-taking penalized. But since it is precisely the taking of risk, the embracing of the unknown and incalculable, that increases the human prospects for the future, we end up harming ourselves. By trying to make life free of failure on the individual level, we create conditions that make general failure inevitable. This is why your first contribution to reconstruction must be the resolution to take a risk—the risk that is inherent when you join with others in the mutual enterprise of reform.

If considered through the narrow-minded arithmetic of risk aversion, it would never make sense to contribute $50 of your resources or a few hours of your time to join in a popular movement to free human action from the forced embrace of dying institutions. No matter how beneficial such a change might be for you, there is always the risk that efforts of reform may fall short. They may in some respects be unpopular. There is a chance that the agents of bureaucracy, rightly perceiving that the opening of life to new possibilities threatens the very principle of their operation, would impose minor or even major retributions upon you if your actions challenge their continued prosperity. And beyond that—beyond the risks inherent in the known loss of time and money which you must commit if a popular movement is to succeed, and beyond the risk that your contribution will fall short—is the risk that you will be spending your effort for nothing because the whole enterprise could have succeeded without you. Seen in the strict calculus of risk aversion, your every action toward the salvation of the progressive way of life is futile, is either too little to matter or superfluous to the final outcome. This is all true, *except under one condition.* You may be the person who makes the crucial difference. The whole enterprise will surely fail unless you believe you are.

That is why we cannot afford to deal with this question of national reform in a spirit which measures only what is known. We must realize that we ourselves are no less contributors to the incalculable realms of the future than anyone to whom we could turn for help. The first reform, then, is to recognize that the probabilities of our long-term success depend upon our individual willingness to become risk-takers ourselves, to look beyond the known costs and the short-term benefits. We must take into account something which we have no way of entering into the accounts of mathematical expectation: our own unrealized potential. If we are to redeem our future from decline and failure, we must borrow the secret of every great enterprise in history—a spirit that is ready to proceed without too close regard for the costs. Only under such conditions do we discover the true extent of human potential.

The whole enterprise of building America depended upon the willingness of those who came before us to strike out without even so much as a good map. They moved their entire households under what would to us be primitive and intolerable conditions of travel out to a frontier fabled as wild and uncivilized. The energy that motivated these pioneers —the same energy which accounts for the slow ascent of man from his former condition as a primordial savage—was built upon hopes that would seem wild and ill-advised upon close scrutiny.

The frontier of American growth has always been a frontier of risk and uncertainty. To restore that condition today, we must embrace risk ourselves and pitch in with our neighbors just as neighbors did to raise one another's homes on the prairie. We must support reforms that aim toward generating new enterprise and a new spirit of adventure in America.

BALANCE THE BUDGET

One institutional reform that would do much to bring the behavior of elected politicians into conformity with the public interest is the proposed constitutional amendment to require that the federal budget be balanced. Such an amendment could be most effective if it were combined with a provision establishing a proportional tax (see below). This would eliminate much of the political profit in inflation and at the same time help foreclose the growth of transcendental capital.

Under current conditions, the politicians have a powerful motive to impose inflationary costs upon the public. Deficit spending enables them to provide increased appropriations to special constituencies while disguising the costs in the form of inflation diffused over large numbers of the rest of society. The beneficiaries of the extra spending are fully aware of the roles that the politicians play in directing the benefits their way. Yet the citizen who is not a beneficiary of the political windfall may not recognize which political actions are the cause of his hurt. Under such conditions, the incentives of the politicians clearly point toward ever-increased spending, with continued inflationary deficits. The political advantage to the politician of approving additional spending far exceeds the political cost when he does so.

A constitutional amendment to require that the budget be balanced would go some way toward correcting this defect in the system. It would at least require that in order for the politicians to siphon additional resources away from the public they would be obliged to levy direct taxes. This would concentrate the costs of the additional spending and mobilize opposition. Under these changed conditions, the chances are remote that a political majority could be mustered to support so unwholesome a growth of transcendental capital as we have witnessed in the last decade. A balance-the-budget amendment would work, which is exactly why politicians have been dragging their feet in opposition.

(To support the balanced-budget, send a contribution or contact the Balance the Budget Amendment Committee, c/o National Taxpayers Union, 325 Pennsylvania Avenue, S.E., Washington, D.C. 20003.)

RESTORE SOUND MONEY

Another way to strike at inflation would be the reintroduction of sound money in America, redeemable in silver or gold. If the history of monetary affairs shows anything, it is that paper money issued only as a circulating instrument of liability must inevitably degenerate to a worthless condition. As the Nobel Prize-winning economist F. A. von Hayek has written: "Practically all governments in history have used their exclusive power to issue money in order to defraud and plunder the people."[1] Only a money supply built upon assets such as silver and gold—which cannot be printed or expanded at the whim of politicians—can maintain value over time.

(The National Committee for Monetary Reform has been working to take control of money out of the hands of politicians and institute a sound currency based on gold. Those who contribute $25 or more in support of this effort receive the Gold Newsletter, which reports monetary developments. For more information contact the National Committee for Monetary Reform, 8422 Oak Street, New Orleans, Louisiana 70118.)

REDUCE TAXES

This means supporting changes in the tax laws to reward risk-taking rather than subjecting it to penalties. Capital-gains taxes, which are clearly taxes imposed upon unexpected success, should be abolished altogether. These taxes are levied almost solely upon the success of new, emerging enterprises rather than upon the established, dominant corporations. Abolishing capital-gains taxes would restore the necessary allure—the rumor of gold in California—that draws people to the frontier of new development.

Removing capital-gains taxation would also have the wholesome consequence of allowing the accumulation of new fortunes and the wider dispersal of capital ownership that is conducive to the widest possible experimentation, not only in commercial enterprises but in philanthropy, education, and the arts. New money brings new forms of activity into being. The chances of some valuable, if completely unforeseen, achievement are far greater when trial and error is encompassing one hundred times the possibilities.

There is no evidence among all the details revealed in the study of the Squeeze on American life to suggest the American people are bad economizers. Quite the contrary, people have shown themselves to be adept at adjusting their personal pursuit of fortune to the opportunities created through the growth of transcendental capital. By eliminating capital-gains taxes on productive investments, the rewards for committing oneself to productive endeavors could be made more commensurate with the service they extend to society.

Instead of making the creation of problems profitable, as we have through the growth of transcendental capital in the form of bureaucratic payrolls and growing welfare payments that subsidize the poor for remaining incompetent, we must make success profitable. The income-tax laws should be changed to substitute a flat proportional tax applying equally to all incomes. If such a tax claimed ten percent of gross income without deductions and without exception, this would be enough and more to finance all the useful activities of government. And it would also spare fantastic sums of time and energy—almost $21 billion in man-hours— currently wasted attempting to comprehend more than thirty shelf feet of the Internal Revenue codes and regulations. If the tax codes were no longer the private resources of accountants, lawyers, and bureaucrats, this would save the typical family more than $400 worth of aggravation per year.

It must be recognized that such a proportionate tax, while lowering the amount taken from everyone, might be in some sense more of a burden to the poor than to the rich. But if that is so, it is merely another way of saying that under such conditions the advantages of escaping poverty would be greater. And this, from the point of view of society, is exactly what is desired. The effect of the current tax rates, as we have already seen, is to immobilize the poor by making it more expensive for many to participate in production than it is to remain on welfare.

The rearrangement of incentives so as to make it once more a matter of profit for the poor to utilize their energies productively would be a

250

fantastic boon to everyone. For too long the poor have been left out. They have been told over and over that they are incapable, even as they were paid to be so. People have a way of growing into the roles that are expected of them. By treating the poor as less than fully human, by shearing away all responsibilities for the conduct of their own lives and vesting those responsibilities in an ostensibly benevolent bureaucracy, we have treated the poor in fact as little better than "industrial animals."

If we are to be responsible ourselves, we must credit others with responsibility. This means more than simply regaling them with slogans. We must make it to their interest, in fact as well as in theory, to provide for their own sustenance, attend to their own hurts, and to participate in the progress of human accomplishment. Lowered taxes levied on a proportionate basis would do more than perhaps any other reform to release the hampered energies of the poor.

The average family, in its working lifetime, is bound under current circumstances to lose a fortune to the costs of politics. But if the taxes, inflation, and regulation which are at fault in this parasitic attack upon the public could be brought even marginally under control—if the costs to the average family could be reduced by as little as 20 percent— that would raise the net worth of this typical family by as much as $100,000. That alone would change the character of American society. It would mean that many more persons would have income, not just from a job, but from capital—it would make them independent. It would diminish what are today disproportionate concerns for maintaining employment, without respect to whether the job contributes to production. Instead of insisting that people be paid to do nothing and, in the process of paying them, consume the capital which could finance the productive endeavors they might otherwise have undertaken, we could let them keep more of the money that is taxed away and allow them to employ themselves in the creation of useful work.

BREAK THE PROFESSIONAL MONOPOLIES

The revival of responsibility inherent in emphasis on risk-taking has as its corollary enhanced individual autonomy over the area of life now monopolized by the professions. For reasons that have already been stated, it is important to eliminate incentives that doctors and lawyers have to befuddle the public and consume productive resources far beyond what their services are worth. This means repealing the licensing restrictions that inhibit free competition in the professions. We should put into practice the suggestion made by John Stuart Mill in his essay *On Liberty* more than a century ago:

> Degrees or other public certificates of scientific or professional acquirements should be given to all who present themselves for examination and stand the test; but such certificates should confer no advantage over competitors other than the weight which may be attached to their testimony by public opinion.[2]

Only a thorough uprooting of the medical monopoly would enable people to see what medical services are actually worth. If anyone who felt called to the art of healing, from the homeopath to the acupuncturist to the charm-school dropout, could set up shop and appeal to the public to minister to a portion of its malaises, several things would happen. First, since there would be more healing services available, there would be a greater opportunity for many individuals to locate the kind of alternative medicine with which they were most comfortable. Because the subjective content in healing is a large measure of the enterprise, even treatments based upon absurd theories would prove successful in some cases in which orthodox treatments would fail.

This would be only one effect of shattering the physicians' monopoly. Another would assuredly be the proliferation of treatments that accomplished nothing or perhaps even inflicted harm. Someone would undoubtedly dust off William Radams' "microbe killer," which was once in daily operation at number 7 Laight Street, New York City, where it was supposed to sizzle any species of "germ, bacteria, or fungus" and thus cure all ailments from cancer to catarrh. There would be new versions of "Nature's Vitalizer"—an electric belt to strengthen the sexual organs. There would be magnetic mittens to cure arthritis, new wonder drugs fabricated from seaweed, psychedelic mushrooms, and the hairs of Castro's beard. Quackery, old and new, would flourish. A public which was gullible enough in the past to believe that a cure for asthma was to have one's hair nailed to an ash tree under the full moon at midnight and cut off would find new ways to get fleeced.

For obvious reasons, most of these would be harmless. No quack with even a smidgen of appreciation for the mysteries of commerce would peddle potions that were too abruptly lethal or even likely to stimulate any strong adverse reaction. What the patients are paying for, after all, is the hope of healing and regeneration. These are definitely associated with pleasant sensations. Almost every quack would know this. As Everett Hughes said, "The quack . . . is the man who continues through time to please his customers but not his colleagues."[3] That is why even self-consciously fraudulent medicine is likely to be no more than a waste of time and money. Of course, that would not be the whole story. Some people would be maimed. Some killed. Some would succumb, as they do today, to Dr. Feelgoods. Some would dawdle over ineffective remedies and thus forgo the opportunity to profit from conventional treatment.

But whatever the ravages of quacks, they could scarcely claim as many victims as does today's monopoly medicine. As already stated, regular physicians now injure and maim hundreds of thousands each year, killing tens of thousands and hastening the deaths of many more. Since their morbid accomplishments are all stamped with the imprimatur of science, their victims yield unquestionably to their fate. The unleashing of quacks would introduce a cautionary note. Even full-time gulls would be alerted to the fact that problematic treatments and possibly dangerous ones were within the repertoire of health practitioners. One contemplating any sort of discretionary medical care would be stimulated to stop and think.

The undoubtedly wholesome consequence of this jarring development would be to reinfuse the individual with a measure of autonomy. He would no longer be facing long odds in a confrontation with monopolistic expertise. He would find the selection of health services a simple commercial choice. And ironically, seeing and comparing results on the basis of open competition, he would be more likely to realize that health is not a commodity that can be bought and sold. It is a state of being, merely the most comfortable of many possible adjustments to the slow loss of vitality and eventual death that are nature's way. To seek health and to find it is a challenge that involves many complicated and even incalculable factors. In the end, no one is more responsible for our well-being than we are. Doctors, competent or not, cannot save us. As Péguy said, "When a man dies, he does not just die of the disease that he has, he dies of his whole life."

By opening the way to genuine self-help, we should be doing no more than recapturing what was the early American tradition. In the interesting book *Medicine Without Doctors: Home Health Care in American History*, Guenter B. Risse and others show that self-doctoring was a vital tradition in early America among all social classes. Even the rich, who could well have afforded the fees of doctors, preferred to take responsibility, whenever possible, for themselves. Most of the time they relied upon known remedies, which were published like recipes in home health books to help cure conditions that would today send us to the doctor. It is unlikely that we will ever recapture that spirit of autonomy and self-responsibility, but expropriating the doctor's transcendental capital—his license to practice—would go a long way toward reviving self-help in one of its more wholesome manifestations.

(An excellent resource of information on the entire medical self-care movement is Dr. Tom Ferguson's quarterly magazine, *Medical Self-Care —Access to Medical Tools*, Box 717, Inverness, California 94937.)

As we saw in Chapter 12, lawyers, as well as doctors, have been squeezing the American public. A popular movement for legal reform such as that which brought a revival of English society in the seventeenth century is needed now to break the legal monopoly. One organization working to that end which is worthy of enthusiastic support is HALT (Help Abolish Legal Tyranny). HALT is moving to undo the lawyer's monopoly privilege which gives him an incentive to confuse property in the economic sense with property in the legal sense. HALT is seeking to save the billions in resources now lost because lawyers are paid $750 to secure an uncontested divorce when, with competition, the papers could be made available to anyone for $7.50. (HALT, 236 Massachusetts Avenue, N.E., Washington, D.C. 20002.)

REDUCE HOUSING REGULATIONS

State and local housing codes, along with federal regulations such as the FHA's Minimum Property Standards, prohibit the availability of the sorts of dwelling that could enable poorer individuals to assume responsibility for housing themselves. In the past, there was a booming business in the preparation of unfinished homes that were often sold as little more than shells. The residents—often the whole family, relatives, and neighbors—then pitched in to gradually improve the quality of the home: to finish unfinished walls, to improve the heating system, perhaps add a bathroom, replace a wooden stove with a gas or electric model, and to effect any of five hundred other improvements that are well within the capabilities of the descendants of pioneers who built their own houses out of logs or planked the wood themselves at the spot, made their own bricks, and built their dwellings piece by piece from the ground up. Where wood was scarce, as it was in the Great Plains, the first families settled into a dugout —little more than a cave scraped out of a low hillside, with a fourth wall made of sod. Grass grew on the roof. Since glass was scarce, these homes often lacked windows, or used improvised panes of waxed paper. Yet, within a few years the pioneers had normally constructed free-standing wooden structures and turned their sod bunkers.

That principle could work today if we would only allow it. The most effective of all inventions to improve housing is the responsibility of the inhabitants for their own dwellings. Today's poor are far richer than the pioneers. They have better tools with which to work, better materials to employ, and a thousand new inventions and improvisations that were beyond the grasp of their ancestors. Yet because the poor do not have scope under the law to take charge of obtaining and maintaining their own shelter, they lose rather than gain competence. As Jack Anderson has astutely noted: "They may well be the descendants of those who cleared the wilderness. Yet they complain listlessly that weeks have passed, and no one has come around from the housing authority to fix the toilet or scrape off the flaking paint."[4]

Unless one is to propose that Americans today are handicapped by some sort of genetic deterioration, which is implausible and outrageous, there is only one explanation for the inability of the poor to improve their housing That is indeed the same explanation that accounts for the overall Housing Squeeze now inflicted upon every American. The laws make improving one's own housing difficult, and the creation of transcendental capital makes it unprofitable.

For proof that more flexible regulations can produce better housing all around, consider the state of housing in modern Japan. The Japanese, despite their phenomenal economic growth in recent years, still average only about 70 percent of the typical American income. As recently as 1960, the average Japanese income was only 10 percent of that then current in America. Obviously, it would have been impossible for the Japanese to have housed themselves according to the same standard that bureaucrats decree for Americans and which, by and large, most Americans have been wealthy enough to afford it. It would have taken almost 100 percent of a typical Japanese income in 1960 to have afforded an American-style home. If American housing codes had been forced into effect in Japan, the result would have been to eliminate economic growth in the country and create the kind of massive chaos that is confined in

255

America to the disruption of the poorer segment of the population. To their credit, the Japanese were not so foolish as to impose a burden on 90 percent of their population, like American bureaucrats did upon 10 percent of ours. They continued to allow construction of new dwellings designed to house people at costs they could afford. In some cases, this meant producing rooms for rental scarcely larger than a single bed. Inhabitants sometimes shared a common bath, a common toilet, and kitchen facilities. In short, they produced a modern, more private version of the tenement housing that was built in American cities in the late nineteenth century to accommodate the influx of impoverished immigrants. The much-noted crowding of the tenements with many individuals living in the same room made use of the principle which the Japanese continue to employ at the present time: reducing the floor space allotted to each inhabitant to a level he can afford.

This, of course, is only one way of mastering the problem of producing shelter to meet the actual ability of people to pay for it. A look around the world confirms that there are no absolute divisions in the quality of housing. Homes are good or bad only according to what their inhabitants can afford. A tar-paper shanty or the makeshift housing one finds in the outskirts of Latin-American cities patched together out of packing crates and cardboard boxes may not be the material for a six-page spread in *Architectural Digest*, but it expresses a necessary step in the evolution out of poverty.

In America today, almost everyone is rich enough to afford something more stately than a shanty. And it must be understood that I do not suggest that the erection of shanties is the solution to the Housing Squeeze. There are other kinds of dwellings that fit somewhere in the range between the tar-paper shack and the palace that would meet the needs of America's poor if the building and housing codes permitted. And it should be borne in mind that to live in housing which does not meet the standards incorporated into current codes is by no means a degradation. Few of history's kings and emperors other than those living in modern times inhabited palaces that could have been certified by an American housing inspector. In addition to lacking plumbing and wiring, the palaces of the past fell short in other ways. They were abysmally heated. Many palaces would fail to meet other modern requirements as well, such as standards for windows, availability of exits, building-material limitations, and requirements for insulation and fireproofing. What this all goes to show is how relative these standards are. What may be a luxury at one point of economic development is quite literally substandard in the next.

PUT BUREAUCRACY ON AN INCENTIVE PLAN

Another item that should be high on the agenda of reform is the introduction of incentives that place the self-interest of the bureaucrat more nearly into accord with the public interest. This means, in the first instance, a freeze on bureaucratic pay and fringe benefits for an indefinite period until the rewards from the pursuit of productive activity clearly exceed those available through committing one's time to the pursuit of transcendental capital. It will be a simple matter to determine when that point is reached. That will be when more persons are leaving their bureaucratic jobs than can be found to replace them. The preposterous criteria employed currently to determine bureaucratic pay levels result in a situation in which bureaucrats are dramatically and persistently better compensated than are persons in the productive sector. At the same time, applications to fill vacancies in the bureaucracy are running higher per opening than in any other area of life, with the possible exception of starting positions on professional basketball teams and starring roles in television series. It is an absolute waste of resources to continuously increase bureaucratic compensation in the face of a deluge of applications.

LIMIT GOVERNMENT SERVICE

Another needed reform to halt the tendency among bureaucrats to settle into a predatory relationship toward the people in the productive sector would be to establish a limit on the number of years that any one individual could serve in civilian government employment. If everyone filling a government post knew that he would hereafter be obliged to find employment that would put his talents to use in productive activity, this would discourage the public's alleged servants from indulging what is otherwise their self-sprung tendency to create problems, and even crises, in order to promote the health of the bureaucracy. If bureaucrats knew that their own fortunes were tied directly to the prosperity of the people upon whose resources they draw, there would be a revolution in the conduct of many agencies.

ABOLISH FUTURE GOVERNMENT PENSIONS

A similar reform that is equally necessary and which aims at the same end is the abolition of future government-pension benefits. If members of the

257

bureaucracy were obliged to invest their savings among the same array of possibilities open to persons outside of government, this, too, would prevent them from becoming a caste apart, able to improve their own well-being while beggaring that of their fellows. If bureaucrats' retirement income were tied directly to the productivity of the economy rather than to the rather less variable powers of the state to levy taxes and print money, their interests would more closely match those of the community as a whole. This reform would be simple to achieve. All the institutional framework necessary is already in place. Bureaucrats who have been on the job for less than a certain period of time, say ten years, or those below the age of forty, would no longer be able to accumulate pension benefits but would instead have to turn to the expedient of an Individual Retirement Account of the sort that persons without pension coverage in the productive sector utilize today. This would reduce dramatically the agitation within the bureaucracy for measures that cause inflation.

BOUNTIES FOR BUREAUCRATIC SAVINGS

Also needed are direct individual incentives for bureaucratic personnel to effect cost savings rather than to spend money. One approach employed in the American past with success still has much to commend it—the bounty program to extend substantial financial incentives to supplement the weak, indeed feeble, hope that bureaucrats will save money, when doing so threatens their career. Anyone who could demonstrate a money-saving improvement in a bureaucratic program would be authorized to obtain a reward of some percentage of the amount saved. Under such conditions billions upon billions now being piddled away would be rescued and put to productive use.

It would also be desirable to alter the incentives which govern the conduct of politicians in their work. Separating the ombudsman function from that of the legislator, for example, would take away the motive for members of Congress to allow the bureaucracy to malfunction. The more havoc bureaucracy creates, the greater the individual congressman's chance of reelection. Unfortunately, one cannot now think seriously of reform of that kind. As difficult as many of the other parts of this agenda are, a direct attack upon the prerequisites of politicians would be impossible. They would be no more likely to vote away their own advantages than a goose is to tow a cargo plane.

ABOLISH THE DEPARTMENT OF ENERGY

There is no aspect of the transcendental capitalist squeeze which would be so easy to end as the gasoline lines and disruption of energy markets. By abolishing the Department of Energy and ending immediately all controls on natural-gas prices, crude-oil prices, retail gasoline prices, and by scrapping the government's program of allocations and entitlements, we would put supply and demand back into balance, thus reducing the real cost of energy to consumers both at home and abroad. Abolishing the Department of Energy would immediately slash overhead costs of energy delivery, saving taxpayers a sum greater than the combined profits of all the major oil companies. Abolishing the Energy Department would end the subsidy for the importation of foreign oil, which as of the summer of 1979 amounted to $1.79 per barrel.[5] It would increase domestic oil production, by allowing Americans to receive as much for a barrel of petroleum as foreign producers are paid for theirs. This alone, according to a study in *Public Interest*, could stimulate enough U.S. production to reduce oil imports to less than one-third of their then current levels.[6] Without the Department of Energy and its arbitrary regulations, there would be no gasoline lines—as there have not been in other countries. Government allocations based not on current usage but on historic usage inevitably fail to take account of shifts in population and differences in economic growth. For example, 800,000 more vehicles were on California roads in May 1979 than a year earlier. Yet energy bureaucrats actually decided to reduce gasoline deliveries below the previous year's levels. Resultant shortages and disruptions were as inevitable as dirty shoes after a walk in the mud. The way to end these problems is to put the energy bureaucracy out of business. Write to your congressman to say that you favor total decontrol of energy, with the elimination of all subsidies, favors, and import quotas. This is the best way of minimizing the costs you will pay to obtain energy in the future.

BECOME A POLITICAL SKEPTIC

An important educational adjustment you can make as an individual is the adoption of an information filter to help make the gaggle of facts and theories surrounding your exploitation by politics intelligible. Given the intensity of the competition for your attention, and the strong incentives which many have to confuse the true stakes of political debate, it is impossible, as I have already suggested, for an individual to investigate all the many political contentions and still have time free to do anything else. Under the circumstances, you must either fall back on an information shortcut such as those which are purely partisan, or you must adapt some other means of making the world intelligible.

I commend to you the advantages of an attitude of acute political skepticism. In other words, be wary of supporting any government growth for whatever reason. No matter how convincing the arguments for creating another bureau may seem, remember that they are advertisements for the growth of transcendental capital, which are financed out of the expected gain of the political entrepreneurs who sponsor them. Because the recipients of transcendental-capital gains can afford to broadcast their perspective on political matters more widely than can anyone else, their ideas are normally found dominating the agenda of public debate. The business that benefits from a new subsidy, or the labor union whose members will be employed in an additional bureaucracy, can, after all, recoup their advertising costs from the transcendental-capital gains they capture. But those opposing the capture of transcendental-capital gains have, by definition, no gains to capture. Thus it is that powerful incentives induce the advocates of government to concoct arguments that direct public opinion along lines which correspond to their selfish interests. As the English author Charlotte Lennox observed: "Such is the Power Interest over almost every mind, that no one is long without Arguments to prove any Position which is ardently wished to be true, or to justify any Measures which are dictated by Inclination."

That bureaucrats and politicians pursuing their own interests could be led to advertise and probably to believe arguments which aggrandize their power and fill their purses is an inevitable feature of life. The only antidote is for you to adopt a posture of skepticism: to disbelieve all claims which result in higher taxes and more government and to support all causes which reduce taxes, take power away from politicians, and consequently reduce the growth of transcendental capital.

Such an attitude on your part will not only lead in the long run toward a reunion of property in the economic sense with property in the legal sense, by tending to reduce the now powerful incentives for individuals to create and profit from confusion, it will also give you more power. It will greatly enhance individual autonomy and even advance the progress of human civilization. This was noted by James H. Breasted in his pioneering and astute analysis of the emergence of the moral sense, published in *The Development of Religion and Thought in Ancient Egypt.* He outlined the role of skepticism in the civilizing process:

> Skepticism means a long experience with inherited beliefs, much rumina-tion on what has heretofore received unthinking acquiescence, a con-scious recognition of personal power to believe or disbelieve, and thus a distinct step forward in the development of self-consciousness and personal initiative. It is only a people of ripe civilization who can de-velop skepticism. It is never found under primitive conditions.[7]

What was true in the history of religion can also apply to the evolu-tion of politics. A skeptical view of political claims would mark an ad-vancement of our culture and an enhancement of your self-control and autonomy. Another means whereby you can contribute to the positive evolution of society is not to rely upon government for anything. This is probably good advice simply from the perspective of getting the most out of your life.

If you plan yourself into a position of dependence, you may find, as Hazel Wiggens did, that politicians and bureaucrats are simply unable to deliver the security they advertise. Ms. Wiggens was unfortunate enough to depend upon political aid for her survival. When a bureau-cratic foul-up interrupted her checks from Social Security at age seventy-six, she fired off an urgent request for help. The bureaucracy answered— five months later. Unfortunately for Hazel Wiggens, by that time she was dead.

That such things have happened, even under conditions which are far more favorable to the competent operation of the system than those you are likely to face in the future, should serve as a cautionary note. But beyond the personal advantage of steering clear of bureaucracy, there is the political advantage. When you withdraw your demand for bureau-cratic services, you withdraw your support of the system. And this weak-ens its power to impose hurt.

(For information about how to maintain your independence, inves-tigate the new publication *Independence*. Issues discuss strategies for independence in all areas of life, including how to find an occupation without renting your time to an employer, how to accumulate capital in spite of the Squeeze, plus tips on how to obtain the best values in travel, how to command higher quality in products and services, ways to find security in old age, how to avoid taxes, and generally how to lead a more intelligent and healthy life in a declining economy. Available for $15 from *Independence*, 10 East Street, S.E., Washington, D.C. 20003.)

TAX RESISTANCE REDUCES TAX RATES

Another possibility for you to entertain is outright tax resistance, or what *The Economist* calls "the private guerrilla warfare of tax-avoidance." Even if you determine after study that the risks are too great to break the law yourself, you should at least extend warm support to those who do. This is radical advice, to be sure. It derives from a close study of the thinking of those radical gentlemen whose early efforts did so much to establish in America a context for a favorable evolution of society. They would have agreed, as Jefferson said explicitly, that there are many advantages when the government is reminded that the people preserve the spirit of resistance. One of those advantages is lower taxes. Contrary to the commonly held conviction which has been employed by government prosecutors with consistent success to sway juries into convicting tax resisters, it is untrue that law-abiding citizens must pay more to make up for the revenues withheld by the resister or the tax avoider. The truth is more nearly the opposite. The more successful and widespread tax resistance is, the greater the number refusing or evading higher tax levies, the lower the rates on the more law-abiding members of the community.

Here is why. Most people do not pay taxes because they wish to avoid breaking the law; they pay taxes to avoid the consequences of breaking the law. The difference is major. It would be readily apparent if the tax laws with all their current provisions were changed in this one particular: remove the penalties for noncompliance in favor of a provision stating that it was the citizen's legal duty to pay his taxes. In other words, if it were merely "the law" that one must pay his taxes, and those who failed to do so suffered no other cost than the knowledge that they had broken the law, it would be doubtful to say the least that the current level of taxation could be collected. What keeps the tax money rolling in is the threat of force. By reducing the credibility of that threat, you reduce the tax rates rather than increase them.

The list of possible reforms that could be supported immediately is long. To learn more about them involves a continuing educational process. Most of the economic reforms, including reducing taxes, making bureaucracy accountable, and balancing the budget, are on the agenda of the National Taxpayers Union, an organization to which I have a long and deep commitment. Their newspaper, *Dollars and Sense*, which goes to contributors of $15 or more, can give you up-to-date information on the progress of these efforts. (National Taxpayers Union, 325 Pennsylvania Avenue, S.E., Washington, D.C. 20003.)

17
A New Vision of Justice

If you have built castles in the air, your work need not be lost; there is where they should be. Now put foundations under them.

—*Henry David Thoreau*

The revolutionary counsel I have offered in the preceding pages is perhaps a fitting prelude to a brief exploration of some of the principles which I believe might be helpful in settling the bases upon which a better society in the future might operate. What we should aim at is no less than to turn Marxism inside out and create a new ideal of social organization which reflects the highest esteem for what is truly social in human relationships and places the pursuit of private interest into a context which rebounds to the public interest. This means eventually abandoning the practice of placing the rules of society within the reach of egotistical manipulation. The greatest damage to society is done through the evolution of transcendental capital that converts the *rules* into private *means* of some individuals, to be employed for their own purposes.

Under today's conditions, the capital value of the rules does not belong to everyone. Increasingly, the rules are becoming mere means in economic terms—the property of private individuals. Just as stock jobbers buy and sell shares of IBM and Disney, so the very rules of society have become, in economic terms, individual assets changed according to the dictates of private greed. To set this matter right, we must make the rules of society public. That is to say, they must be the property of no man. They must be organized so they are not economic assets enabling some individuals to perform certain actions that are not legal for others. Only by freeing the laws from private ownership in the economic sense can we really put the primordial, even instinctual, human disposition to act according to self-interest to a fully social use. As long as we have institutions that provide for private ownership of the capital value of the rules, it is a logical necessity that we create incentives for some individuals to harm the public in pursuit of their particular private gain.

What we should aim at, therefore, is a socialism of *rules* and a capitalism of *means*. This would involve a long-range adjustment to make all laws apply equally to everyone by eliminating all discrimination between individuals which the rules now establish. It would automatically expropriate most remaining transcendental capital and redistribute its value to everyone in the form of lower prices. This would once again unite property in the economic sense with property in the legal sense. It would make the operations of every kind of establishment more intelligible and thus open to the participation of individuals who are presently excluded by their inability to penetrate the murk disguising the operations of the current system.

Freeing the rules from private manipulation would radically reduce both the number of rules and the frequency of their alteration. This would do more to help achieve social justice than any other reform. It is far more difficult for an individual to adjust to a change in the rules than to a change in the means. In fact, a change in one's means, of even the most pronounced sort, seldom poses a challenge to comprehension, even among persons of low intellectual capacity. That this is true may be judged from consideration of a few simple possibilities. Imagine, for example, that you have left your wallet at home, and failing to realize this, have gone shopping. When you discover that your available means are less than you anticipated, this does not cause a crisis of understanding. It is at worst an embarrassment. Almost anyone can readily adjust to the slight intellectual difficulties posed by fluctuations in the material means available to him as he conducts his life. This is not so with changes in the rules. Go out shopping and discover that the automatic blender you sought is not on the shelf because of price controls, and this does pose a genuine intellectual difficulty. Finding what you want is no longer merely a matter of obtaining additional resources, it is a challenge to attain a better understanding of the way the world works. And this is all the more true because when individuals expropriate the rules as their private means they have an incentive to obscure the information you need rather than make it handy.

A *socialism of rules* would bring the end of this tendency. It would also free billions in resources now consumed unnecessarily by persons attempting but failing to comply with unintelligible rules, or taking counterproductive steps to avoid being snared in the mesh of laws and regulations that are directed to private purposes. The rules that could really apply to everyone would necessarily be simple, clear, and complete. As already suggested, there could not be one tax rate for you and another tax rate for your neighbor. Whatever tax collected would be strictly proportionate.

There are many more respects in which a *socialism of rules* would purge society of many of the adverse consequences arising from the current system in which the rules become de facto assets of particular individuals. The dramatic slashing of taxes, combined with the termination of needless bureaucracy and inflation, would purge life of another of its contemporary evils—the control of property by nonowner management. A host of factors resulting from the confusion of property in the economic sense and property in the legal sense have deprived nominal owners in many cases of effective control over the operation of enterprises and transferred that control to managers. The interests of the owners and managers largely overlap. But when they diverge, the owners are more likely to be interested in seeing their resources put to productive use, whereas the self-interest of the managers may tend in some circumstances toward the wasting of resources. The manager, for example, has an incentive to squander vast sums of money on plush offices and other "fringe benefits" that may be of little productive significance. He may take long lunch breaks and send the bill to the owner, travel to conventions in resort areas, or even place subordinates to work in his personal service. And such behavior is merely the most obvious of a long-noted and well-documented tendency of hired hands to convert the resources under their control to their own use. Even when there is an overlap of interest between the owner and the manager, the manager at certain points may have incentives to suppress productive efforts. Such is the case when he fears the growth of business beyond a certain size would lead to his replacement. The same may be true when his talents are associated with a certain kind of production. He may under those circumstances resist innovation and keep the business's assets locked into an antiquated use. The owner, on the other hand, would prefer to see the assets placed in their most productive use.[1]

The restoration of effective control to the legal owners of productive assets would have the effect of reducing waste and increasing the value of output. This, in turn, would lead to a better quality of product and service at a lower price.

A new synthesis between property in the economic sense and property in the legal sense would revolutionize American society. It would help bring self-interest into conjunction with the public interest. It would dampen the now hot incentives which individuals find to impose costs on their fellow beings in the pursuit of transcendental capital. Individuals, and government employees in particular, would no longer hold property rights in their posts. Resources would be committed to their most productive known use, not to the satisfaction of the selfish interests of those who happen to find a job somewhere in the productive process. The relationship between employment and output would be restored to its proper balance—with the employee serving because of his contribution rather than the job existing as an excuse to drain resources into the employee's pocket regardless of his contribution.

Not everyone would like the results as they applied to himself, but we should enjoy the social consequences. And those, after all, should be the object of social policy. Only then can we properly explore the meaning of Baruch Spinoza's dictum, which should be the underpinning of our public philosophy: "The primary and sole foundation of virtue, or of the proper conduct of life, is to seek our own profit." In recognizing this, we will do no more than bring into account primordial facts of human action. By pretending otherwise, we have created institutions ostensibly liberated from the profit motive but which in fact provide incentives for individuals to create public wrongs.

There can be little doubt that it would require a renaissance of courage and responsibility to reorganize the circumstances of action in order to truly place the interest of society first. This is so for reasons I have broadly discussed. Nor do I gloss over the fact that one of the chief motivations for support of rules with differential impact is to direct benefits to those individuals who are the objects of our pity. When we see a starving person, we wish that the law would provide some special imperative to keep this individual from starvation. And we are usually content that this be done, even if the effect of feeding one known individual is to induce the starvation of ten unknown individuals. Indeed, it is an obvious fact, though one which is little remarked upon, that the imperatives of charity are peculiarly selfish. The knowledge that tens of thousands, hundreds of thousands, perhaps even tens of millions of persons are starving somewhere in the world produces far less of a charitable urge in most individuals than the direct confrontation with a single starving person. So it is with much else that involves imperatives to action. responsible. What all this comes down to is a realization which journalist Phil Tracy explored in the April 19, 1976, issue of *The Village Voice*: If we are to be sober and unselfish in our desire to see society placed upon a footing which is beneficial for all, we cannot be willing to impose a hurt upon ten unknown persons in order to satisfy our desire to direct a benefit to one known individual. In other words, in a socialism of rules, no one would be able to expropriate the rules in order to satisfy any selfish cause, including the alleviation of his private conscience at public expense. And besides, we cannot be truly compassionate without being

> You see, the dirty little secret Washington is hiding from us is that we can't pay people to be compassionate for us. We either do it ourselves, as individuals, or we don't do it at all.

Of course, we must do it. We must be responsible, as we would be without the lure of bureaucracy promising us the selfish benefits of compassion with none of its responsibilities.

What we should gradually point toward is an evolution of society in which everyone is encouraged by circumstances to organize and support his own charitable endeavors. Since these would involve greater individual responsibility in an environment of incomparably greater productivity, I, for one, do not doubt that a *socialism of rules* would leave almost everyone better off. It would guarantee the continuation of progress with all it entails. This would mean the rewarding of success, rather than failure. It would bring the capital value of the rules equally to everyone and bring everyone greater returns from the means. This would be of more real value to the poor than all the alleged benefits from the current bureaucratic system. But even a one-percent increase in productive growth would direct greater riches to the poorer segment of the population than any conceivable redistribution of wealth.[2]

What has been outlined here is admittedly ambitious and complex. It is far easier to state what has to be done than it is to see who will do it and under what circumstances they could be successful. It would certainly be reasonable for one to pause and wonder whether it is practical to stake out an agenda in such bold terms. I think it is. Nothing that has been canvassed here is impossible. If you, and enough others like you, join me in a resolve to act to free America from the Squeeze, it can be done. It must be worth more than a little struggle to rescue progress, competence, and self-realization, all of which are now imperiled by the growth of transcendental capital.

The Squeeze has gripped what is best in American life to the point of suffocation. Now we must rise to defend the American Dream. In the process, we are defending more than what exists in America. We are defending the rational hopes of human beings, the quest for freedom and personality, what French theologian Jacques Ellul calls "the great western venture." We not only can succeed, we must succeed. We must prove that separate individuals, acting on their own sense of discipline and responsibility, can build "an invisible community" that can achieve a kind of miracle: reform of a system that has gone out of control.

We have the means to do so: the access to democratic institutions, including, in many locales, the rights of initiative, referendum, and recall. We can work through state legislatures to convene limited constitutional conventions. We can redress the imbalance of power which leads to domination over Congress and the Presidency by special interests. And perhaps, most important, we can join with others in supporting organized action in pursuit of all the available means of reform.

The new American Revolution begins with you. It must arise first with your resolve to accept risk into your life; to reach out into the unknown by joining with other individuals, persons whom you may never know; to recompose the balance in our system; to set right what is wrong and perhaps in the process to create something better than we now know.

Notes

CHAPTER 1
Awakening from the American Dream

1. Reston, James, "A Personal Communique from Robert Frost," *The New York Times*, October 27, 1957, p. 8E.

CHAPTER 2
The Rise and Fall of Progress

1. Mackay, Charles, *Extraordinary Popular Delusions and the Madness of Crowds* (New York, Farrar and Straus, 1932), p. 260.

CHAPTER 3
The Information Deficit

1. For more information, see Lee Benham and Alexandra Benham, "Regulating Through the Professions: A Perspective on Information Control," *Journal of Law and Economics*, XVIII: 421–47 (October, 1975).

2. Whitehead, Alfred North, *Introduction to Mathematics* (New York: Oxford University Press, 1948), p. 42.

3. Adult Performance Level Project, University of Texas at Austin, Division of Extension, Industrial and Business Training Bureau, *Adult Functional Competency in Texas*, prepared for the Texas State Manpower Services Council and the Texas Education Agency (Austin: The Project, 1975).

4. Williams, Raymond, *Key Words: A Vocabulary of Culture and Society* (New York: Oxford University Press, 1976), p. 127.

NOTES

CHAPTER 4
The Illusions of Politics

1. Plamenatz, John, *Democracy and Illusion* (London, Longman, 1973), p. 26.

2. Douglas, William O., quoted during the "Douglas Convocation on the State of Individual Freedom," held by the Center for the Study of Democratic Institutions, Washington, D.C., December 7–9, 1978.

3. Fiorina, Morris P., *Congress—Keystone of the Washington Establishment* (New Haven, Yale University Press, 1977), p. 39.

4. Bajt, Aleksander, "Property in Capital and in the Means of Production in Socialist Economies," *Journal of Law and Economies*, XI: 1 (April, 1968).

CHAPTER 5
The Three Species of Capital

1. Barber, Benjamin R., *The Death of Communal Liberty: A History of Freedom in a Swiss Mountain Canton* (Princeton, N.J., Princeton University Press, 1974), pp. 152–3.

2. Schumpeter, Joseph, *Capitalism, Socialism, and Democracy* (New York, Harper and Brothers, 1942), p. 198.

3. Kitch, E. W., et al., "Regulation of Taxicabs in Chicago," *Journal of Law and Economics*, XIV: 285–350 (October, 1971).

4. "Koch Threatens to Fire City Welfare Cheats," *New York Post*, October 15, 1978, p. 27.

5. "Costly Pensions: Fire, Police Disability Payments Escalating," *The Washington Post*, January 8, 1978, p. A1.

6. *Ibid.*, p. A18.

CHAPTER 6
The Money Squeeze

1. Hayek, F. A., *Individualism and Economic Order* (Chicago, University of Chicago Press, 1948), pp. 86–7.

2. *The Cambridge Ancient History*, Volume XII: "The Imperial Crisis and Recovery AD 193–324," edited by S. A. Cook, F. E. Adcock, M. P. Charlesworth, and N. H. Baynes (Cambridge, Cambridge University Press, 1939), p. 266.

3. Groseclose, Elgin, *Money and Man: A Survey of Monetary Experience* (New York: Frederick Ungar Publishing Co., 1967), pp. 74–5.

4. *Ibid.*, p. 117.

5. *Ibid.*, p. 118.

6. Hayek, F. A., *The Constitution of Liberty* (Chicago, Henry Regnery, 1972), p. 331.

7. *Ibid.*, p. 332.

8. New money in the form of bank deposits allows banks to enjoy windfall profits because they can loan the new deposits and collect interest on the loans. The fact that banks are able to lend out most of their deposits, keeping only a fraction in reserve, gives them this unearned windfall. The government guarantees depositors, through the Federal Deposits Insurance Corporation, that their money is not in jeopardy. To the depositor, the money in banks is as safe as if it were held in reserve and none were lent out. Without such an arrangement, banks would be unable to lend out most of an individual's deposit and retain his confidence. Thus banks need the backing of the government, and, with it, have an incentive to push for a continuing inflation. Bank stock can therefore be considered as a prime example of transcendental capital. The price of the stock has been bid up on the stock market to reflect its high returns. Thus, the present owners of the stock are receiving normal returns on investment, but they have a vested interest in seeing that inflation continues.

9. Cited by John A. Pugsley, "How to Survive Runaway Inflation," *The Inflation Survival Letter*, July 13, 1977.

10. Hayek, *op. cit.*, p. 331.

11. Many economists contend that there is no economic distinction between operating on borrowed and invested funds. They neglect the structural consequences of indebtedness, and particularly the extent to which the corporate indebtedness biases the system toward inflation. Further, neglect of the distinction between owners and managers dismisses a partial conflict of interest which is firmly based in the logic of choice and which is evident even to casual observation.

12. Chou, Shun-hsin, *The Chinese Inflation, 1937–1947* (New York, Columbia University Press, 1963), p. 261.

13. Martin, Robert P., "China in the '40s," *U.S. News & World Report*, October 2, 1978, pp. 37–8.

14. *Ibid.*, p. 38.

15. Naipaul, V. S., "A Country Dying on Its Feet," *New York Review of Books*, 1974, April 4, pp. 21–3.

CHAPTER 7
The Tax Squeeze

1. Calhoun, John C., *A Disquisition on Government* (New York, Liberal Arts Press, 1953), pp. 16–18, cited by Murray Rothbard, *Power & Market: Government and the Economy* (Menlo Park, California, Institute for Humane Studies, 1970), pp. 12–13.

2. Roberts, Paul Craig, "Disguising the Tax Burden," *Harpers*, March, 1978, pp. 35–6.

3. Nelson, Michael, "Where Do All the Taxcuts Go?" *The Washington Post Magazine*, March 5, 1978, p. 30.

4. Feldstein, Martin, and J. Slemrod, "Inflation and the Excess Taxation of Capital Gains," *National Tax Journal*, 31: 107 (June, 1978).

5. Clark, Colin, *Welfare and Taxation* (Oxford: Catholic Social Guild, 1954), p. 51.

6. Roberts, Paul Craig, "Bursting the Balloons of Income Tax Reform," *San Francisco Chronicle*, May 13, 1978, p. 34.

7. A more typical estimate would be 20 percent by the turn of the century. For a defense of the 60 percent figure see E. C. Harwood, *The Money Mirage* (Bermuda, 1976), p. 16.

CHAPTER 8
The Quality Squeeze

1. Melman, Seymour, "American Technology: The Big Machine Breaks Down," *The Nation*, March 20, 1972, p. 364.

2. Main, Jeremy, "They Don't Make Things Like They Used To . . . Or Do They?" *Money*, December, 1976, p. 66.

3. Marvin, Mickey, "My Favorite Jokes," *Parade*, December 17, 1978, p. 20.

4. Kamen, Joseph M., "Controlling 'Just Noticeable Differences' in Quality," *Harvard Business Review*, November–December, 1977, p. 16.

5. Melman, Seymour, *op. cit.*, p. 364.

6. Interview with Calvin Trillin, "Ways to Find Good Food in America," *U.S. News & World Report*, December 18, 1978, p. 70.

7. I am indebted to William Bonner for pointing this out.

8. Kamen, *op. cit.*, p. 16.

9. *Ibid.*, p. 16.

10. Cole, David E., Interview with author, December 7, 1978.

11. Estimate of Ralph Carter, Body Shop Manager, Peacock Buick, Vienna, Virginia.

12. Dole, Charles E., "Auto Recalls: Uphill Fight for Quality," *The Christian Science Monitor*, January 4, 1973, p. 9.

13. Andreason, Allen, and Arthur Best, "Consumers Complain—Does Business Respond?" *Harvard Business Review*, July–August, 1977, pp. 93–101.

14. "The Angry Consumer: 'No Words Can Express My Disgust,' " *U.S. News & World Report*, July 15, 1974, p. 43.

15. *Ibid.*, pp. 42–3.

16. "When Dream Homes Turn into Nightmares," *U.S. News & World Report*, December 11, 1978, p. 43.

17. "Report Complains About the People Who Handle Complaints," *The Washington Star*, December 6, 1978, p. A6.

18. *Ibid.*, p. A6.

19. "Towards a Keynesian Friedmanism," *The Economist*, June 17–23, 1978, p. 38.

20. Jacobs, Jane, *The Death and Life of Great American Cities* (New York, Random House, 1961), p. 4.

CHAPTER 9
The Underemployment Squeeze

1. Burns, Scott, "National Parenting and the Capital Gains Tax," *Dollars and Sense*, July–August, 1976, p. 4.

2. "Paychecks, Here and Abroad," *The Washington Post*, November 11, 1978, p. A16.

3. It may not be accurate to assume that the extent of transcendental capital in various societies can be measured by comparing the government shares of GNP. Indeed, the crucial issue as far as growth rates are concerned may be forms of transcendental capital (i.e., regulations, restrictions, trade barriers, collusive agreements, "due process" claims, union monopoly privileges, etc.) which largely protect income streams of private persons. There is reason to believe that only Great Britain among industrialized countries compares to America in the growth and extent of these forms of transcendental capital. See Mancur Olson, "The Political Economy of Comparative Growth Rates."

4. "The Breakdown of U.S. Innovation," *Business Week*, February 16, 1976, p. 56.

5. Melman, Seymour, "American Technology: The Big Machine Breaks Down," *The Nation*, March 20, 1972, p. 364.

6. Crowe, Kenneth, *America for Sale* (Garden City, N.Y., Doubleday, 1978).

7. Simon, John, "Teacher, Heal Thyself," *Esquire*, March 1, 1978, p. 38.

8. "Board Agrees to Pass 2 of 4 Who Failed Math at College," *The Washington Post*, May 12, 1977, pp. A1, A4.

9. Hoffman, Nicholas von, "Reversing the Laws of Supply and Demand," *The Washington Post*, June 6, 1978, p. B4.

10. Anderson, Sherwood, *Winesburg, Ohio* (New York, The Viking Press, 1960), pp. 87–8.

11. "Challenge to U.S.: 72,000 New Jobs Needed Every Week," *U.S. News & World Report*, June 28, 1976, pp. 20–4.

12. "Value of a College Diploma: Center of Growing Debate," *U.S. News & World Report*, October 13, 1975, p. 37.

13. Jencks, Christopher, *Inequality: A Reassessment of the Effect of Family and Schooling in America* (New York, Basic Books, 1973).

14. Bird, Caroline, *The Case Against College*, ed. by Helene Mandelbaum (New York, David McKay Company, Inc., 1974), pp. 64–5.

15. Vaizey, John, *The Political Economy of Education* (London, Duckworth, 1972).

16. Melman, Seymour, *Pentagon Capitalism: The Political Economy of War* (New York, McGraw-Hill, 1970), Chapter 8.

17. Lachmann, Ludwig M., *Capital, Expectations and the Market Process*, ed. by Walter E. Grinder (Kansas City, Sheed Andrews and McMeel, 1977).

18. "Value of a College Diploma: Center of Growing Debate," *U.S. News & World Report*, October 13, 1975, p. 37.

19. Reed, Fred, "More Jobs for More People Doing Much Less," *The Washington Post*, December 2, 1978, p. A19.

20. Anderson, Martin, "The Roller-Coaster Income Tax," *The Public Interest*, 50: 17–28 (Winter, 1978).

21. Williams, Walter E., "Government Sanctioned Restraints That Reduce Economic Opportunities for Minorities," *Policy Review*, Fall, 1977, p. 20.

CHAPTER 10
The Health-Care Squeeze

1. Illich, Ivan, *Medical Nemesis: The Expropriation of Health* (New York, Pantheon Books, 1976), p. 16.

2. Bjorksten, Dr. Johan, "The Relevance of Research to Preserve Vitality," *The Relevant Scientist*, 1:29 (November, 1979).

3. Crapsey, Edward, *The Nether Side of New York* (Montclair, N.J., Patterson Smith, 1969), p. 155.

4. McNeill, William H., *Plagues and Peoples* (Oxford, Basil Blackwell, 1977), p. 175.

5. "Yes, Clean Living Does Pay Off," *U.S. News & World Report*, November 10, 1975, p. 58.

6. U.S. Bureau of the Budget, *Special Analysis K: Health Special Analysis* (Washington. D.C., U.S. Government Printing Office, 1977), p. 208.

7. Cousins, Norman, and Susan Schiefelbein, "Mysterious Placebo: How Mind Helps Medicine Work," *Saturday Review*, October 1, 1977, pp. 8–12.

8. Illich, *op. cit.*, p. 26.

9. "What Hospitals Are Doing to Cut Down Accidents," *U.S. News & World Report*, March 29, 1976, p. 37.

10. Winchester. James H., "The Shocking Truth About Medical Lab Reports," *The Reader's Digest*, July 1976, pp. 57–8.

11. Illich, *op. cit.*, p. 31.

12. "Death Rate in LA Fell in Slowdown by Doctors," *The Washington Post*, October 20, 1978, p. A6.

13. "Senate Probe Finds 'Rampant' Medicaid Fraud," *The Washington Post*, August 30, 1976, p. A1.

14. Thomasson, Dan, and Carl West, "Our Multi-Billion Dollar Medicaid Scandal," *The Reader's Digest*, May 1977, p. 88.

15. Illich, *op. cit.*, p. 22.

16. MacKay, William, as told to Maureen Mylander, *Salesman-Surgeon: The Incredible Story of an Amateur in the Operating Room* (New York, McGraw-Hill, 1978).

17. Illich, *op. cit.*, p. 59.

CHAPTER 11
The Housing Squeeze

1. According to Vordal Granlee, head of the National Association of Home Builders.

2. The year of *Ladies' Home Journal* issues which included the pieces about saving for your home was 1903, Volume 20. Here are some of the titles of that year:

January, 1903: "How We Saved for a Home," pp. 18–19.

February, 1903: "How Some Young Couples Have Saved for a Home," pp. 20–21.

March, 1903: "How Some Young Couples Have Saved for a Home," pp. 22–23.

April, 1903: "How Some Young Couples Have Saved for a Home," pp. 26–27.

May, 1903: "How Some Young Men Saved for a Home Before Marriage," pp. 24–25.

June, 1903: "Houses Saved for on Less than $15 a Week," pp. 22–23.

July, 1903: "Four Families' Different Ways of Saving for Homes," p. 27.

August, 1903: "From Practically Nothing to Their Own Homes," p. 27.

September, 1903: "Houses Saved for on Less than $15 a Week," pp. 20–21.

October, 1903: "How Some Families Have Saved for Homes," p. 22.

October, 1903: "How Women Have Saved for Homes," p. 23.

3. Seidel, Stephen R., *Housing Costs and Government Regulations* (New Brunswick, N.J., The Center for Urban Policy Research, 1978), p. 88.

4. Cited by Mayer, Martin, *The Builders: Houses, People, Neighborhoods, Governments* (New York, Norton, 1978), p. 73.

5. Cited by *Ibid.*, p. 111.

6. For more details, see *Ibid.*, pp. 67–9.

7. Siegan, Bernard, *Land Use Without Zoning* (Lexington, Mass., Lexington Books, 1972), p. 87.

8. Hearing before the Subcommittee on the Environment, of the Committee on Interior and Insular Affairs, House of Representatives, on H.R. 10294, April 23, 25, and 26, 1974 (Washington, D.C., U.S. Government Printing Office, 1974), pp. 110–11.

9. Perrin, Noel, "The Possibility Tax," *Inquiry*, February 6, 1978, p. 31.

10. Breckenfeld, Gurney, "Is the One-Family House Becoming a Fossil? Far from It," *Fortune*, April, 1976, p. 89.

11. In Mayer, *op. cit.*, p. 72.

12. Mandel, David J., "Zoning Laws: The Case for Repeal," *Architectural Forum*, December, 1971, pp. 58–9.

13. Mayer, *op. cit.*, p. 75.

14. *Ibid.*, p. 221.

15. *Ibid.*, p. 226.

16. Hartman, Chester, "The Politics of Housing: Displaced Persons," *Society*, July–August, 1972, p. 61.

17. Hearings before the Committee on Banking, Housing, and Urban Affairs, U.S. Senate, on the Management of Federal Housing Programs by the Federal Housing Administration and the Department of Housing and Urban Development, July 14, 1975 (Washington, D.C., U.S. Government Printing Office, 1975), p. 4.

18. Hospers, John, "A Plague on All Your Houses," *Reason*, December, 1978, p. 32.

19. Meyer, Herbert E., "How Government Helped the South Bronx," *Fortune*, November, 1975, p. 144.

NOTES

CHAPTER 12
The Legal Squeeze

1. Silberman, Lawrence H., "Will Lawyering Strangle Democratic Capitalism?" *Regulation*, March/April, 1978, p. 21.

2. Scoles, Eugene F., and Edward C. Halbach, Jr., *Problems and Materials on Decedents' Estates and Trusts*, (Boston, Little, Brown and Co., 1973).

3. Kaus, Robert M., "How the Supreme Court Sabotaged Civil Service Reform," *Washington Monthly*, December, 1978, p. 44.

4. Gilmore, Grant, *The Ages of American Law* (New Haven, Yale University Press, 1977), p. 111.

5. Quoted by Donald Veall, *The Popular Movement for Law Reform, 1640–1660* (Oxford, The Clarendon Press, 1970), p. 121.

6. "A Washington Lawyer Thrives by Negotiating in a Bureaucratic Maze," *Wall Street Journal*, August 14, 1978, p. 1.

7. "Why Everybody Is Suing Everybody," *U.S. News & World Report*, December 4, 1978, p. 52.

8. "Joan Little's Lawyer Scorns Legal System and Says He 'Bought' Her Acquittal," *The New York Times*, October 20, 1975, p. 23.

9. Bloomfield, Maxwell H., *American Lawyers in a Changing Society 1776–1876* (Cambridge, Harvard University Press, 1976), Chapter 5.

10. McCarthy, Eugene, *America Revisited: 150 Years After Tocqueville* (Garden City, New York, Doubleday, 1978), p. 118.

CHAPTER 13
The Bureaucratic Squeeze

1. Rosenbloom, Richard S., "The Real Productivity Crisis Is in Government," *Harvard Business Review*, September–October, 1973, p. 156.

2. Schuck, Peter H., "Why Regulation Fails," *Harper's*, September, 1975, p. 16.

3. Friedman, Milton, "Gammon's 'Black Holes,' " *Newsweek*, November 7, 1977, p. 84.

4. 'Why OSHA Should Be Dissolved," a *Factory* Special Report, *Factory*, August, 1976, p. 18.

5. Marx, Karl, *Critique of Hegel's Philosophy of Right*, translated from the German by Annette Jolin and Joseph O'Malley, ed. by Joseph O'Malley (Cambridge, Cambridge University Press, 1970), pp. 47–8.

6. The Bureaucracy Task Force, *The Whistle Blowers: A Report on Federal Employees Who Disclose Acts of Governmental Waste, Abuse, and*

Corruption, prepared for the Committee on Governmental Affairs, U.S. Senate (Washington, D.C., U.S. Government Printing Office, 1978).

7. Gonzales, J., "Great Leap Backward for Civil Service," *The Washington Star*, December 18, 1978, p. A11.

8. Moynihan, Daniel Patrick, "Government and the Ruin of Private Education," *Harper's*, April, 1978, p. 29.

9. *The Washington Post*, "Bishops Decry Government 'Incursions'," November 17, 1978, p. A3.

10. De Tocqueville, Alexis, *Democracy in America* (New York, Alfred A. Knopf, 1966), Vol. II, p. 318.

11. Quoted by Fiorina, Morris T., *Congress—Keystone of the Washington Establishment* (New Haven, Yale University Press, 1977), p. 42.

12. *Ibid.*, p. 48.

13. Bethell, Tom, "The Wealth of Washington," *Harper's*, June, 1978, p. 60.

14. Kline, Bennett E., and Norman H. Martin, "Freedom, Authority and Decentralization," *Harvard Business Review*, May–June, 1958, p. 70.

CHAPTER 14
The Energy Squeeze

1. Ferguson, Adam, *An Essay on the History of Civil Society* (Edin- and It Agrees," August 24, 1979, p. A6.

CHAPTER 15
The Imperative for Reform

1. Ferguson, Adam, *An Essay on the History of Civil Society*, (Edinburgh, University of Edinburgh Press, 1967), p. 279.

CHAPTER 16
What You Can Do

1. Hayek, F. A. von, *New Studies in Philosophy, Politics, Economics, and the History of Ideas* (London, Routledge & Kegan Paul, 1978), p. 224.

2. Mill, John Stuart, *On Liberty* (New York, W. W. Norton, 1975 ed.), p. 100.

3. Hughes, Everett Cherrington, *Men and Their Work* (Glencoe, Ill.: Free Press, 1958), p. 98.

4. Anderson, Jack, "A Society Lulled by Bureaucracy," *The Washington Post*, December 31, 1978, p. B7.

5. Figure supplied by William S. Pitcher, Koch Refining Company.

6. Hall, R. E., and R. S. Pindyck, "Conflicting Goals of National Energy Policy," *Public Interest*, 47:3–15 (Spring, 1977).

7. Breasted, James H., *The Development of Religion and Thought in Ancient Egypt* (New York, Charles Scribner & Sons), 1912, p. 181.

CHAPTER 17
A New Vision of Justice

1. For more information on the long history of abuse by nonowner management, see Jae H. Cho, "Moral Implication of Acquisitive Instinct Under the Separation of Ownership and Control," *Review of Social Economy*, No. 35, October, 1977, pp. 143–8.

2. See comments of Henry C. Wallich, *Yale Review*, XLVI (1956), p. 67, quoted by F. A. von Hayek, *The Constitution of Liberty* (Chicago, Gateway), 1960, p. 428.

About the Author

James Dale Davidson is chairman of the National Taxpayers Union and is the driving force behind the Constitutional Convention to Balance the Budget. He was born in Washington, D.C., and was educated at the University of Maryland and Pembroke College, Oxford, England. He lectures all over the country and has written for several publications including the *Wall Street Journal* and *Playboy*.